'The Light of Asia.' Andhakarena onadha padipam na gayesatha— Dhammapada, v. 146 (*Surrounded by darkness, seek ye not for light*). *The Buddha-image reproduced above is peculiar to Siam. It shows the Buddha, up from a bath, setting out on his preaching round. The image is popularly known in Siam as the 'Bathing Buddha'. The dynamic urge He imparted to the religion is perhaps more accented here than in other standing and static images.*

Buddhism in East Asia

FOR MY WIFE

SAVITRI

With love and gratitude

for all kinds of help in my travels

Buddhism in East Asia

An outline of Buddhism in the history and culture of the peoples of East Asia

Sukumar Dutt

Originals
(an imprint of Low Price Publications)
Delhi-110052

First Published by ICCR, March 1966
Reprinted with Permission 2004

ISBN 81-88629-27-8

Published by
Originals
(an imprint of Low Price Publications)
A-6, Nimri Commercial Centre,
Near Ashok Vihar Phase-IV,
Delhi-110052

visit us at: www.lppindia.com

Printed at
D K Fine Art Press P Ltd.
Delhi-110052

PRINTED IN INDIA

PREFACE

THE present work is in fulfilment of a commission given to me by the Indian Council for Cultural Relations for the study of Buddhism in the history and culture of Buddhist countries in East Asia. It was in the fitness of things that the Council should interest itself in a work of this kind, for India's relations with other Asian countries began a long way back in the past with the spread of Buddhism in the Continent.

The subject was one capable in its scope and treatment of being indefinitely extended, but the condition laid on me by Professor Humayun Kabir, then President of the Council, was that the book should be such as to hold the general reader, without too much critical apparatus or scholarly dissertation and the subject should be presented in broad outline. I have tried to conform to this condition.

The work does not pretend to be one of 'fundamental research', and my main purpose has been to collate, arrange and evaluate facts which specialists in this line have discovered already.

Buddhism was born in India—died also as an institutional religion in India. But India has a keen awareness of the role it played in her political and cultural history during the seventeen and odd centuries (B.C. 5th—A.D. 12th) it existed here as a living faith. The sense and awareness of it is emblazoned in the designs of her National Flag and State Insignia. Though outside the fellowship of Buddhist countries today, it cannot be impertinent for an Indian to ask—How fared this religion of India under other skies?

Unfortunately I found the materials available in this country scarcely enough to satisfy this natural curiosity. The Council, however, was ready to help and financed a tour for me of South-east Asia and the Far East where, besides the privilege of seeing Buddhism in practice, I had a lot of relevant materials to consult and collect. The countries visited were Burma, Thailand, Cambodia, Japan and Ceylon. For reasons, mainly political, China and Tibet had to be cut out of the itinerary. My wife who accompanied me on the tour and I were treated in all these countries with the utmost cordiality and warmest friendship. Nowhere did it strike us for a moment that we were strangers in a strange land and spontaneous help was forthcoming everywhere,—from purchasing a railway ticket to reading and translating a text in foreign script and tongue.

For this, our gratitude is to our hosts in different countries and the scholars on whose time and patience we levied a rather heavy tax.

Our hosts in South-east Asia were—the Ramakrishna Mission (Rangoon); Mr. M. K. Ghosh (Bangkok); the Ministry of Cults, Government of Cambodia (Siamreap and Phnom-Penh); in Ceylon, the Vidyalankar University and its Registrar, Mr. Abeykoon (Colombo and Paradeniya); in Japan, Mr. P. K. Guha of the Indian Embassy, the Mainichi Press, the International House of Japan, and the Indo-Japanese Friendship Association (Tokyo, Kyoto, Nara and Tenri).

Among the scholars we contacted were—Dr. G. H. Luce and Dr. Pe Maun Yin (Rangoon); Prince Dhaninivat (Bangkok); Rev. Pong Khat and other monk-scholars of both Mahānikāya and Dharmayutt sects (Phnom-Penh); Dr. H. Kishimoto and Dr. J. Takaseki of the Tokyo University (Tokyo); Prof. J. Fujiyoshi and Dr. G. Nagao of the Kyoto University (Kyoto), besides the world-famous Zen scholars of Japan, Dr. D. Suzuki (Kamakura), Mrs. Ruth Sasaki and Prof. Hisamatsu (Kyoto); and lastly, Dr. N.A. Jayawickreme, Dr. W. Pachow and Mr. D. T. Devendra (Peradeniya).

To obviate difficulties for the general reader, I have used diacritical marks only for Sanskrit and Pali words and avoided them, as far as possible, for words of other languages, as their diacritical systems are not quite settled and agreed upon by scholars yet.

What has been done by me leaves a good deal undone. I regret having to leave out Indonesia, Korea and Mongolia. But the histories of these countries have not yet been so clarified and periodized by modern scholarship as to enable one to appraise the exact place of Buddhism in the different stages of their evolution.

NEW DELHI SUKUMAR DUTT

December, 1963.

ACKNOWLEDGEMENTS

Apart from scholars in other countries, my grateful thanks are due to Mr. S. K. Chowdhury, Lecturer in Japanese in the School of Foreign Languages, Ministry of Defence, Government of India for help in writing the chapter on Japan; to Miss Latika Lahiri for the chapter on China; to Mr. S. H. Vatsyayan, Editor of *Din Man* for procuring a number of photographs; to Mr. Inder P. Verma for the map; and lastly to my daughter Miss Krishna Dutt for preparing the Index.

For the views and opinions expressed in this book the Author takes full responsibility.

CONTENTS

LIST OF ILLUSTRATIONS

Text Illustrations :

Chapter I

INTRODUCING THE BUDDHIST COUNTRIES

A Geographical Perspective

EAST Asia, though not a current geographical name, is the major geographical division of the Continent, covering nearly two-thirds of its whole area. From countries to its west, it is separated by a vast non-descript region full of mountain-ranges, plateaux and wide stretches of uninhabited and trackless desert. This region may be said to be Asia's 'Great Divide'.

But the physical division is not all. It connotes also a separation of two zones of culture that sprang from two opposite faiths. To its east are the Buddhist countries; to its west the Moslem. To pass from the temples and pagodas of the eastern lands to the mosques and minars of the west is like stepping out of one pattern of life and culture to a different one. Islam was born in West Asia, but it established itself in several parts of the east from the 9th to the 14th centuries, ousting their pre-Islamic Buddhist faith.

To the ancients of Asia, East Asia seems to have been known as a Union of Buddhist countries, the chosen home of Buddhism on the Continent. It was destined by a prophecy of the Buddha to be the region where his religion would most grow and prosper. To this prophecy the King of Kudara (in Korea) drew the attention of the Mikado of Japan in his despatch of 552 A.D., inviting the latter to join the Buddhist countries and add more strength to the faith. Whether it was due to divine dispensation or the existence of better facilities for travel and transport, it was in East Asia that Buddhism was extensively propagated.

With the solitary exception of Tibet, the countries of East Asia fall into three main groups :

(*i*) *South-East Asia* which includes Burma, Thailand (Siam), Laos, Cambodia, Vietnam, Malay, Indonesia and the Philippines (unknown and unexplored till modern times), to which Ceylon should be added not only for the south-eastern slant of the island, but also because of the position it holds among the peoples of south-east Asia in Buddhist history. The name, *South-East Asia*, was invented during the last world-war as a term of military usage, but has now become geographical.

(*ii*) *Mid-Asia* or *Central Asia* includes the whole of China and the region called Sinkiang, now a sizable Soviet republic.

(*iii*) *The Far East*, a term current since its use by the early explorers of the East from Europe, includes Korea, Japan and a part of Mongolia.

Tibet does not fall into any of the above sectors, being, as it were, 'stand-offish' in its geographical isolation on the highest table-land of the world.

With the exception of the Philippines which has no ancient history, the entire East had been Buddhist until the picture changed largely in the 9th and 10th centuries A.D. and after.

"With the *Koran* in one hand and a sword in the other", as the saying goes, Islam emerged towards the end of the eighth century from West Asia and carved its way from the west to the east of the Continent, bent on conquest and conversion. So totally were the countries that lay in its path, from West Asia through Mid-Asia to the Indonesian islands, overrun and converted to Islam that no living roots of their pre-Islamic culture were left in its trail.

Among East Asian countries that fell to the advance of Islam were the oasis-states of Mid-Asia, the Malay peninsula and most of the Indonesian islands. Archaeological researches in these countries have proved their pre-Islamic faith and culture to have been Buddhist.

The explorers of Mid-Asia of the last century, chiefly Aurel Stein, brought to light not only a mass of Buddhist terra-cottas, manuscripts and paintings but also uncovered the sand-buried foundations of many a temple and convent from the vanished oasis-states round the Taklamakan desert and in the valley of the Tarim river. Malay also yielded Hindu and Buddhist images along with allied cult-objects. In Indonesia, more spectacular Buddhist remains exist like the ancient temples called *Menduts* and one magnificent Buddhist structure in Java, the Borobudur Stūpa, carved out of a hill by the Buddhist Sailendra kings. Besides, Indonesian historical works known as *Babat* are found to contain legends of the later Buddhist times in Indonesia.

In these countries the Moslem faith now prevails and their pre-Islamic Buddhism is purely a matter of archaeology. But aside from these countries of obliterated Buddhism, it is a living faith and traditionary influence on culture in the other countries of East Asia, viz., Ceylon, Burma, Thailand (Siam), Cambodia, China, Japan and Tibet dealt with in Part II of the present work, with Mid-Asia added mainly for its importance in the early history of Buddhism in China.

The Coming of Buddhism into East Asia

A slogan raised in Japan on the eve of the Russo-Japanese War of 1904-'05 ran—'Asia is one'. A political slogan, popular in a country then ambitious of the leadership of Asia, it found an aesthetic and philosophical interpreter in Kokuso Okakura whose popular work, *The Ideals of the East*, was first published in England in 1903. The author in this work sought to show that the East (i.e. Asia) was one in respect of its cultural and aesthetic ideals. The conclusion, however, that Asia was one, though neither answering to reality nor a scientific summation, was yet a *possibility* of Asian history. If the movements of Buddhism in Asia over different centuries could have reached a consummation, 'one Asia'— a Buddhist Asia—might have been the outcome. But the diffusions of Buddhism occurred to its east and they came neither from a single source nor in a single movement. Yet behind them, forming a unifying background, was the history of Buddhist development in India in the south.

We can distinguish an early diffusion of the religion direct from India in the 3rd century B.C., in the reign of the Indian Buddhist emperor Asoka (B.C. 269-239 ?) about which there is an ancient legend—one that seems to have taken shape round a historical kernel. Preserved by one school of Buddhism, viz., the Theravāda, it forms a sort of prologue to the history, recorded in Ceylonese chronicles, of the first introduction of Buddhism into the island. But the legend itself is larger in its scope and content, describing nine missions, sent to different parts of India and East Asia in Asoka's reign, of which one mission achieved the conversion of Ceylon. Whatever its historicity, the legend points in fact to the first outward move of Buddhism out of its homeland into the wider continental scene.

In the reign of Asoka, Buddhism was hardly more than two centuries and a half old. It had only passed the first stage of its development, had not bifurcated yet into its two main schools, Hīnayāna and Mahāyāna, and the school of Buddhism named in Ceylon *Theravāda* ('The School of the Elders') was the leading form of it in northern India. Its position, however, was not without a challenge from an emergent rival school called *Mahāsāṅghika*. Some Buddhistic scholars are of the opinion that this rival school was the nidus out of which the Mahāyāna emerged in a later age. The doctrines and monastic regulations of the religion were yet perhaps in the making—anyway they had not been fixed in a canon yet.

About three centuries later, somewhere round the beginning of the Christian era when the next movement of Buddhism into East Asia began, this primitive picture of Buddhism no longer held good. The Mahāyāna branch of it had developed; a Hīnayāna school called *Sarvāstivāda* (a school of realist philosophy, holding the doctrine that 'all exists') which found many votaries in East Asia, had come into existence. Their stronghold had been in Gandhara and Kashmir. New forms of rites and rituals, supplementing with ceremonial image-worship the old symbol-worship of the *Stūpa* and the Bodhi tree, had become incorporated in the religion. The Buddha-image was now the cult-object of worship. The scriptural literature was in a far more developed condition; writing had come into practice and, while the Hīnayāna had begun to be developed with exegetic works and commentaries, the Mahāyāna also was being amplified with works on logic and metaphysics and on the doctrines and dogmas of the school.

The second diffusion was of this developed Buddhism. It started in the early years of the Christian era and there are reasons to suppose that its pioneers were monks from India's north-western provinces,—from Kashmir and Gandhara. About their peregrinations and activities, our information, however, is extremely scanty except for a little that is known from Chinese legend and literature, particularly the *Kao-sen-chuan*[1] which gives glimpses of some Indian monks who toured parts of Mid-Asia and China in the second and third A.D. centuries.

There is clear evidence, though circumstantial, of the presence in Mid-Asia of these pioneer monks from India's north-western provinces which the Kushan kings ruled over in the early Christian centuries. The Kushans had entered India through Mid-Asia and, though settled in the country, they never broke off all their past connections with Mid-Asia. Trade-routes existed between Mid-Asia and India's north-western borders and it was possible for outgoing Indian monks to accompany the caravans along these routes.

Both Mahāyāna Buddhism and the Hīnayāna Sarvāstivāda had centres in Mid-Asia at Khotan (for Mahāyāna) in the south and at Kucha (for Hīnayāna Sarvāstivāda) in the north. Their first beginnings must have been made by Indian monks from India's north-west. The texts recovered from these centres by the Chinese in ancient times and European explorers like Stein and others in the last century are manuscripts which are all in Indian script, and they must have been brought by Indian monks from India.

During this second period of diffusion of Buddhism which spread over several centuries, it was not from India alone that the Buddhist countries of East Asia received their Buddhism. The older Buddhist countries at different stages transmitted it to the younger. The sources were various, as shown in the following table :

i. Burma from India and Ceylon.
ii. Thailand (Siam) from Burma and Ceylon.
iii. Cambodia from Siam (?) and Ceylon.
iv. Malaya from India and Ceylon.
v. Indonesia from India (Buddhism now extinct).
vi. Mid-Asia from India (Buddhism now extinct).

[1] It means 'Lives of Eminent Monks'. Incorporated in the Chinese Tripitaka, it is in three series written in different centuries and the whole will be found in the 50th volume of the Japanese Taisho edition.

vii. China from India and Mid-Asia.
viii. Korea from China.
ix. Japan from Korea and China.
x. Tibet from India and partially from China.
xi. Mongolia from Tibet and China.

Later in the history of Buddhism, two countries became the accredited sources of the religion to the others, viz., China for Mahāyāna Buddhism and Ceylon for Hīnayāna. These two countries came to be regarded as the well-springs respectively of the two systems. There is a well marked division along this line among Buddhist countries in East Asia, some holding on to one system and some to the other. China, Korea, Japan and the Buddhist part of Mongolia are Mahāyānist, while the countries of south-east Asia with the possible exception of Vietnam are Hīnayānist. The first group have their faces turned to China, while the second to Ceylon. The regional histories in Part II will show the respective influence of China and Ceylon in the two groups of countries.

The Initial Historical Periods

In the countries where Buddhism still flourishes, the introduction of the religion in different centuries was followed, sooner or later in each, by an historical period when the religion, from whatever source derived, became an established regional faith and was recognised as such by the State. For each country, it was the 'first glad confident morning of Buddhism'. These periods, longer or shorter in duration, were as follows:

(i) 'Anurādhapura period' of Ceylon (3rd century B.C.—12th century A.D.... a long period during which Buddhism was firmly established as the religion of Ceylon)
(ii) 'Han period' of China (Ist century B.C.—220 A.D.)
(iii) 'Nara period' of Japan (710 A.D.— 784 A.D.)
(iv) 'Pagan period' of Burma (C. 1044 A.D.— 1287 A.D.)
(v) Reign of Rama Khamheng in Siam (C. 1275 A.D.— 1318 A.D.)
(vi) Reign of Jayavarma Paramesvara in Cambodia (1327 A.D.— 1353 A.D. ?)

In these initial periods of history, Buddhism was not alone in the field. Side by side were —(i) unorganised animistic faiths and magical cults, afterwards replaced or absorbed by Buddhism; (ii) more firmly-rooted and more or less organised indigenous cults, like *Nat*-worship in Burma and *Shinto* in Japan, which co-existed as rival or competitive cults throughout the history of Buddhism in the country; and (iii) lastly in China, two systems of indigenous thought, philosophy and practice, viz., Confucianism and Taoism.

What made Buddhism the paramount faith in each country was not so much its superior quality, consistency and organisation, as the fact of its adoption by the rulers preferably for what we may call 'reasons of State'. Some of the rulers were Buddhist by personal faith, but what chiefly moved them to assist in its propagation and promotion was probably the awareness that, more than any other faith in the realm, it was calculated to strengthen the bases of State and Society.

Buddhism was not a mere cult or credal faith: it was a developed ethical and religious system. It inculcated standards of social behaviour, stressed virtues that were conducive to peace in social life; it preached peace and good-will in a world unsettled and prone to outbursts of cruelty and violence. The practice of this religion also involved activities that introduced the rudiments of civilization. Literacy was encouraged by the teaching and learning of scripture ; sculpture by the making of images for ritual worship; architecture by the building of temples and pagodas and convents. Refinements of life came in the wake of Buddhism. Those rulers who cared for a stable State and its advancement in civilization preferred to raise it to the status of a State Religion in their domains.

China was the only exception to this.

Buddhism as a potentially civilizing agency was not likely to occur to the Han rulers about the time of its introduction. North China was the *Chin Kuo* (Central Kingdom) of the Celestial Empire. Here was a settled type of civilization, geared to Confucian doctrines, with a state and society that felt secure of its own stability till, in the second half of the 2nd century, A.D. the Han order began to collapse. Buddhism first obtained recognition in China as a new philosophy, a new school of thought, though of 'barbarian' origin: it was as a philosophy that it was taken up and investigated by the scholar gentry of the Han period. It had to wait for its affiliation to China's indigenous civilization for five to six centuries before it could be an active influence on Chinese life.

The Bahujana in Buddhism

The *Bahujana* is a canonical expression, interpreted by the great Theravāda commentator Buddhaghosa as 'the unconverted, the masses' and occurs significantly in some of the canon-reported sayings of the Buddha. It connotes all the lay people of the world, all those who have not gone like the monks from 'home into homelessness', but who live in the world, rearing families, engaged in the ordinary vocations of life. They form in every country the vast majority of the population.

It is commonly believed that Buddhism is a religion not intended for them, but exclusively for monks, the world-forsakers, for whom the culture of religion is the be-all and end-all of life. In Buddhist scripture, irrespective of school, there is hardly any recognition of the collectively functioning life of the *Bahujana* or the consequences that flow from it, viz., society, culture, the arts of civilization or the happiness of men living together in pursuit of common ends.

But if Buddhism were really a religion of this character and intent it would be somewhat difficult to understand how among people who accepted it as a way of life it became, instead of a school for ascetic practices and monkish virtues, a rich seed-bed for the growth of socially oriented activities, like literacy and learning, artistic and literary pursuits, and the uplift of society by infusing into it the higher values of life inculcated by Buddhist teaching.

Mrs. Rhys Davids in several of her writings suggested with almost passionate emphasis that the religion as presented in the Buddhist scripture was a 'monk-made' version of it, having been composed by monks who formulated the faith into a system of their own. They themselves, forsakers of the world, made the religion completely other-worldly and essentially individualistic in its spiritual discipline. They made *Nibbāna* (Extinction of the Ego) the highest attainment of the religion and the elimination of all motives of action the precondition for spiritual advancement. Taking their notion of Buddhism from its scripture, scholars like Kern and others were persuaded that Buddhism was a 'religion for the monkhood and the laity was but accessory'.[2]

From some of the canon-reported utterances of the Founder, the truth seems to lie the other way about. The Founder's own notion seems to have been that his religion could find its fulfilment only in its acceptance by the *Bahujana*, meaning all people of the world, not the monk-community alone.

It seems that from the beginning of his ministrations to the end, it was the *Bahujana* that the founder of Buddhism had at the end of his vista. In his first exhortation to the monk-followers, he enjoined them to propagate the religion among the *Bahujana*,[3] not keeping it to themselves: in his argument with Māra on the Cāpāla Cetiya only three months before the 'great decease', he declared his unwillingness to depart from life before the religion had become not only well expounded to men, but *Bāhujaññā*, i.e. the property of all men,—not a faith merely of monks.[4]

Perhaps the monks themselves were not unaware that the aim and the discipline they accepted and prescribed for themselves were impossible to adopt for those who were not avowed world-forsakers but house-holders

---

[2] Kern's *Manual of Indian Buddhism*, p. 72.

[3] See quotation, *infra*.

[4] *Mahaparinibbana Suttanta*, iii, 8.

only, being the largest number among people. So in their religious ministrations they made a perfectly intelligible distinction between monkhood and laity.

Thus monks were enjoined not to expound the religion (i.e., the religion of the canon) 'clause by clause' to lay men,[5]—and the restriction could not have been because the religion was supposed to be an esoteric one, this being emphatically denied in several passages of the canon.[6] The only presumption possible is that it was felt that the inner discipline of the *Dhamma* and the ideal of *Nibbāna* were only for those who were committed to them by their vow of ordination.

It is illustrated by the *Uposatha* service, one of the oldest institutions of the earlier Hīnayāna Buddhism. The day of *Uposatha* provided an occasion for a get-together of monks and lay men. On this day the custom for monks was to recite among themselves the *Pātimokkha*, the monks' code of 'Thou-shalt-nots', and to instruct the assembled lay men separately in the teachings of the religion. This was done by rehearsing to them the canonical Buddha-legends, that is the *Suttas* of the scripture.

It is significant that a number of *Suttas* are rubricated in the canon as 'for Householders only' and captioned in it as *Gahapativaggas* (*Suttas* for householders). It is also significant that these *suttas* without exception relate only to ethical concepts and the practice of morality (*Śila*); and obviously they were believed to represent so much of the system as was deemed to be the *dhamma* for the lay man. Just so much, it is said, would lead him to *Svarga* (Heaven), a goal quite distinct from *Arhatship* (Perfection in Sainthood) set as the goal for monks. And one of the monk's specific duties prescribed in the canon was to show the laity 'the way of Heaven.'[7]

In the light of this differentiation made between monks and lay people, the famous passage in the Pali canon which purports to give the Buddha's first exhortation to his monk-followers, being at the same time the canonical sanction for the proselytising character of the faith, becomes really meaningful :

> "Go forth, O Bhikkhus, on your wanderings, for the good of the *Bahujana*, for the happiness of the *Bahujana*,—in compassion for the world—for the good, the welfare (*Hita*) and the happiness (*Sukha*) of gods and men. Let not two of you go the same way.

---

[5] It would be an ecclesiastical offence for a monk to do so. See *Patimokkha, Pacittiya* p. 4.

[6] See passages cited in Dutt's *The Buddha and Five After-Centuries*, p. 93.

[7] See *ibid*, p. 145.

O Bhikkhus, proclaim the Dhamma which is beneficent at the beginning,—beneficent in the middle and beneficent in the end".[8]

Weighing what is explicitly said in this passage and what is kept implicit, it seems clear that the Founder's injunction to his ordained monk-followers was not to make efforts to convert the laity to monkhood, but through the teachings of the religion help them attain their own 'well-being' (*Hita*) and 'happiness' (*Sukha*). It would be far-fetched to attribute to *Sukha* and *Hita* in this context any exclusively spiritual signification : *prima facie* they were secular concepts, applicable to those in secular life. In the Buddhist faith alone they could secure their 'welfare' and 'happiness',—and it was this feeling no doubt that made Buddhism a way of life among people in the lands where it spread. Where it was taken as a 'philosophy', as in China by the scholar-gentry, it was tardy in its diffusion.

The monks, as distinct from the *Bahujana*, were, however, an inalienable part of the religion. The Three-Jewel (*Triratna*) creed of Buddhism places the *Saṅgha* (Monkhood) on a par with the *Buddha* and *Dhamma*,—the three concepts completing the cycle of the faith.

At every seat of Buddhism, therefore, the existence of a Saṅgha, a fraternity of monks, was indispensable. The building of monasteries was an act of piety and sometimes the monastery was a considerably large establishment. The *Saṅgha* life functioned and flourished there and a monastery became also a centre of religious studies and discussions. Seeing that the formation of a sect in Buddhism was easy and was not under inhibition by the rules of the canon,[9] it is not surprising that this intellectual occupation of the cloisters led to proliferation in the monk-community of sects and schools. Sects grew up in all Buddhist countries among monks,—the largest number, nearly 150, in Japan. Sectarianism however was purely monkish in origin.

The life of lay people was neither expected to be subject to monastic discipline nor directed to the ideals of monastic life. Living with fellowmen in society, their business was to encompass their own *Hita* and *Sukha* consistently with the teachings of the *Dhamma*. The *Dhamma* was not meant to be their all-absorbing occupation in life, but only a normative and regulative principle in the conduct of life.

The Founder's injunction had bound the life of the monks with the life of the laity and it was never the object of Buddhist monachism to shun society, to live a segregated life, indifferent to the activities of lay people. In

---

[8] Mahavagga, I, II, 1.

[9] About sect-formation and the facilities offered for it under Vinaya rules, see Dutt's *Early Buddhist Monachism* (Indian Ed.), pp. 158-163. Also in the same book, section IX on *Sects and Schools* pp. 123-139.

every Buddhist country, monks are seen to come into relation in certain recognised capacities with the people's day-to-day life. Normally they are regarded as "teachers", "instructors of religion", priests and "custodians of religious rites", "social workers" and "promoters of the people's *Hita* (well-being) and *Sukha* (happiness)".

Variety of Patterns in Buddhism

A remarkable feature of Buddhism as it developed in different countries is the variety of patterns under which it was practised. In theory or in the philosophy of the religion, there were points of contact or lines of affiliation among different sects and schools. Speaking schematically, however, some countries follow Hīnayāna and some Mahāyāna and Tibet follows Vajrayāna. The actual practice of the religion is so different in different countries that a Hīnayānist Buddhist from Ceylon or Burma or Thailand would be loth to hail a Lamaist Buddhist from Tibet or a Zen Buddhist from Japan as brother in faith. This is because in every country it is not so much the monks as the people that have had the shaping of religious practice in their hands. Naturally there entered into the regional development of Buddhism factors of group-psychology, of pre-conditioned tendencies, predilections and prejudices, or what is called the 'native genius of the people', making one form of development different from another. The mental conditioning of the people had a large part to play in it.

Thus the striking difference in Buddhist development between China and Japan, although Japan was indebted to China for all her Buddhist Schools (except Nichiren), was at bottom a matter of 'ethno-psychology'.

The concept of ethno-psychology is based on the notion that an ethnic group may have a distinct psychology of its own which, though not a 'concomitant of culture', 'enters into culture as an integral constituent'.[10]

The Chinese and the Japanese are ethnically different and the latter have a pronounced 'ethno-psychology' of their own. It entered integrally into their culture of Buddhism. Its peculiar expression is aestheticism,—an intuitive seeking for the beautiful in religion, in art and in life. The Japanese borrowed the Chinese schools of Buddhism, but won little or no advance on their philosophical side: on the other hand they converted them into sources of art, of aesthetic principles, of the culture and expression of the beautiful.

The Japanese Shingon was borrowed in the Heian Period (714-1184 A.D.) from China. It was a Buddhist school derived originally from Indian *tāntric* philosophy, and the peculiar mode of exposition of this philosophy

[10] *Theoretical Anthropology* by David Bidney. Columbia University Press, New York, 1953, p. 79.

was to reduce cosmic truths to graphic and pictorial representation. Painted symbols, figures and diagrams called *Maṇḍalas*, were pressed into its service oftener than textual matter. From this figurative mode of expounding Shingon, Japanese painting derived its first impulse to growth. The philosophy did not develop, but the pictorial art of Japan grew out of the characteristic mode of Shingon exegesis. Also in later mediaeval times, Zen, which had nothing to do with art or its culture, became prolific in producing those purely artistic qualities which mark Japanese tea-ceremony, domestic decor, *Noh*-drama and *Haiku* poetry and which have passed into Japanese culture to make it so unique a phenomenon in the culture-history of the world. China was wedded to the philosophy of Buddhism: Japan, conditioned by her own psychology, to its aesthetic possibilities.

Buddhism as a Crucial Tradition

If culture means, as stated by the eminent anthropologist Carlton Coon of America, "the sum-total of things people do as a result of having been so taught,"[11] all the higher forms of culture in East Asia may be said to have stemmed from Buddhism and its teachings.

The Buddhist tradition in most countries is now centuries old, though with set-backs and periods of temporary eclipse as the regional histories in Part II will show, and it lives in these countries today side by side with urges, more or less pronounced, for modern progress. Historical experience from the west makes it a paradox that tradition and progress can keep house together and people who cling to tradition can desire progress. It is a dogma of history that tradition and progress pull in opposite ways and that a people cannot cherish tradition and be progressive at the same time. But it is a question how far this dogma is supported by the history and evolution of peoples that belong to the East.

No country in East Asia has throughout its history been more tenacious of tradition than Japan. Thoroughly traditionalist in faith and culture, she has demonstrated, since 1854 when Commodore Parry's fleet cast anchor in the Edo bay, that traditionalism was no check on her enterprise and her quest for things without tradition in her history.

Progress in the histories of western peoples starts with the breaching of tradition—by unfixing what has stood too long in thought and action; in the east it starts with efforts to reconcile what has newly come by way of history with what has remained established by long acceptance. Tradition is not regarded as an opposing but a regulative force: the new if it has to live has to come to some sort of terms with it.

[11] Carlton S. Coon's *The History of Man*, London, Jonathan Cape, 1958 p. 5.

Buddhism is the main tradition in Buddhist countries where an innovation or progressive measure is tested against this touchstone to find out how it would affect the 'welfare' (*Hita*) and 'happiness' (*Sukha*) of the people.

Of this, a few instances within recent memory and culled from different countries may be cited in illustration. They show not only how the Buddhist tradition acts in practice, but also its dominating, persistent and resilient power.

The first World-War of this century shook several countries of Asia, and Siam had need to raise an army of defence. But the Buddhist Siamese king in this emergency thought fit to look for sanction for such a step in Buddhist scripture. When two modern universities were incorporated in Ceylon in 1958, they were introduced in the official act, not as modern innovations, but as revivals of the *Pariveṇa* tradition of Ceylonese Buddhist monasteries. When in 1956, the former Buddhist Prime Minister of Burma, U Nu, wanted to build an assembly-hall for monks, foregathered at Rangoon to hold the 25th centenary celebration of the Buddha's 'Great Decease', he turned for its plan and model to the primitive Saptaparni Cave at Rajagaha (in India), wishing to link it with the tradition of *Saṅgītis* (Monks' assemblies for canon recitation) celebrated in Buddhist history. The *Noh*-drama and the *Haiku* poetry, mediaeval outgrowths of Zen Buddhist culture, maintain their popularity in Japan to this day as dramatic entertainment and literary exercise.

These occasional harkings back to tradition even in modern times, which have behind them no urge either of reason or necessity, though seemingly small and disparate, are nonetheless meaningful. They are not the mere manifestations of a common Buddhist faith. 'These heterogeneous items of behaviour' point to the shape of the culture and the resiliency of its tradition. "A culture like an individual", observes Ruth Benedict, "is a more or less consistent pattern of thought and action. With each culture there comes into being characteristic purposes, not necessarily shared by other types of society. In obedience to these purposes, each people further and further consolidates its experience, and in proportion to the urgency of these drives, the heterogeneous items of behaviour take a more and more congruous shape. Taken up by a well-integrated culture, the most ill-assorted acts become characteristic of its peculiar goals, often by the most unlikely metamorphoses. The forms that these acts take we can understand only by understanding first the emotional and intellectual mainsprings of that society".[12]

[12] *Patterns of Culture*, Mentor Book, published by The New American Library, 1951, p. 42.

Chapter II

THE LEGEND OF THE 'NINE MISSIONS'

THE urge to propagate itself among the *Bahujana* was, as we have seen[1], planted in the religion by the Founder himself. He had enjoined his monk followers to strive to that end and expressed his desire not to pass into his 'Great Decease' before his religion had become successful (*iddhaṁ*), prosperous (*phītaṁ*), wide-spread (*vitthārikaṁ*), available to the *Bahujana* (*bāhujaññaṁ*), great (*puthubhūtaṁ*) and well proclaimed to men (*manussehi suppakāsitaṁ*).[2]

From the foundation of the *Saṅgha* (Monk-organization) in a small corner of northern India, this dynamic urge instilled into the religion by the Founder increased in tempo. Within a couple of centuries of the 'Great Decease' the religion spread from its original home in Magadha over a whole region of northern India named *Puratthima* ('Eastern Tract') in the legends of the canon.[3] The boundaries of this region are indicated in the canon from which it appears that it was hardly 150 square miles in extent.[4] Perhaps when Asoka was on the throne in 269 B.C. of an empire the most extensive in the history of India, east to west from 'sea to sea' and north to south, from Gandhara to Mysore, the extent of the incidence of Buddhism in India was not much beyond the ancient *Puratthima*.

Asoka who embraced Buddhism was the first Buddhist emperor of India. Perhaps it was felt by those who were leaders of the Buddhist community in India in his time that it was an anomaly that the empire ruled over by a Buddhist sovereign should be so vast while the religion professed by him so small in its incidence. The feeling must have given a spurt to the Buddhists' desire to spread and propagate the religion all over the empire, and in other countries then accessible from its borders.

The tradition of a planned missionary movement in Asoka's reign has been preserved by one school of Buddhism, viz. the Theravāda. It is historically connected with the first introduction of Buddhism into the island of Ceylon.

The story briefly is that during the reign of Asoka (c. 260-239 B.C.),—sometime after the emperor had embraced Buddhism,—a great prelate and

[1] See pp. 6 to 9.

[2] *Mahaparinibbana Suttanta, III, 8.* See SBE Vol. XI (Buddhist Suttas), p. 43.

[3] In the *Mahavagga* and the *Cullavagga* of the Pali Theravada canon.

[4] See Dutt's *Buddhist Monks and Monasteries of India*, pp. 101-103.

Buddhist leader of that time Moggaliputta Tissa, conceived the idea of organizing nine missions to propagate Buddhism not only within Asoka's empire, but also beyond. Three of the countries mentioned in the legend were outside India,—Ceylon (with the king of which country Asoka is said to have had some previous diplomatic contact), the 'Yona country' which means the country of the Yavanas and points perhaps to Bactria, and "Suvarṇa-bhūmi", a region, not exactly located, either in Burma or in Siam.

The story of these nine missions is restricted to the literature of Theravāda Buddhism. The traditionary legend that grew out of it was so shaped by its Theravāda narrators as to reflect glory on the school they represented,—to set it up as the purest form of Buddhism and recognised as such by the first Indian Buddhist emperor. In its Theravāda rendition, we have a consistent narrative in which Asoka is represented as a champion of Theravāda: is said to have expelled all non-Theravādins from the *Saṅgha* (monk-organisation) and, as the religion was getting mixed up with heresies, to have given the cue to Tissa to take steps to bring about its purification. A great work in the Theravāda canon entitled *Kathāvatthu*, is ascribed to the latter. In this work current heretical doctrines and notions are refuted by Tissa from the Theravāda point of view. It is said that after completing this work he organised nine missions to propagate what he believed to be the really genuine form of Buddhism, viz., the Theravāda.

The oldest version in which the tradition of these missions has come down to us is in the Ceylonese chronicle, *Dīpavaṁsa*, and in Buddhaghosa's historical introduction, *Samantapāsādikā*, to his Vinaya commentary. These two works belong to the end of the 4th century, i.e. about six centuries later than the events reported. In the preceding centuries, it may be presumed, the tradition had developed to its present form and got imbued with its Theravāda colour. The tradition, more or less in this form, is taken up in the other and more extended Ceylonese chronicle *Mahāvaṁsa* and carried on into various Theravāda works of later date. The monk-writers of south-east Asian countries who have dealt with regional histories of Buddhism and who all belong to the Theravāda school are piously committed to this legend as the unimpeachable source of our knowledge of the first emergence of Buddhism out of India and of the conversion of the first Buddhist country in East Asia, Ceylon.

But no historical perspective on it can be gained unless (i) it is straightened out of its Theravāda slant and (ii) salvaged out of the inconsistencies and improbabilities that have clustered round it on account of the narrators' lack of historical sense and their preconceived notions. For this purpose it is necessary to examine the legend in its nexus,—its different but interconnected parts, viz., the part assigned to Asoka, the story of the missionaries and their assignments and the supposed work and achievements of these 'Nine Missions'.

Buddhaghosha's Version: its Theravāda slant

Buddhaghosha's version, which is perhaps the earliest record in point of time, is most elaborate in its circumstantiality. It is at the same time a closely consistent narrative which is briefly as follows:[5]

> The munificence of Emperor Asoka, after his conversion to Buddhism, to the monk community had the effect of drawing into the Saṅgha a large number of heretics whose adherence to the religion was doubtful. Moggaliputta Tissa, then at the head of the Saṅgha, protested against this state of things by relinquishing his charge and retired.
>
> The Vinaya rule requiring that any 'act of the Saṅgha' (*Saṅghakamma*) must be gone through by the Saṅgha in its entirety, genuine monks, unwilling to associate with the intruders, gave up due performance of ecclesiastical acts including the *uposatha* with the result that the royal monastery, *Asokārāma* at Pātaliputta, was practically defunct for seven years.
>
> The emperor sent a minister of his to the monastery to investigate the situation. This minister, to make short work of it, killed off a number of heretics who were believed to be trouble-makers. Asoka was deeply aggrieved over this cruel act he had never authorised and sent for Tissa for consultation. The latter gave the verdict that the emperor was not to blame for the minister's inhuman and unauthorised deed. On this the emperor took matters into his own hand.
>
> Assembling the monks at Asokārāma and dividing the dissidents into several groups, he called each group by turn to declare to him what, in its opinion, the true teaching of the Buddha was. Not satisfied with their answers, he deprived them of the clerical robe. He summoned the other monks last and posed to them the same test question. They answered unanimously that the Buddha's teaching was *Vibhajjavāda* ("*Kimvādī bhante sammāsambuddho' ti? Vibhajjavādi mohārāja 'ti*").

Vibhajjavāda is a mode of exegesis by which the *Buddhavacana* (Words of the Buddha) was interpreted by the Theravāda School. *Vibhajjavāda* is used synonymously with Theravāda. The Buddha is said to have declared himself a *Vibhajjavādin*[6] and hence its authenticity. The Vibhajjavādin or Theravada monk was therefore indicated as the true bearer of the Lord's teaching. The emperor, satisfied with the answer, retained only monks of that school in the Saṅgha.

---

[5] Summarised from the *Samanta-Pasadika* extracts given in Oldenberg's *Vinayapitakam*, vol. III.

[6] See Subha Sutta (*Majjhima Nikaya*); *Further Dialogues of the Buddha*, ii, pp. 113-114.

The purge and the simultaneous declaration that the Theravāda was the only genuine form of Buddhism spurred Tissa to further activity. He is said to have composed thereafter his great polemical work, *Kathāvatthu*, to refute heresies and clarify Theravāda standpoints in doctrine. After this work he sent out nine missions to propagate 'true Buddhism'.

This version of incidents that led to the missions of Moggaliputta Tissa is, however, made doubtful by two considerations. First, it is completely out of accord with the character of Asoka as reflected in his edicts, and secondly, it attributes to Asoka the performance of a prerogative act, viz., *Sodhana* (Purification of the Order), claimed only by the kings of Ceylon.

In the edicts, there is nowhere the remotest allusion to this purge.[7] It also seems unlikely and quite out of character that Asoka would 'unfrock' so large a number of monks, simply because they did not adhere to a rule of interpretation of *Buddhavacana* current in the Theravāda school. The edicts on the other hand show him more keenly interested in the ethical side of Buddhism than in its dogmas and doctrines, for even in the selection of scriptural texts recommended by him to monks,[8] he includes none of the outstanding *suttas* on doctrines like, for example, the *Brahmajāla* and the *Sāmaññaphala*.

Asoka's purgation of heretics from the Saṅgha as described by Buddaghosa was virtually a *Sodhana* (purification) ceremony. In Ceylon, in Buddhaghosa's time, Theravāda Buddhism was the State Religion and the kings of Ceylon had to see that it was maintained in its purity. It was a constitutional duty on the King's part to cast out heretics from the *Saṅgha* to safeguard its purity and, above all, to maintain its *Samaggatta* (integrity). Hence the kings of Ceylon in different eras held what were called *Sodhana* ceremonies.

About a couple of centuries before Buddhaghosa, a *Sodhana* had in fact been carried out by Vohārika Tissa (A.D. 269-291) and there are certain parallelisms, significant though not essential, between the legend of Vohārika Tissa and Buddhaghosa's story of Asoka.

Vohārika, like Asoka, sent, it is said, a minister of his for preliminary investigation when he felt called upon to effect a *Sodhana*. But while

---

[7] Prof. N. A. Jayavickrame, however, has argued in two articles (*University of Ceylon Review*, Vol. XVII, Nos. 3 and 4) that the theory of purge by Asoka is corroborated by the expression *Samghe Samaje Kate* occurring in some of his *Sanghabhedaka* edicts. By the purge of the dissidents the emperor actually brought about unity in the Sangha. But the expression may mean the 'Sangha which was made by the Founder to be a united body', rather than the 'Sangha which has now been united by the Emperor's efforts'. Prof. Jayavickrame's argument rests on the interpretation of this one dubious phrase.

[8] See A. C. Sen's *Asoka's Edicts*, pp. 132-133 (Calcutta Bairat Edict) for the texts recommended to monks by the emperor.

Vohārika's minister dutifully reported to the king on the situation, Asoka's took unauthorised action. The heretics in Asoka's time were the self-mortifying ascetics, fire-worshippers, sun-worshippers and bogus proponents of the Dhamma,—those in Vohārika's time were heterodox Mahāyānists (*Vaitulyavādins*, as they were called in Ceylon) who were recusants from the Theravāda. In both cases a *Samagga Uposatha* ceremony (i.e. an *uposatha* held by the entire body of monks) was aimed at and this was made possible as alleged by the expulsion of the heretics.

The Missionaries and their Assignments

Having reviewed the part assigned to Asoka in the legend—the purge of non-Theravādins from the Saṅgha and the virtual declaration by him of the genuineness of the Theravāda—let us turn to the missions organised by Moggaliputta Tissa to carry Buddhism in this form to the *Bahujana* in the south of Asoka's empire and outside. The missions were in nine groups, assigned to nine different regions and they tally perfectly in the different sources.

1. *Dīpavaṁsa* version (Ch. VIII)—

(i) Majjhantika and four others to the Gandhara region
(ii) Mahādeva to Mahisamandala
(iii) Rakkhita to a region not named
(iv) Yonaka Dhammarakkhita to Aparantaka
(v) Mahā-Dhammarakkhita to Mahārattha
(vi) Mahā-Rakkhita to Yonaka region
(vii) Majjhima, Sahadeva and Mulaka to Himalayan region
(viii) Sona and Uttara to Suvarṇabhūmi
(ix) Mahindra and four others to Ceylon (Laṅkā)

2. *Mahāvaṁsa* version (Ch. XII)—

(i) Majjhantika to Kashmir and Gandhara
(ii) Mahādeva to Mahisamandala
(iii) Rakkhita to Vanavāsa
(iv) Yoñaka Dhammarakkhita to Aparanta
(v) Mahā-Rakkhita to Yona country
(vi) Mahā-Dhammarakkhita to Mahārattha
(vii) Sona and Uttara to Suvarṇabhūmi
(viii) Majjhima, Sahadeva and Mulaka to Himalayan region
(ix) Mahinda and four others (Itthiya, Uttiya, Sambala and Bhaddaśila) to Ceylon

3. *Samantapāsādikā* version—

(i) Majjhantika to Kashmir and Gandhara
(ii) Mahādeva to Mahasamandala
(iii) Rakkhita to Vanavāsa
(iv) Yonaka Dhammarakkhita to Aparanta
(v) Mahā-Dhammarakkhita to Mahārattha
(vi) Mahā-Rakkhita to Yona country
(vii) Majjhima to Himalayan country
(viii) Sona and Uttara to Suvaṇṇabhūmi
(ix) Mahinda and four others (Itthiya, Uttiya, Sambala and Bhaddaśila) to Ceylon.

The tradition of Tissa's missionaries must have come down to after-generations as a genuine historical tradition. Their names were not regarded as figments of fancy. It was in the belief that these men, sainted now, had once lived and preached the religion that people of after times set out to collect their supposed body-relics and tried to envisage their physiognomy.

At Sanchi (in India) a *stūpa* (sacred mound) yielded on excavation two caskets of body-relics, probably deposited there in the 1st or the 2nd century, B.C. On these appear the names of Majjhima and two of his associates, viz., Kassapagota and Dundubhissara (out of four named in the *Samantapāsādikā* as having accompanied him on the mission, viz., Kassapagota, Alakadeva, Dundubhissara and Sahadeva).

At Anurādhapura (in Ceylon), a king named Kūtakaṇṇa, a successor of Devānampiya Tissa, in whose reign the missionaries had arrived in Ceylon, set up their images with an epigraph for recognition, about 200 years after the event.[9]

The Geographical Names

The countries to which the missions are said to have been assigned were both within the limits of Asoka's Indian empire and outside. They are all vaguely described by Buddhaghosa as 'Border Tracts' (*Paccantima Janapada*).

But this is not accurate. Some of the regions were within Asoka's empire; others far from its borders. The Yona country, the Himalayan country and the Aparanta ('Border country')[10] are purely descriptive names,

---

[9] Ambatthala Inscription discovered at Mahintale (in Brahmi script and in the old Sinhalese language). See Paranavitana's *Sigiri Graffiti* (Oxford University Press, 1956), pp. XLVII and LXV, where he assigns the inscription to King Kutakanna Abhaya (43-21 B.C.).

[10] The word 'Aparanta' occurs in Asoka's Rock Edict No. 5 where the context indicates that it means 'people of the borders'. In after use, it was sought to be applied to some definite regions on the west coast of India.

supplemented by the proper names, viz. Mahārattha, Mahisamandala and Vanavāsa. These last were regions within India. The first of the three stands for modern Maharashtra; the second either for Mysore or for the ancient Mahīsmatī (in the Madhya-Pradesh), and the third for a district of North Kanara,[11] all in southern India, across the Vindhya hill-range.

Two missions are said to have been assigned outside India—one to Ceylon and the other to Suvaṇṇabhūmi. Ceylon is well-known in the ancient and modern geography of Asia, but the other has completely disappeared from it. It literally means the 'Land of gold' to which Sona and Uttara were deputed.

Scholars have long debated about the location and identification of Suvarṇabhūmi. The name occurs not only in Indian literature, but also in Greek, Latin, Arabic and Chinese. Dr. Majumdar, on a detailed survey of the uses of the term in all these contexts, comes to the following tentative conclusions:[12]

"*Suvarṇabhūmi* (Gold-land) and *Suvarṇadvīpa* (Gold-island), names of oversea countries, were familiar to the Indians from a very early period. They occur in the old popular stories such as have been preserved in the *Jātakas*, *Kathākośa* and *Brihatkathā*, as well as in more serious literary works, mainly Buddhist",—and in all these references to Suvarṇabhūmi, its accessibility from India by a sea-voyage is indicated. In the compound name, Suvarṇabhūmi, the term 'bhūmi' has the general sense of land or territory, without any allusion to its configuration,—whether island, peninsula or inland territory. Both the names, *Suvarṇabhūmi* and *Suvarṇadvīpa*, were geographical designations which are applicable to Burma, Malay Peninsula and Malayan Archipelago (modern Indonesia).[13]

In Burmese and Siamese Buddhist legends, Sona and Uttara are claimed to have been the pioneers of Buddhism in these countries and, as the traditional field of their mission was *Suvaṇṇabhūmi*, the Buddhists of Burma and Siam point to certain definite localities within their regional borders as representing the Suvarṇabhūmi of ancient tradition.. These legends are to the following effect.

When Anawrahta, the first Buddhist ruler of Burma, annexed Lower Burma (known later as *Ramaṇṇa-deśa*, populated by the Mons) round the middle of the 11th century, he found Buddhism thriving in its capital city, Thaton. He brought from there to his own capital, Pagan, some fragments of Theravāda scripture along with a large party of Mon monks. This Mon seat of Buddhism in Lower Burma came to be regarded by the Burmese as

[11] See B. C. Law's *Historical Geography of Ancient India*, pp. 171-172 and 199.
[12] See R. C. Majumdar's *Suvarnadvipa*, Part I, p. 37.
[13] *Ibid*, p. 43.

Suvaṇṇabhūmi and is recorded as such in the Burmese chronicle. "Seeing that the account of the arrival of the missionary elders, Sona and Uttara, in the reign of Jotakuma Siridhammāsoka, grandson of King Upadeva, (ancient king of Thaton, mentioned in the *Thaton Chronicle*), agrees with the statement in the books that the elders Sona and Uttara were sent on mission to Suvaṇṇabhūmi, only Thaton should be understood by Suvarṇabhūmi".[14]

Sona and Uttara are also claimed as the first apostles of Buddhism in their country by the Siamese. Different localities in Siam are believed to represent the venue of their missionary activities.

The site of the present city of Prapatom, according to a local legend, was covered in ancient times by another, no longer existing, called Chaisuri or Sirichai and that ancient city is said to have been visited by Sona and Uttara in Siam. Also the town of Sapunburi had the ancient name of U-tong which is the Siamese equivalent of Suvaṇṇabhūmi. The name Subaṇṇabhūmi occurs also in the stele of Rama Khamheng as of a place lying to the east of U-tong.

Some scholars suggest that Suvaṇṇabhūmi was a name given anciently to an extensive land-block of East Asia extending from Burma to Indonesia and that the name now survives only in modern Sapunburi (ancient U-tong) of Siam.

The strangest version, however, of the geographical names is found in a Pali work *Sāsanavaṁsa*, purporting to be a 'history of the Buddhist religion' written by a Burmese monk named Paññaswamī of Maun Daung, in 1861. Ḥis 'history' is meant to be a comprehensive account of the spread and development of Buddhism in 'nine places' (that being the traditional number of missions), viz., Siṁhala, Suvaṇṇabhūmi, Yonaka country, Vanavāsa, Aparanta, Kashmir and Gandhara, Mahiṁsaka (Mahisamandala?), Mahārattha and China. He leaves out the 'Himalayan country' and, adding China, makes up the total number of nine. The tradition of Tissa's missions is of course taken as the starting-point of his 'history'.

The geographical names are strangely misconceived and misapplied by Paññaswamī. Mahārattha is said to lie near the Siyama (Siam) country where Dhammarakkhita preached the doctrine and made them 'drink the essence of deathlessness'; Burma is identified with Aparanta where the elder Yona Rakkhita 'made all the inhabitants of the Mranma country (Burma) do the same'. The realm of Haripunjiya (in northern Siam) is identified with the Yonaka country and Sirikhetta (in Lower Burma) with Vanavāsa (in India).[15]

---

[14] The *Glass Palace Chronicle*, tr. by Tin and Luce, 1960, p. 49.

[15] See *Sasanavamsa* (Ed. by B.C. Law), pp. 54, 59 and 169.

The Appraisal of the Missions in Ceylonese Legends

If we accept the tradition of the 'nine missions', it is still permissible to doubt whether they ever reached the countries of their assignment. We can be certain only about the mission to Ceylon. Sona and Uttara figure no doubt in the legends of Burma and Siam, but scarcely more than as lay figures. About their missionary activities, nothing in particular is said in the legends.

In the 3rd century B.C., Buddhism would have had a poor chance to grow in the regions to which the missions are said to have been sent. Except in Ceylon where there was a large mass of immigrants from India, they had no contact with Indian thought or philosophy. Besides, there was little chance of exchange between the missionaries and the local people for lack of a common linguistic medium. There were insuperable difficulties of other kinds too. For one thing, the world-view presented by Buddhism must have been more or less unintelligible to those unfamiliar with Indian ways of thought. The first lessons in Buddhism would be wasted on them.

The glowing accounts, therefore, in the Ceylonese chronicles of the achievements of these missions in different regions,—of thousands of people converted and hundreds ordained,—may be bypassed as fanciful.

The Ceylonese tradition has it that all Tissa's missionaries gave to people readings from the *Suttas* (Holy Legends), but we are told in particular of the method employed by Mahinda in Ceylon.

Many of the *Suttas*, of which the Theravāda canon is made up, must have been composed earlier and in Asoka's time. From the report in the Ceylonese chronicles, it appears that Mahinda while preaching would select a *Sutta* and base a sermon on its text. The first *Sutta* he preached to his Ceylonese audience (among whom King Devānampiya Tissa was present) was the *Cūla-hatthipadopama Sūtta*. It is *Sutta* No. 27 of the *Majjhima Nikāya*. It contains the parable of blind men trying to guess the shape and size of an elephant's leg. Just as it would be impossible for them to make a right guess without actually touching the animal's leg, so the greatness of the Buddha's *dhamma* would never be realised without actually practising it. The appropriateness of the *Sutta* to the occasion is unmistakable. It was a call for the adoption of the religion in the practice of life, not simply to understand it in theory.

From the tradition of Mahinda's preaching method, it is supposed by the Ceylonese chroniclers that it must have been the typical method followed by all the missionaries of Tissa. In naming the missionaries, they also specify the particular *Sutta* preached individually by them in different countries.

The Historicity of the Legend

How far does this legend of the Nine Missions carry us in our enquiries about the first appearance of Buddhism in the East Asian world?

It is hardly possible to deny that in the reign of Asoka there was a missionary movement among Buddhists in India and that Buddhism reached Ceylon in consequence. Whatever the part played by Asoka and whatever the antecedent circumstances as alleged, it is a highly plausible supposition that, after Asoka's conversion, the Buddhist religion gained a certain prestige and superior status among the many faiths and creeds current in India in his time.[16] To leaders of the Buddhist community in India like Moggaliputta Tissa, it must have seemed an anomaly, something not in the fitness of things, that while the empire should be so vast, the religion professed by the emperor was so small in its incidence, existing only in parts of northern India. The emperor's religion should be, to their thinking, the paramount religion of the empire. The idea must have given a fillip to the desire for expansion of Buddhism all over India and its further expansion even outside to accessible regions and kingdoms.

To implement this desire and take it to fulfilment, monks would not be lacking,—those prepared to brave all hazards and hardships and venture into parts of the country difficult to reach and beyond them to countries across the seas. It was the monks' allotted task to bring the *Bahujana* within the fold of the religion. Perhaps in the time of Asoka when Buddhism had received a new access of vigour under a Buddhist emperor, there were monks who actually took the holy burden on themselves. Memories of some of them survived; people in after-ages sought for their sacred body-relics, which they thought fit to enshrine in a Stūpa (holy mound). The three names on the casket-relics discovered at Sanchi (Stūpa II) occur also among Tissa's missionaries, though the legend must have been made up several centuries after the enshrinement, probably in the 2nd century, B.C.

But what is doubtful is whether these missionaries actually formed organised bands under Tissa and were assigned to specified regions for their proselytising activities, as told in the legend. This seems somewhat questionable as there happens to be no tradition in Buddhism of this kind of organised preaching, that is, by appointed bands of missionaries, with areas assigned for each band. The Founder's injunction to preach and proselytise was based on individual efforts ("Let not two of you go together"), nor is there any direction in the canon about joint and organised missionary effort. The idea of such 'missionary' propagation never took root in Buddhism, and, although in its later history, we hear of 'parties' of

[16] See the Rupnath, Maski, Gujarra and other edicts in which divers creeds and sects current in India in Asoka's time are referred to.

monks going from Ceylon or some other seat of Buddhism to another country, their object always was to take part in the decision of some ecclesiastic matter which concerned the *Saṅgha* (monk-body) only. Though a proselytising religion, Buddhism is not, in the same sense as Christianity is, a "missionary" one. The legendary story of the organising of nine missions by Tissa must therefore be rather suspect. But a movement with the specific object of spreading the religion within the country and abroad in the reign of Asoka is circumstantially believable. The movement found missionary workers but its schematisation, as described in the legend, is hardly as credible.

The introduction of Buddhism into the south-east Asian countries by some of Tissa's missionaries seems also to lack historical evidence except in the case of Ceylon. In the legend, the countries outside India except Ceylon are indicated only by descriptive names. The legends of Sona and Uttara in Burma and Siam seem to have been borrowed from the stock-legend of Theravāda provenance to give a faked antiquity to Buddhism in these countries.

But among the missionaries of the legend, Mahinda, who took Buddhism to Ceylon, stands out as an undoubtedly historical figure. The ancient chronicles of the country describe in detail his ministrations and activities. His advent at Mahintale and the respectful support he received from the Ceylonese king, who had previous diplomatic relations with Emperor Asoka and was advised by the Indian emperor to propagate Buddhism in his kingdom, is a fixed peg on which hangs the whole after-history of Buddhism in the island.

Chapter III

CEYLON

CEYLON'S national chronicle, the *Mahāvaṁsa*, dilates on the long prehistory and proto-history of the island. But its authentic historical era begins in the reign of Devānaṁpiya Tissa (247-207 B. C.) who succeeded to the throne of his father Mutasiva, the last of the line of Ceylon's legendary kings. The kings before Tissa are shadowy figures: they all belong to the realm of myth, legend and folklore.

The *Dīpavaṁsa* and the *Mahāvaṁsa* with its continuation known as the *Cūlavaṁsa*, along with amplifications and additional data contained in subsidiary commentarial literature, represent the indigenous chronicles of Ceylon. The writers of these chronicles and their commentaries were monks who were not clear-eyed historians. They write from their own angle, and to them the chequered story of Buddhism is the core of the island's history. In telling the story, they also bring into play prejudices and prepossessions bred in their cloisters.

The chronicles, left off and re-started at different points, have never been wholly discontinued, and even after the last work composed in the 18th century in the reign of Rājasiṁha, Ceylonese scholars have tried to bring these chronicles up to modern times.[1]

The point at which authentic history begins in these source-books is the arrival from India of one of Moggaliputta Tissa's missions, headed by Mahinda. The King was perhaps expecting its arrival. So he received the mission ceremonially at Mahintale, an upland eight miles east of the capital Anurādhapura. Cetiyagiri was its ancient name: it had been so named when Buddhism spread in the island, after Asoka's great Stūpa at Sanchi anciently known as Cetiyagiri.

Political Background of the Mission

The reason why the mission was expected was that there had been some previous negotiations about certain matters of state between the Ceylonese king and the Indian emperor. About the status of the 'King of Ceylon' there had been some vagueness. Tissa wanted to clear it up once for all and had, for that purpose, approached Asoka through his envoys for advice and guidance.

1 *Mahavamsa, the Third Part* by Yagirala Pannananda, Colombo, 1935 and *Dipavamsa, the Second Part* by Ahungalle Vimalakirti, Colombo, 1939.

By right of inheritance Tissa had risen from a *Gāmaṇi* (local chief) of the southern province of Rohana to the royal throne of Anurādhapura, but even on elevation to the throne, his old title Gāmaṇi was not changed and his royal prerogative was indicated only by the old Ceylonese custom of a new *jasthi* (rod) being handed over to him as symbolical of his penal authority and power. Tissa wanted his sovereign status to be consecrated by a proper coronation ceremony as the custom was in India.

The emperors of the Maurya dynasty had the honorific designation *Devānampiya* ('Beloved of the gods', equivalent to 'His Majesty') and ascended the throne after a ceremony of coronation. Tissa, wishful to introduce the Indian custom into Ceylon,—and also perhaps to cultivate friendly relations with the Indian emperor, —had sent a mission with costly presents to Asoka's capital Pātaliputra. The envoys were welcomed and some of them were invested with titles of honour and dignity.[2]

Through the envoys, Asoka advised the Ceylonese king to hold a proper coronation ceremony and sent him the articles used at a king's coronation in India. As regards the overseas kingdom's relations with his empire, he touched upon his state-policy of *Dhamma-vijaya* (conquest through Dhamma), telling the envoys that it was 'the *dhamma* of the Sākyaputta' that he had adopted and his relations therefore with other states would be regulated by that state-policy. His message to the Ceylonese king was: "I have taken refuge in the Buddha, the Dhamma and the Saṅgha. I have declared myself a lay disciple in the religion of the Sākyaputta (vide Minor Rock Edict, No. 1; A.C. Sen's *Asoka's Edicts*, pp. 52-53). Seek then, even thou, the best of men, refuge in these three best of gems (*Triratna*—Buddha, Dhamma and Saṅgha), converting thy mind with believing heart". The suggestion was that the desired *entente cordiale* could be established through adoption by Ceylon of 'the religion of the Sākyaputta'.

It was some time after this diplomatic exchange that the mission assigned to Ceylon by Tissa consisting of Itthiya, Uttiya, Bhaddaśila and Sambala with Mahinda as leader arrived in the island.

Consequences followed: the king, dropping the humble title of *Gāmaṇi*, adopted the dignified Maurya title of *Devānaṁpiya*; he had a regular coronation, and embraced the religion recommended by the Indian emperor. The title *Devānaṁpiya* was kept up by the kings of Ceylon till the middle of the 6th century, A.D.[3] The conversion of the Ceylonese to Buddhism went on with vigour under Mahinda's guidance.

In these proceedings on the part of the king, it is difficult to assess how

---

[2] See *History of Ceylon*, vol. I, Pt. 1 (Ceylon University Press, Colombo, 1959), pp. 133-135.

[3] See Rahula's *History of Buddhism in Ceylon* (Gunasena and Co., Colombo, 1956), p. 28.

much was prompted by diplomatic and political considerations and how much by pure religious zeal, but the conversion of Ceylon must have been hailed by the Indian emperor as a signal instance of *Dhammavijaya* to the empire's south (among the Colas and Pandyas up to Tammapanni, Ceylon).[4]

Mahinda's Missionary Activities

The existence of Buddhists in Ceylon before Mahinda's appearance on the scene is not inherently improbable. In the population there was a large number of Indian immigrants, both before and after the arrival of Mahinda, mostly from the lands of the Colas and Pandyas in south India. Buddhism was presumably not unknown in Ceylon. But under Mahinda's initiative and guidance mass conversions took place.

Not only did the faith spread among the people, the capital city itself was so altered in lay-out and ensemble as to be a Buddhist city in all appearance, with an array of temples, monasteries and assembly-halls within sanctified boundaries called *Sīmā*. All the structural innovations and alterations were planned by Mahinda and readily carried out by the king.

The activities recorded in the chronicles were ably seconded by a distinguished nun from India, supposed to be a daughter of emperor Asoka, who arrived later with a company of nun-followers. She is credited with having brought from India a sapling of the Bodhi Tree of Gaya and planted it at Anurādhapura. The nun sorority, founded by Saṅghamittā, disappeared from Ceylonese Buddhism only in the 12th century, A.D.[5] but the Bodhi sapling she planted survives as a great many-branched banyan tree and receives worship to this day at Anurādhapura as the centre of an annual religious festival.

The *Mahāvaṁsa*, and also the *Dīpavaṁsa* to some extent, describe the day-to-day activities of Mahinda, specifying the sacred texts he used to base his sermons on, the reactions of the audience, the mass conversions that followed the sermon, etc. The historical value of these details is questionable, though the memories of men were more retentive before writing was invented to aid memory. But they certainly call up a general picture of Mahinda's work and achievements in Ceylon.

They seem to have been guided by two correlated aims—first to make Buddhism not only a popular but a 'national' religion in Ceylon, and

---

[4] See Rock Edict, No. 13—— A.C. Sen's *Asoka's Edicts*, p. 102. Mookerji is of opinion that the edict could not be a reference to Ceylon's conversion to Buddhism, as it was earlier than Mahinda's mission. See Mookerji's *Asoka*, p. 36.

[5] See *The Polannaruva Period* (Special Issue of the *Ceylon Historical Journal*, 2nd Ed. 1958) p. 124.

secondly, to establish it as the religion of the State, a desideratum hinted at by Asoka in his talks with Tissa's envoys.

It seems from a legend recorded in the *Samantapāsādikā*, which gives a traditional history of Buddhist development in Ceylon, that Mahinda was not satisfied even when he found all people of Ceylon eagerly accepting the Buddhist faith. He felt there was something wanting yet: it was a faith that had come to the Ceylonese from a foreign source and needed to be naturalised on the soil. When asked by Tissa whether he thought that the *Dhamma* had been well-established in the country, he replied that it had been established no doubt, but its roots did not go deep. It could be deep-rooted only when 'a son born in the island of Tambapanni became a monk here (i.e., in the capital city of Anurādhapura), studied the Vinaya here and recited it here'. If we can rely on this legend, Mahinda's idea undoubtedly was that Buddhism in Ceylon, to be deep-rooted, must become *Ceylonese* Buddhism. So it eventually became and remained so through all the centuries.

The acceptance of Buddhism by the king and the people and the replanning of Anurādhapura as a city sacred to Buddhism with amenities provided for the holding of ecclesiastical assemblies by monks virtually made Buddhism the state-religion though without any formal edict or proclamation.

Mahinda: Maker of Buddhist Ceylon

Prior to Mahinda's arrival, Ceylon had neither a *Saṅgha* (monk community) nor a monastery (*Āvāsa*). It is said that when he and his companions first came to Anurādhapura, they were accommodated in caves on a hill-side,—a cave being one of the five *lenas* (approved dwellings for monks).[6] It was hardly suitable for community purposes,—for performance of the 'acts of the Saṅgha' (*Saṅghakamma*), which required the bringing together of all members of the *Saṅgha* at one place.

The king met this felt need by donating a spacious garden, called Mahāmeghavana (the wood of great clouds), to the south of Anurādhapura, for construction of monasteries therein. The site was soon covered with a cluster of them. When the main building was being raised, an earthquake is reported to have taken place, as though to mark an event of momentous importance, the first beginning of Ceylon's long and eventful ecclesiastical history. "In the most excellent island of Lankā, this was the first monastery", reports the *Dīpavaṁsa*.[7]

---

[6] See Cullavagga, VI, 1, 2.

[7] *Dipavamsa*, 13. 36——
Imam Pathamaṃ viharam Lankadipe varuttame sasanaruhanatiya pathamam pathavikampanam ("In the most excellent island of Lanka, this was the first monastery. For the growth of the religion, there was the first shaking of the earth" —B.C. Law's translation.)

It came to be known as the *Mahāvihāra* ('Great Monastery'). Here settled the first Saṅgha of Ceylon, and into its hands passed the direction and administration of the new State-religion.

Devānampiya Tissa predeceased Mahinda who died in 192 B.C. at Mahintale where he had been spending the *vassa* (rain-retreat). It was eight years after the coronation of the king's successor Uttiya. Mahinda died at the age of 60, having come to Ceylon in his early thirties, and had a befitting funeral.

Long after Mahinda, founder of the Mahāvihāra, and king Tissa, its donor and builder, had passed away, the monk-community of this foundation acquired such authority and prestige that it was entrusted with the performance of the king's coronation ceremony. This gave it the consequential right to decide, in a case of disputed succession, who the rightful sovereign was. Its approval or disapproval of the king's administrative measures was supposed to articulate the voice of the people and had considerable effect on the determination of state-policies in times both of peace and of war. It pulled its weight in settling the question of accession when there were rival claimants to the throne. It became a principle of the constitution that the king of Ceylon should be a Buddhist and his accession should have the approval of the *Mahāsaṅgha*, i.e., the monk-community of the Mahāvihāra. Throughout the ancient period of Ceylon's history, as long as the capital was at Anurādhapura, the Mahāsaṅgha resident at the Mahāvihāra enjoyed these privileges. When a king went wrong it could flout him with the act of 'turning down the bowl'[8] as was done once in the case of Dathopatissa II (650-658 A.D.). The king, on the other hand, had a royal prerogative in respect of the monk-community: he could perform a ceremony called *Sodhana* (Purification) on the monastic site and in accordance with the Vinaya rules, and unfrock monks who were heretics or unworthy of the robe. This prerogative was exercised several times by the kings of Ceylon.

In short, since Tissa had raised Buddhism to a State-religion, it became gradually a power in the land to which the king's secular power had to bow its head. Towards the end of the Anurādhapura period in the 10th century A.D., Mahinda IV was for a space of years on the throne of Ceylon. He declared in an epigraph the constitutional practice that had developed between the State and the Church: "The kings of Lankā who are *Bodhisattas* are to serve and attend on the Mahāsaṅgha on the very day that they celebrate the coronation festival after attaining to the dignity of kingship. It

[8] It means refusal to accept alms. It is an act sanctioned by the Vinaya rules (vide *Cullavagga*, v. 20, 6-7) to express monks' disapproval of a householder's character or conduct.

is bestowed by the Mahāsaṅgha for the purpose of defending the bowl and the robe".[9]

For considerably over a millennium, the Mahāvihāra functioned at the capital city of Ceylon. Its prestige stood so high in Buddhist countries that monks from the Mahāvihāra, who were presumed to represent the true line of succession from the first masters, were sought after in Burma and Siam as the most efficient instructors of the religion.

But its long history was full of vicissitudes.

The Māhāvihara-Abhyagiri Dispute

From 43 B.C. to 17 B.C., the Anurādhapura throne was occupied by Tamil rulers.

The Tamils from India were an unassimilated part of the Ceylonese population. They were fanatical in their Hindu faith and tried to demolish all the institutions of Buddhism. They not only demolished the *vihāras* (monasteries), but reduced the country by their misrule to such a condition of famine that people were driven by hunger to cannibalism. They even fed upon the corpses of dead monks. Chaos prevailed, and it was after a dozen years of tough and strenuous struggle (B.C. 29-B.C. 17) that king Vaṭṭagāminī Abhaya could recover the throne from the usurpers. The Mahāvihāra at Anurādhapura was deserted during this period, and the new king, on coming to the throne, built a new monastery which was called after him *Abhayagiri Vihāra*. On restoration of peaceful conditions under his rule, the abandoned Mahāvihāra was repopulated. The king dedicated the new Abhayagiri Vihāra to a *thera* (venerable old monk) named Mahātissa.

Mahātissa had helped the king during his years of struggle and had on one occasion brought about a reconciliation between the king and some of his disaffected generals. Mahātissa seems to have been more a man of action than a pious monk: perhaps he was not too strait-laced in the observance of the Vinaya. His abbotship of Abhayagiri was resented by the Mahāvihāra monks and they carried out against him the 'act of *ukkhepanīya*' which was tantamount to suspension from the Order.[10] The offence alleged against him was that of mixing too freely with lay people.

One of his disciples, who had the nickname of 'Big-bearded Tissa' sided with his master, and the same body of monks expelled Tissa too by the *ukkhepanīya* act. He left the Mahāvihāra with a large following and settled permanently at the new monastery of Abhayagiri.

---

[9] See Rahula's *History of Buddhism in Ceylon* p. 70. It occurs in the Jetavana Slab Inscription of Mahinda IV.

[10] See Cullavagga, 1, 25 ff. The sentence has to be proclaimed at all the *avasas* (monk settlements).

Mahātissa, the abbot of Abhayagiri, though a Theravādin, was perhaps not strictly orthodox in his religious persuasion. To the monk-community of Abhayagiri he imparted a tone of liberalism in religion, an attitude of open-mindedness, which was repugnant to the hide-bound orthodoxy of the Mahāvihāra monks. They were steadfast in the religion with which the Mahāvihāra had started and would brook no change. The monks of Abhayagiri who were not so orthodox were regarded by them as representing a different sect of Buddhism and were named by them the 'sect Dhammaruchi' or called 'Vajjiputtakas' after the name of the first secessionists from the Theravāda in Buddhist history. They kept up contact with the sectarian developments in India and welcomed the concepts and doctrines of Mahāyānism which were known in Ceylon as *Vaitulya-vāda*. They studied both the Theravāda and the Mahāyāna, while at the Mahāvihāra the study of the Theravāda alone was permissible.

The subsequent ecclesiastical history of Ceylon is concerned mainly with the rivalry between the two establishments. The episodes of it are described in a Pali work entitled *Nikāya-saṁgraha* written towards the end of the 14th century. The kings, for different reasons, patronised one or the other of the two establishments and the one enjoying royal favour flourished for a time.

The Buddhist *sāsana* (regime) had become a state-department; both Mahāvihāra and Abhayagiri had permanent official staffs to look after their maintenance; the king had the prerogative of *Sodhana*, i.e., the weeding out of the monk community of those who were heretics or 'impure' and, during the Anurādhapura period, the prerogative was exercised several times from the 3rd century on by Vohārika Tissa (269-291), Goṭhābhya (309-322), Mogallāna I (496-513), Moggallāna III (513-522), Silāmeghavaṅṅa (617-626), Aggabodhi VII (766-772) and lastly Sena II (853-887). The *Sodhana* used to be disguised in the form of a *Saṅghakamma* (Act of the Saṅgha), but the monks carried out only the king's orders. The test of 'purity' was adherence to the Theravāda, the approved form of the State-religion. Sometimes bitter persecution followed a *Sodhana*. Thus after a *Sodhana* by Goṭhābhaya, sixty heretics were marked with a brand and banished from Ceylon. The author of *Samaya-saṁgraha*, from whom we have this story, belonged to the Mahāvihāra and he eulogises the king as one who has "glorified the Order of the Buddha".

The brandished and banished monks were of Abhayagiri. They left Ceylon in a body and took asylum in a monastery called Kaveripattana in the Cola Kingdom in South India.

Among the Ceylonese monks at Kaveripattana was one who had a devoted disciple living with him in the same monastery. The disciple was Saṅghamitta. One day when his master had stripped himself for a bath, he saw brand-marks on his body and came to know how they had been caused. He took a solemn oath to wreak vengeance on the Mahāvihāra and see it destroyed. With this resolve in mind, he crossed over to Ceylon from Kaveripattana. Goṭhābhaya was still on the throne at Anurādhapura.

He met king Goṭhabhaya and managed by wily means to ingratiate himself with the king and was appointed tutor to the king's two sons. The elder prince did not receive the teachings favourably and when he succeeded to the throne after the king's death, Saṅghamitta disappeared from Ceylon. But when the other prince Mahāsena, who was more favourable to him, acceded, he appeared again and became the stoutest champion of Mahāyanism in Ceylon. Under his influence Mahāsena's relations with the Mahāvihāra steadily deteriorated and the king stopped by an ordinance the giving of alms to the Mahāvihāra monks. For nine years the monastery was deserted and parts of its architecture were broken off and applied to decorate the rival Abhayagiri monastery. The Mahāvihāra site itself was sown with beans. At the same time the king, over-riding opposition from the Mahāvihāra monks, built a huge monastery adjacent to the Jetavana Stūpa and installed in the new monastery as abbot a monk named Tissa who belonged to an independent sect named Sāgaliya. Against him too the Mahāvihāra monks carried out an *ukkhepanīya* act. So the orthodox sect of the Mahāvihāra called the *Mahāsaṅgha*, the heterodox Abhayagiri and the independent Sāgaliya sects were the three divisions of the Ceylonese monk-community till the end of Anurādhapura period. Among them there was no accord.

The Cola Devastation

The Anurādhapura period was a whole age during which Buddhism in Ceylon passed from its dawn to its noon. Firmly planted in the island, functioning as a State-religion, though unproclaimed as such, adopted in the country's constitutional frame, the only shakings it had received so far were from the bitter long-drawn rivalries between Mahāvihāra and Abhayagiri. It was a ding-dong battle over centuries between the forces of orthodoxy and of heterodoxy, but it did not affect the fortune of Buddhism itself. But the violence and disaster, which closed this age, spanning about 13 centuries, were a shattering blow, only short of a death-blow, to Buddhism in Ceylon.

Colas from the Indian mainland invaded Ceylon and took the reigning king Mahinda V captive in 1017. These Colas professed Brahmanical faith and had scant respect for Buddhism and its symbols and institutions.

The chronicle *Cūlavaṁsa* contains lurid descriptions of the violence perpetrated on Buddhism by the Colas: "In the three fraternities (i.e., in the three establishments of the three sects, the Mahāvihāra, the Abhayagiri and the Jetavana) and in all Lankā, they broke open the relic-chambers and carried away many costly images of gold, and while they violently destroyed here and there (i.e., in different parts of the area of their occupation) all the monasteries. Like the blood-sucking *Yakkhas*, they took all the treasures of Lankā for themselves".[11] The area under Cola conquest is indicated thus: "With Pulatthinagara as base, the Colas held sway over Rājaraṭṭha as far as the locality known as Rakkhapāsāṇakanṭha".

To the south of this area was the province of Rohaṇa. The Cola sway did not extend over it. Dethroned kings, deposed chiefs and princes with no prospects, disaffected military officers, adventurous careerists, gravitating to Rohaṇa, made it a formidable pocket of resistance to Cola rule. Vijayabāhu, at the spear head of the resistance movement, was of Rohaṇa: it was then the 'home of lost causes and impossible loyalties'.

The Cola conquerors set up the seat of their government at Polonnaruva under the changed name of Jananāthapura. They made the conquered portion of the island a province of the Cola empire and ruled over it from India. The loot and revenues gathered from Ceylon were sent from the island to their capital in India to keep up the magnificence of South Indian Hindu temples.

The Cola power in Ceylon, however, was dependent on support from India. The Ceylonese were in revolt and the Cola army in their clashes with them met with two major reverses. When the Cola king in India, Kullattunga Cola (1070-1122) heard of these defeats, he decided to abandon the island and made no further attempt to reconquer it. The Colas had ruled over the greater part of Ceylon for 77 years and their last inscription is dated in 1070. In 1073 Vijayabāhu, leader of national resistance to Cola rule, came to the throne and with his enthronement, Buddhism in Ceylon came to life once again.

Vijayabāhu : His romantic career and Rehabilitation of the Saṅgha

Round the early life of Vijayabāhu rests a halo of romance.

When he brought the resistance movement to a successful close, he was hailed as Ceylon's rightful king, It was not from the old line of the Anurādhapura kings, however, that he could trace his descent. The line had in fact been extinct with the death of Vikkamabāhu (between 1037 and 1041), son of Mahinda V. But Moggallāna, Vijayabāhu's father, was a descendant in a collateral line from Meghavaṇṇa who had been king at Anurādhapura in 684 A.D. and whose dynasty had lasted for three centuries. It is not definitely known whether Moggallāna ever wore the crown, but his son Prince Kitti, whatever his right by descent to the throne, was accepted

[11] *Culavamsa*, 55. 20.

universally as the rightful king when, after withdrawal of Cola rule, he occupied the throne as Vijayabāhu.

For nearly eight decades, the country had been in a turmoil with the royal family dispersed and in hiding. Warfare of the guerrilla kind had been on between the alien conquerors on one side and the people and chieftains of Rohaṇa on the other. About 1050, an army chieftain named Loka or Lokissara took over the government of Rohaṇa. Moggallāna's son Prince Kitti was then growing up to adolescence amid the hills and jungles of Rohaṇa, where the crownless king Moggallāna and his family were in hiding. They went in constant fear of life though under the protection of one Buddharāja.

Buddharāja had set up his own armed camp at the foot of the Malaya mountain in the central uplands of Ceylon and collected a following. Prince Kitti joined Buddharāja's party and the chronicle (*Cūlavaṁsa*) says that he distinguished himself in a battle even at the age of 14. When he came to the throne as Vijayabāhu, he remembered wistfully the hardships of his early life to which he makes a feeling reference in one of his inscriptions: "At the time we were remaining concealed in a mountain-wilderness........ (Buddharāja) brought us up in our tender age; he nurtured us with the sustenance of (edible) roots and green herbs from the jungle; (he) concealed us from enemies who were prowling about seeking us wherever we went; engaging himself in battle in (this) place and (that) place, (he) secured once again the territory of Rohaṇa and took us out of the mountain wilderness and established us in our own kindgom".[12]

A trial of military strength went on for two years between Loka, Governor of Rohaṇa, and his successor Kassupa on one side and Buddharāja and Kitti on the other. Buddharāja ultimately secured undisputed control over Rohaṇa and Kitti became his successor in his eighteenth year in 1055—1560. "He was now on the threshold of manhood and, though of royal lineage, he had known neither Palace nor Court."[13]

Thereafter the war-toughened soldier, young in years but veteran in action, gave the last push-over to the Cola power which was breaking up already and, after a series of alternate military successes and failures, laid seige to the Cola capital Polonnaruva. It capitulated after a spell of stiff resistance. From there he marched on in triumph to Anurādhapura to be crowned king of all Ceylon.

But what an Anurādhapura met his eager expectant gaze! Pillaged and destroyed, with no ringings of temple-bells and chantings of monks, all the old monasteries and stūpas laid in ruins, it was but a skeleton of the

---

[12] For this inscription of Vijayabahu, see *Epigraphia Zeylanica*, vol. V, pp. 24-25.

[13] *History of Ceylon*, vol. II, p. 423.

ancient holy city. The *vihāras* of Ratnavaluka, Jetavana, Mirisaveti and Abhayagiri "were all overgrown with great trees; bears and panthers dwelt there and the ground of the jungle scarcely offered a foothold by reason of heaps of bricks and earth".[14]

Yet king Vijayabāhu, as he was now called, set his heart on having his coronation there. A structure was rapidly erected; the ceremony was somehow gone through, but the Mahāsaṅgha that used to chant their benedictions on the new king at his coronation had ceased to exist. No monks had been ordained at all for decades past, for it had been difficult to collect even five monks whose presence at an ordination was required by the Vinaya rules. The two cherished traditions of the country,—the primacy of Anurādhapura as Ceylon's capital and holy city and the monk-organisation which had played over the centuries such a prominent part in the city's civic as well as religious life,—had gone into complete eclipse.

Vijayabāhu retained Polonnaruva, the Cola capital, for the functions of government. It had a strategic importance. "From Polonnaruva the southern province of Rohaṇa was easy of access, and Rohaṇa was always a source of trouble to the Sinhalese kings; it was difficult to control at the best of times, and often the stronghold of rebellious princes and chiefs".[15] It was also the most convenient approach for invaders from the south to the interior and hence the control of Rohaṇa needed Polonnaruva as its base. Anurādhapura also was the city of his soul.

To revive the holy city, the first thing needful was to replenish its *Saṅgha* life, then at its lowest ebb. The rite of ordination itself having been in abeyance for several decades, the monk-community had dwindled, was gone down to the very dregs. Vijayabāhu looked for foreign aid to re-introduce Buddhism. It had by then become nearly extinct in India, but was flourishing in Burma under the rule of the pious Buddhist king Anawrahta (1044-1077).

Burma was known to the Ceylonese by way of commerce. In exchange for the island's raw materials, cargoes of merchandise came to entrepots in Rohaṇa from Burma in Indonesian trading vessels. Vijayabāhu started a cultural intercourse with Burma with a request to Anawrahta to send to Ceylon a batch of monks, who were pious and learned and of recognised standing, from Rāmañña (Lower Burma). "When they arrived in Ceylon, he had them perform repeatedly the necessary ceremonies so that numerous new Sinhalese monks could be admitted to the Order and the Saṅgha become competent in number and learning to resume its position in the religious

[14] *Culavamsa*, 78. 100 ff.

[15] Per Dr. A.L. Basham. See *The Polonnaruva Period* p. 11

life of the people".[16] Hinduism in the meantime had raised its head in Ceylon.

Even in the 7th century, there was a large Tamil element in the population of northern Ceylon. In the succeeding centuries, in consequence of more Tamil invasions, ending with the Cola conquest, from 993 to 1070, it must have naturally very greatly increased. This Tamil element has never been thoroughly assimilated in the island. The Tamils had been staunch in their adherence to Hindu faith; with the Tamil immigrants had come numerous Brāhmanas to act as their priests; they had established *Devalas* (Hindu temples) and introduced Hindu rites and ceremonies of worship to which even the Buddhists of Ceylon were drawn. Popular Buddhism of the island thus received an unmistakable tincture of Hinduism. It is perceptible even today in a Buddhist religious establishment of Ceylon where the worship of the Buddha or of a Bodhisattva is held side by side with that of Skandha or Shiva.

With this new development, however, Vijayabāhu did not interfere nor did he aim at purging the heterodoxies that had crept in the interim into the Buddhist faith. His sole concern was to rehabilitate the *Saṅgha.* But his efforts bore fruit only in the reign of his more illustrious successor Parākkamabāhu.

Stability, unity and good government were still to be established in the state when Vijayabāhu died in 1110-11. The next three decades were full of turmoil. Civil war was on, and, in its intervals, were rampant intrigue, dissension and a state of 'cold war'. The revenues of the three principalities, Rajarāṭṭha, Rohaṇa and Dakkhiṇadesa, sufficed only for their military expenditure. These lean years however, led to a burst of glory, unprecedented and unmatched in the history of Ceylon, when his successor Parākkamabāhu, having defeated rival claimants to the throne and suppressed adventurous chieftains and rebellious rulers, came to the throne in 1153 to hold sovereignty for 36 years of peace.

Parākkamabāhu : His Saṅgha reforms : Revival of Buddhism : Tooth-relic cult

His reign is celebrated in epic style in the *Cūlavaṁsa*, and the hero of the epic figures as a mighty warrior, a firm and able administrator, a liberal patron of arts and letters, a great builder of secular and religious edifices and sundry works of public utility and benefit.

At the same time Parākkamabāhu proceeded bravely to complete the work of Saṅgha rehabilitation, started by his predecessor. The *Cūlavaṁsa* says that when Parākkamabāhu came to the throne, he desired the fulfilment

[16] See *History of Ceylon* vol. II, p. 430.

of four kingly aspirations—to effectuate (i) the happiness of the masses, (ii) the stability of the religion, (iii) the protection of nobility, and (iv) the support of those in want.[17] Of these, the second one was for him the most difficult to achieve.

The *Saṅgha* had to grow again in number and importance since Vijayabāhu had re-established the rite of ordination with the help of the Rāmañña monks sent by Anawrahta. But the *Saṅgha*, to be effective in the service of the state and the people, had also to be reformed and placed on a sounder footing.

The evils Parākkamabāhu found rampant in the *Saṅgha* were, first, the abundance in it of monks who were thoroughly unworthy of the robe; and second, the dissensions between the orthodox monkhood of the Mahāvihāra and heterodox sects both within it and outside. Aiming to remedy these two evils, he convened in *circa* 1165 a synod with a highly learned ecclesiastic Udambaragiri Mahākāssapa to preside over it. It is said that the synod was held in the *Latāmandapa* (The Pavilion of Creepers) where Mahākāssapa brought together the members of the heterodox Dhammaruci, Sāgaliya and Vaitulya sects, and for their edification had the Theravāda canon read to them all night. He afterwards expelled 'miscreants' which means perhaps those who refused to subscribe to the sanctity and authority of the canon.

There is a reference to this synod in one of the inscriptions of Parākkamabāhu. The Vinaya or the regulative laws of the *Saṅgha* seems to have been the main theme of discussion and debate in the synod. The king, to set matters at rest, issued what is called a *Kathikāvata*, a set of disciplinary rules for monks under his own primatur. He had it published in an inscription known as the Gālvihāra inscription.[18] It enjoins on teachers and instructors at a monastery to see that monks under them learn the main rules of monastic discipline, and prohibits monks from going out of monastic bounds except in an emergency and from divulging to outsiders disputes that occur in the monk-community.

These disputes had grown almost into a traditional feature of Saṅgha life in Ceylon. They were not always confined to matters of doctrine and rule, but spilt over to unsavoury personalities, deleterious to the prestige and authority of monkhood. The king, wishing to settle them once for all, took the first step of trying to reconcile factions *within* the Mahāvihāra. But the dissensions between the Mahāvihāra on one hand and the Abhayagiri and the Jetavana on the other remained untouched, for they had stemmed from the Mahāyānic doctrines: and these doctrines had been the *raison d'etre*

---

[17] *Culavamsa*, lxxiii.

[18] See *Epigraphia Zeylanica*, vol. II, No. 41.

of their separate existence. These irreconcilable sects, however, were made to cease to exist as corporations. But certain monk-colleges at Abhayagiri, instead of closing, continued to exist for three to four after-centuries.

The chronicler describes the unity thus achieved as 'mixing of milk and water': "From the days of Bhattagāmiṇi Abhaya, the three fraternities (viz., of Mahāvihāra and Abhayagiri and Sāgaliya) had lost their unity, despite the great efforts made in every way by former kings. But the all-wise ruler (i.e. Parākkamabāhu) achieved the union whereby he had to endure double as much toil as in his efforts for royal dignity. And he made the Order as uniform as milk and water so that it could last in purity for five thousand years".[19] But the 'milk-and-water' uniformity, if it had been really achieved, did not last even for a hundred years, nor, for the matter of that, the 'purity' of the *Saṅgha*, for we find Parākkamabāhu's successor Nissaṅka Malla (1186-1197) undertaking over again the task of his predecessor in purifying and uniting the *Saṅgha*.

Parākkamabāhu was a great builder and he augmented immensely the architectural wealth of Ceylon. He built a large number of temples and *vihāras* of which a list is given in the *Cūlavaṁsa*. Their general architectural style and workmanship are significant, betraying the linkage of the renascent Buddhism of Polonnaruva with the ancient traditions of Anurādhapura. Dr. Paranavitana points out that "it is a natural development, if not a continuation of the Anurādhapura period".[20]

The renascent Buddhism shaped also the literature of the period. It ushered in a spell of intense literary activity in Pali, particularly in Buddhist philosophical analysis. Some assign to it the name of the 'Augustan age of Ceylonese Pali literature'.

The three illustrious kings of Polonnaruva—Vijayabāhu, Parākkamabāhu and Nissaṅkamalla,—had all been protagonists of Buddhism. Anurādhapura and the glory of Buddhism in that holy city were the source of their inspiration and the main-spring of their action.

The growth to unwonted popularity of the old Buddhist 'Tooth-relic cult' of Ceylon was significant of the spirit of the Polonnaruva age.

The question must have haunted the minds of the people of Ceylon when Cola rule spread over Rājaraṭṭha and adjoining parts,—to whom was their loyalty due? The thought took colour from Buddhism; it expressed itself concretely in the 'cult of the Tooth-relic'.

The legendary history of the relic is given in a Pali work (based on an earlier Sinhalese work), entitled *Dāṭhāvaṁsa*, written near the beginning of the 13th century by Rājaguru Dhammakitti. The 'cult of the Tooth-relic'

---

[19] *Culavamsa*, 73. 18.

[20] *The Polonnaruva Period*, p. 74.

was on the ascendent at the time. It is said in this work that this body-relic of the Buddha had been brought into Ceylon in the reign of Kittisiri Meghavaṇṇa (362-369). It became an object of worship and used to be taken in a solemn procession from one great monastery to another with an outburst of popular enthusiasm. Fa-hsien has described a 'Tooth-relic' procession he saw when he was in Ceylon sometime in 411-413. But the Tooth-relic attracted to itself other ideas than that of mere worship and reverence. It grew into a national symbol.

The destiny of kingship in Ceylon was supposed to be bound up with it: the relic was a divine guarantee to the possessor thereof that his ascension to the throne was divinely ordained. Hence the possession of the relic was sharply contested, and the rape and recovery of it from different possessors form many an episode in Ceylon's political history. It was last recovered from Rohaṇa by Parākkamabāhu, and during the Polannaruva period the Festival of the Tooth Relic was an expression of Ceylon's religio-political consciousness. The festival used to be held at the capital with lavish expenditure and high pomp and ceremony. After the capture of Polonnaruva by Māgha (1214-1235) and his notorious assault on Buddhism, the cult of the Tooth-relic seems to have gained a fresh accession of strength in the island.

There is no king of Ceylon now, but to the devout Buddhist the possession of the relic is a guarantee for the future of the race and the religion. Preserved in the Temple of the Tooth at Kandy, it is a magnet that draws Buddhist members of the Ceylonese Parliament to the temple to offer worship to the relic, an act symbolical of self-dedication to the country's service.

After the Cola occupation of 77 years, Buddhism revived in Ceylon, not merely on its ecclesiastical side, but with a large extension of activities,—all inspired by Buddhism,—in literature, both religious and secular, and in the arts. Nationalism found a centre in the cult of the Tooth-relic which linked to Buddhism the kingdom's political destiny.

Māgha's assault on Buddhism: Lean After-centuries

But the Polonnaṛuva period, so great in its achievements, closed with another spell of foreign rule and a fresh assault on Buddhism more disastrous than that of the Colas.

An Indian prince named Māgha from Kalinga (Orissa in India) invaded Ceylon with a huge army, captured Polonnaruva and ruled Ceylon from that capital city for 21 years (1214-1235). He was a sworn enemy of Buddhism and his cruelties to the monks and vandalism on temples, stūpas and vihāras are described in lurid colours in the *Cūlavaṁsa.* The decadence of religious sculpture was remarkable, there being few examples of Buddha-images in stone of post-Polonnaruva times.[21] The *theras* left the monasteries to their fate and led by one Vãcissara, crossed the sea and found refuge in the Cola and Pandya regions of south India. Shattering as the shock was to Ceylonese Buddhism, it did not succeed in crushing its vitality. Still it drained away so much of its strength that never again was it able to rise to the height attained in the Polonnaruva period.

Nearly three centuries of depression followed.

During these centuries, several factors, —the chief being the increase of Tamil immigrants from India,—combined to make Hinduism a rising tide in the Buddhist country. The result was not the submergence of Buddhism but a somewhat strange intermixture in practice and ritual of the two different religions. Neither doctrine nor philosophy was affected on either side, but in temple-worship the intermixture became manifest. A Hindu temple called *Devale* (i.e., Sanskrit— *Devālaya*) and a Buddhist temple called *Vihāra* accommodated indiscriminately images of deities of both religions. In the reign of Parākkamabāhu II a temple was built near Ratnapura which had the curiously composite name *Mahā-samana Devale*, i.e., a *Devālaya* dedicated to the Buddha, the Mahā-samaṇa. The mixed folk-worship had its repercussions also higher up.

"Parākkamabāhu IV built a temple for Vishnu........Aḷagakkonara, when he fortified Kotte, built for its protection four temples dedicated to Hindu deities. Hindu gods began to be worshipped also either in *devales* attached to the Buddhist *vihāras* or in the *vihāras* themselves. In the Laṅkātilaka Vihāra, near Gampola, images of Hindu gods are placed between the inner and outer walls of the building. Sinhalese writers, after paying their homage to the Buddha, the Dhamma and the Saṅgha, begged Hindu gods, such as Brahmā, Shiva and others, for their blessing. The Bodhisattvas *Nata* and *Saman* began to be identified with the Hindu god Rāma and his brother Lakshmaṇa............. The Gadatadeniya Vihāra was built...........with the help of a South Indian architect and has the characteristics of the Vijayanagara (Hindu) style of architecture".[22]

Ceylon lost also its political integrity during these lean centuries. There was no king of Ceylon and no central capital. Round the turn of the 16th century, the island was divided into three kingdoms with their capitals respectively at Kotte, Gampola (afterwards Kandy) and Nallur (near Jaffna). Attached to each of them were several vassal states, each ruled by a *Vanniar* (chieftain) owing allegiance either to the Tamil kingdom of Jaffna in the north or the Sinhalese Kandyan kingdom in the central uplands.

[21] See *History of Ceylon*, vol. II, p. 788.

[22] Per Dr. Mendis. Cited in James Cartman's *Hinduism in Ceylon* (Gunasena and Co., Colombo, 1957), p. 39-40 (slightly abridged).

In this political situation of Ceylon began the impact upon it, lasting over nearly four centuries and a half, of three western powers, the Portuguese (1505-1658), the Dutch (1658-1796) and the British (1796-1947). They knew little of the past Buddhist traditions of Ceylon, but were interested witnesses to the prevalence of that religion on the island. Each power determined its attitude towards it according to its own tradition of dealing with the 'pagan' religion of an oriental people come under its subjection.

Buddhism in 'Ceylon of the Three Kingdoms'

The Portuguese who landed in Ceylon in 1505 could occupy only some coastal regions from where they made forays into the interior. But their claim was tall and they posed as rulers of the country. Fanatical in their Christian zeal, they did all that lay in their power to suppress the 'pagan' religion even to the destruction of images, temples and monasteries. The Dutch, who came after them, were more tolerant and some of the deserted monasteries were repopulated during their regime. The British who followed were committed to their traditional policy of 'laissez faire'. Till the nineties of the last century, Buddhism was just 'carrying on' in Ceylon but it received a fresh spurt of life from a new Sinhalese generation taking up a re-oriented study of its scripture, its history and its doctrines and teachings.

Kandy continued, however, to be under Buddhist Sinhalese rulers till the 'Kandyan Convention' of 1815. The death-knell of Kandyan independence was then rung here by the British rulers of Ceylon.

In 1628, Rajasinha, the youngest son of the king of Kandy, had been formally assigned the Kandyan kingdom as his portion by the Portuguese. Here, in spite of the adverse circumstances, the old *Saṅgha* tradition was alive and the *Cūlavaṁsa* records the attempts of the kings of Kandy to strengthen the *Saṅgha* with the help of monks from Burma and Siam.

It is said that during the reign of Rajasinhe in Kandy (1580-1592) the Saṅgha had so much declined that only a handful of *samaneras* was left in it and they were engaged in lay pursuits and some even had families. Even a chapter of monks could not be collected to hold the rite of ordination. The king, however, got together about ten monks and had *upasampadā* (ordination) conferred on intending Ceylonese monks at a place called Gatambe on the Mahāvali Gangā river. The monks who ministered the rite had to be brought from Rakkhaṅga (Arakan) in Burma. In the reign of the next Kandyan king Vimala Dharma Suriya I, envoys had again to be sent to Rakkhaṅga to bring 33 monks, and an ordination ceremony was held again at the same place, only 120 Sinhalese entering the Order on this occasion. Another Kandyan king, Sri Vijaya Rajasinha sent a fresh party of envoys with a similar mission to Siam but, the Siamese king having died before their arrival, the commission proved abortive. The last

1. *Sigiriya Frescos: Sigiriya art holds pride of place in Ceylonese sculpture.*

2. *The Thuparama Temple at Polannaruva.*

3. *The Taluwil Buddha, Anuradhapura.*

4. *The embellished flight of steps to the ancient Viharas of Anuradhapura, with the guardstones at the sides and the moonstone in the foreground.*

commission sent from Kandy to Siam was by Kirti Sri Rajasinha round the middle of 18th century when the greater part of the maritime provinces of the island were under Dutch power.

Theravāda Buddhism and extant Ceylonese Sects

The form of Buddhism introduced by Mahinda into Ceylon is known by the name of Theravāda. Perhaps the name originated in Ceylon.

It is said to be the earliest form of the religion, settled, shortly after the Buddha's decease, at an assembly at Rājagaha where his disciples recited from memory what they knew of the Founder's teachings. The texts (imparted by word of mouth and preserved in memory) were settled and made definitive by the most venerable and learned monks in the assembly who were known as *theras* (Elders); "By these and other elders numbering five hundred who performed their duties properly, the collection of *Dhamma* and *Vinaya* was made," says the *Dīpavaṁsa*. "It is called the Doctrine of the Elders (Theravāda) because the collection was made by the Elders (Theras)".[23]

Upāli, as the tradition has it, first recited the Vinaya, the rules to be followed by monks in the conduct of life and organisation of the Order. These rules, according to Buddhaghosa, were transmitted by a succession of Teachers (*Ācariya-paraṁparā*), viz., Upāli, Dāsaka, Soṅaka, Siggava and Tissa. Tissa, who was the last in the line of the Vinaya masters, sent Mahinda at the head of the missionaries deputed to Ceylon.

Whatever the historicity of this ancient tradition, it is doubtless that it was Buddhism of this pristine pattern,with its emphasis on monkhood and Vinaya, that was propagated by Mahinda in Ceylon. The Dhamma-Vinaya had already been systematised by the *theras*; the *Saṅgha* was made its repository and the monks were its dispensers to lay people. Hence 'Monastic Buddhism' is an apt name for it.

The fact that the earliest form of Buddhism was a monk-made system which assigned to the *Saṅgha* leadership in the religion is betrayed by the reaction against it which materialised in the rise of the rival school *Mahāsaṅgha*. It was an ancient school of Buddhism, going back perhaps to the 4th century B.C. The meaning of *Saṅgha* is well-known,—it denotes the fraternity of monks. But *Mahāsaṅgha* is a coined expression, a correlative name, meaning a body not conterminous with, but wider than the *Saṅgha*.

The real significance of the name is brought out by the tradition about the origin of the School reported by Hsüan-tsang from an obviously Mahāsāṅghika source :

> "Going west from this point (in Magadha).......................
> is a *stūpa* built by Asoka Rājā. This is the spot where the Great

[23] *Dipavamsa*, 5. 10.

Assembly (*Mahāsaṅgha*) was held. Those who were not permitted to join Kasyapa's assembly (Note: the Theravāda tradition is that all but the adherents of his school were expelled therefrom), whether learners or Arhats, to the number of 100,000 men, came together to this spot and said: 'While the Tathāgata was alive, we all had a common master, but now that the King of the Law is dead, it is different. We too wish to show our gratitude to the Buddha and we also will hold an assembly for the collecting of the scriptures. On this the common folk with the holy personages came to the assembly,—the foolish and the wise alike flocked together. And because in this assembly both common folk and holy personages (*Arhats*) were mixed together, it was called *Mahāsaṅgha*".[24]

In the tradition Hsüan-tsang draws upon, the rise of the Mahāsāṅghika school is represented as post-Asokan, but we find a number of doctrines said to have been held by Mahāsāṅghika monks refuted in the *Kathāvatthu* of Tissa, Asoka's contemporary.

The Mahāsāṅghika movement thus seems to have been a revolt against the 'cloistering of the Lord's teachings',—reducing them to a purely monkish religion.[25]

But even if the *Mahābheda* (the Great Schism between the Theravāda and the Mahāsāṅghika) had taken place before Asoka's time, the Mahāsāṅghikas had not yet time to grow and the Theravāda stood in Magadha as the great banyan tree, as the *Dīpavaṁsa* puts it,[26] from which Mahinda took a graft to plant in Ceylon. It struck deep roots in Ceylonese soil; it grew to be a tree so stout and hardy that all the storms that shook it in its history of twenty-three centuries and all the milder winds of change have not dislodged it from the island.

The Theravāda scriptures are all in Pali and the entire collection has been recovered from Ceylon. It is impossible to distinguish how many of them originated in India and how many in Ceylon. Pali itself is an ancient Indian language, which Ceylonese monk-scholars of old believed to have been the current language of Magadha. Modern Indian philologists, however, are inclined to point to ancient Avanti (in India) as its original speech-area. There is a tradition that Mahinda introduced Pali into Ceylon, but it is based only on the legend that he with his party had spent some time at

---

[24] Beal's *Buddhist Records of the Western World* (Popular Ed.), vol. II, pp. 164-165.

[25] See discussion of this point in Dutt's *The Buddha and Five After-Centuries* (Luzac and Co., 1957), pp. 132-133 and pp. 139-140.

[26] Dipavamsa, 5. 52——Nigrodha va maharukkho theravadanam uttamo.
(Tr. This good Theravada is like a banyan tree, a great tree the best to Theravadins).

Vidisā (in the same area) and made themselves conversant with Pali before leaving India for Ceylon. The adoption of Pali as the sacred language of Theravāda Buddhism is probably not earlier than Buddhaghosa.

Buddhaghosa lived for a number of years in Ceylon,—was certainly at Anurādhapura round 400 A.D.,—assiduously rendering the scriptural commentaries (*aṭṭhakathā*) from the Sinhalese language into Pali which was supposed to be the 'original language' of Magadha, as the *Cūlavaṁsa* says:

> "Parivattesi sabbā pi sīhalaṭṭhakathā tadā sabbesaṁ mūlabhāsāya māgadhāya niruttiyā". (37.244)
> (Tr. He will render all the Sinhalese commentaries and restore them to the original language, the speech-form of Magadha).

Round 411 Fa-hsien was in Ceylon. The object of his pilgrimage was to observe the Vinaya practices of the monks and also to collect texts on Vinaya. But the texts he could collect in Ceylon were the *Mahāśāsaka Vinayapitaka*, the *Dīrghāgama*, the *Saṁyuktāgama* and the *Sannipāta*,—none of them in Pali. It seems to indicate that the canonical literature of Ceylon in Pali had not developed by the time of Fa-hsien's visit to Ceylon.

In any case, our knowledge of the character of Theravāda Buddhism is confined almost exclusively to Pali Ceylonese scriptures. Their contents leave no room for doubt that the Theravāda was purely "monastic Buddhism" in which the *Saṅgha*, functioning under the Vinaya laws of the canon, is vested with supreme control of the religion.

The monk-organisation of Ceylon was founded by Mahinda; it was followed up with an organisation of nuns founded by Saṅghamittā. But the latter became extinct in the Polonnaruva period.[27]

So long as Buddhism functioned as the State Religion in Ceylon, its administration vested in the central monk-organisation called the Mahāsaṅgha at the Mahāvihāra of Anurādhapura. The monastery was several times destroyed or deserted. But its prestige was great; in its *pariveṇas* (academies) were the most learned monks of Ceylon; it was supposed to preserve the grand old line of Ceylonese monkhood since Mahinda. Ordination by the monks of the Mahāsaṅgha was believed in the countries of south-east Asia to carry the true and authentic stamp of monkhood. But the Mahāsaṅgha suffered constantly from internal dissensions, the rivalry of the Abhayagiri monks and the heterodoxies (*vaitulyavāda*) that were spreading in the island from Indian Mahāyānist sources. But it kept the torch of Theravāda undimmed till the establishment was effaced in the wholesale depradations on Buddhist establishments in the early part of Māgha's reign (1214-1235).

[27] See *The Polonnaruva Period*, p. 124.

A sect in the *Saṅgha* is called a *Nikāya* in Ceylon and at present there are only three *nikāyas*, none of which originated earlier than the mid-18th century viz., the Siyām Nikāya, the Ramañña Nikāya and the Amarapura Nikāya.

The first came into existence in Ceylon in the reign of Kirti Sri Rajasinhe who came to the throne of Kandy in the sixties of the 18th century. The second was formed by the coalescence of two groups of monks,—one led by Ambagahawatta Siri Sarṇaṅkara and the other by Puvakdandave Siri Paññānanda. The third was established later in the 'hill country' by Dhammajyoti who had gone to Amarapura (in Burma) and been ordained there.

Modernised Pariveṇa tradition

Buddhism is professed by about seventy per cent. of the population of Ceylon whose culture is predominantly Buddhist, with the exception of pockets, large and small, of Hindus, Christians and Moslems. All the higher culture of the island has been so organised in recent times as to fall in line with the old Buddhist tradition of *Pariveṇa.*

"A *pariveṇa* (Sinhalese—*Piriven*) originally meant a monk's cell; later, the term denoted a monastic residence founded by the king, a noble or some other rich individual and endowed with a regular income for the maintenance of its inmates. A monk (*bhikkhu*) who had received a *pariveṇa* as a benefice could devote his time to religious pursuits and studies without any anxiety with regard to his personal needs."[28]

In Ceylon there had been since the time of King Bhaṭikābhaya (31-66 A.D.) two distinct classes of monks, *Ganthadhura* and *Vipassanādhura,*—monks devoted to learning and monks devoted to *Vipassanā* (Meditation). Some of these *pariveṇas,* occupied by *Ganthadhura* monks, became abodes of famous teachers who had pupils living in the same residence and the word '*pariveṇa*', by a semantic change came to denote a 'seat of learning'. Many of these *pariveṇas* were named after their founders and the recipient of the benefice was known by the name of the institution. The persons to whom such benefices were granted had to be monks who had passed the stage of probation under a preceptor (i.e. of *nissaya*) and thus become qualified to teach novices.

The *Pariveṇa* tradition of monastic education probably dates back in Ceylon to the first monastic foundations in the island. The Mahāvihāra, the Abhayagiri and other famous old foundations all had their *pariveṇas* or residences of learned teachers. The system of education that first developed probably at the Mahāvihāra spread to all parts of the country resulting in the establishment of a large number of seats of Buddhist learning.

---

[28] *History of Ceylon,* vol. I. Pt. 2, pp. 748-749.

When two modern universities were incorporated in Ceylon by the 'Vidyodaya and Vidyalankara University Act', No. 45 of 1958, in December of that year, this ancient *parivena tradition* was sought to be embodied in them.[29] Each of these modern universities has a large number of monk teachers and monk inmates as well as lay students, with a learned *Thera* at the head. They have faculties for the study of Buddhism and research in Buddhist learning. Across the sea and across the centuries, it recalls memories of the Buddhist monastic universities that functioned and flourished in India under the Gupta emperors and the Pāla kings.[30]

---

[29] See *Second Anniversary Souvenir* of the Inauguration of the Vidyodaya University of Ceylon (18th February, 1861).

[30] See Dutt's *Buddhist Monks and Monasteries of India* (Allen and Unwin 1962). Part V.

Part Two

LATER DIFFUSIONS IN EAST ASIA

(Post-Christian Centuries)

Chapter IV

BURMA

Burmese Legends of Buddhist Beginnings in the Country

A GIFT of the two rivers, the Chindwin and the Irrawaddy, Burma was hardly at the dawn of her history a geographical unit. Within its ill-defined borders was a population drawn from different racial stocks and living at different levels of culture. It was not before its conquest in the 11th century by a Thai people called Mranma that the ethnic name Burma ('Land of the Mranma') was adopted to indicate its territorial integrity.

The mountainous north was peopled by a number of nomadic tribes of whom we get glimpses in Chinese records; the central plains were occupied by colonies of agricultural tribes; only the south was held by a people called the Mon among whom Buddhism had spread, though from what source is unknown, and led them to civilized ways of life and society.

These Mons of the south were part of a settled community of people that lived in a series of small States. The Mon States extended south-westwards from Burma into Siam and were so united by racial and cultural bonds that they formed a whole, regarded in later times by Arab geographers, as making up a territorial unit, known as *Ramañña-desha* ('The country of the Mons').

The political history of Burma begins from its Thai conquest. But the history of Buddhism within its physical boundaries goes back beyond it by a few centuries. The existence of Buddhism in Burma, in faith as well as in institutional forms, long before the coming of the Thai, is confirmed by archaeological finds. But the question, how long before? is obscured by a number of Burmese legends investing the first coming of Buddhism into the country with a faked antiquity. They are dispersed and local legends, but have edged themselves into Burma's national chronicles, their object being to show that Buddhism in Burma was coeval with the Founder's lifetime.

One of these legends, reported by almost all the chronicles, represents the Buddha as having come in person to Burma and visited a village in its west named Lekaing.[1] Two local merchants are said to have started building a monastery of sandal-wood in the village, and till its completion the

[1] For this legend, see the *Glass Palace Chronicle* tr. by Maung Tin and Luce, Burma Research Society, 2nd printing, 1960, pp. 6-7.

Buddha himself along with his disciples used to come periodically to the village, as the legend has it, to supervise the construction. He stayed for some time in this sandalwood-monastery of Lekaing, converted local people to his religion and is said to have uttered the prophecy that Burma in the ripeness of time would become a Buddhist country. Buddhism in Burma, according to this legend, began at the village of Lekaing in humble surroundings, among local folk, and from this centre spread all over the country. Thilawuntha, a Burmese poet of the 15th century, makes the proud boast that Buddhism in Burma is older than in Ceylon: "In our land the religion arose since the time the Lord came to dwell in the Sandalwood monastery" (*Celebrated Chronicle*).

The Glass Palace Chronicle speaks of some early kings of Burma as being 'Sakiyan', i.e. descended from the Sakya clan to which the Buddha himself belonged.[2] But of these Sakiyan kings there is no mention in the other chronicles, except casually in the *New Pagan Chronicle* only.[3]

The Shwedagon Pagoda of Rangoon derives its holiness from a legend that it was founded over a lock of hair from the Buddha's head that had been gifted by the Buddha himself to two Burmese merchants and brought by them to Burma. The two merchants are named Taphussa and Bhallika. This legend, however, is not original: it is a tendentious Burmese version of the canonical story of the first two *upāsakas* (lay worshippers) of the Buddha, described as two merchants, Tapussa and Bhallika.[4] But they are called '*Ukkala*', i.e., coming from Utkala (Orissa in India) and there is no mention in the canon itself of the gift of any lock of hair to them.

There is also the legend identifying Thaton with Suvaññabhūmi to which Tissa's missionaries, Sona and Uttara, were assigned, but, alongside, there is a somewhat different legend that Suvaññabhūmi was actually Chiengmai in Siam and that Sona and Uttara came to Burma from there.[5]

We may put on one side these picturesque legends of the chronicles, obviously inventions of pious monks wishful to claim an impossibly high antiquity for Buddhism in their country. In the perspective of history, however, the first appearance of Buddhism in Burma is seen among the Pyu people. What their original habitat was before their settlement in Burma is unknown; they do not seem to have been of Indian origin. It is evident, however, from the relics they have left at Hmawza (Old Prome) and round it

---

[2] The early kings of Tagaung,——Abhiraja, Dhajaraja and their dynasties. See *Ibid*, pp. 1-3, 30, etc.

[3] The *New Pagan Chronicle* omits Abhiraja, but mentions Dhajaraja. See *Ibid*, Intro. p. xv.

[4] Mahavagga, 1, 4.

[5] See *Historians of South-east Asia*, School of Oriental and African Studies, University of London, Oxford University Press, 1961, p. 54.

that they had at some stage of their history come under the influence of Indian civilization.

The Ancient Pyu

The Pyu have been so completely absorbed and merged in the Burmese population that there are no representatives of them in the country now. Yet they were the real 'ancients' of the land, that is, so long as they retained their identity as a people.

They were known in China under the Tang dynasty. Dr. May cites an interesting passage from the Tang Annals (covering A.D. 609-918)[6] in which Burma is described as 'containing 18 States and 9 walled towns' which belonged to the Pyu. The Pyu people are said to have been Buddhists, having a hundred richly decorated monasteries and a huge image of a white elephant worshipped by the devout. Their capital is described as a great walled city of twelve gates with a pagoda at each of the four corners, abounding in wealth. The name of this Pyu capital city is known from Burmese sources: it was Śrīkshetra, same as that of the city of god Jagannāth in Orissa (in India),—Tharehkittara in Burmese.

In the 7th century it was a famous seat of Buddhism. Hsüan-tsang was in East Bengal (Samtata) in 640 A.D., and standing on the shore of the Bay of Bengal, he was curious to know what Buddhist settlements existed on the other side of the water. He was told of Śrīkshetra (Chinese—Shih-li-chata-lo) and some other places. Being far off his route, Hsüan-tsang was unable to visit them, but he has recorded the names of these places in the *Si-yu-ki.*[7]

The Pyu archaeological remains unearthed at Hmawza and round about it leave no doubt that the people had acquired elements of civilization: developed literacy and practised architecture and sculpture which were concomitants of the Indian religions, Brāhmaṇical and Buddhist, professed by them. But the art of music also was cultivated by them.[8] Round 801 a band of Pyu musicians was taken to the Chinese capital to entertain the emperor. It is said that the latter, without 'pressing the cap-strings to his ears', listened attentively to that music from 'the land of P'ias' brought to his ears from 'the Great Ocean's south-west corner'.[9]

---

[6] Reginald Le May's *The Culture of South-east Asia*, Allen and Unwin, 1954, pp. 45-46

[7] See *On Yuan-chawng* by Watters and Rhys Davids, Vol. II, p. 188.

[8] "I-mon-hsun, Kolofeng's grandson and successor, sent a present of Pyu musicians to the Tang Court in 800. In 801-2 a Pyu king sent a formal embassy, accompanied by thirty-five musicians, to China via Nanchao"—Hall's *History of South-east Asia*, MacMillan and Co. 1961, p. 121.

[9] Dorothy Woodman's *Making of Burma*, Cresset Press, London, 1962, pp.

About three decades after this pleasant function with Pyu musicians at the Chinese court, disaster overwhelmed the Pyu in Burma. There was an invasion from Nanchao in 832. Their capital was ruthlessly sacked and destroyed; about 3,000 people were taken captive, and those who survived the event continued to live in utmost wretchedness. But it seems that the language and script of the Pyu were understood in Burma at least till 1113 A.D.[10]

Lost as a people and their culture become a story, the Pyu still lived on in traditional memory, with a glamour lent by the passage of time. When later the Burmese chronicles take up the story of the Pyu, it is with this glamour upon it.

The old Pyu city Tharehkittara (Śrīkshetra), the centre of Pyu culture, has become in them a 'holy' city. There is a legendary chronicle of the city describing its foundation in ancient times and its mythical line of kings.[11]

Its foundation, it is said, was laid by God Śakra; it was built as a 'golden city', "noble and glorious as the Sudassana city, Śakra's own abode, marvellously graceful and having all things needful for a city,—main gates, thirty-two small gates, thirty-two moats, ditches, baribicans, machicolations, four-cornered towers with graduated roofs over the gates, turrets along the walls, and so forth; the whole being one *yojana* in diameter and three *yojanas* in circumference".[12]

It is a purely imaginary picture, for Tharehkittara vanished long back, destroyed about 1058 by Anawrahta for political reasons.[13] Yet placing it by the side of the more realistic one in the Tang Annals, certain common features and landmarks leap to view.

The site of the Pyu kingdom which lay round Old Prome in Central Burma has been surveyed and explored by archaeologists. A large assortment of Pyu artefacts has come into their possession. These confirm the following broad conclusions:

(i) The Pyu had a distinct language of their own (of Tibeto-Burman stock), written in a South Indian script;

(ii) They had absorbed a good deal of Indian cultural influence and professed both Brāhmaṇism and Buddhism; and

(iii) Their Buddhism was from a Hīnayānist source, probably Theravāda Buddhism, and its Pali scriptural texts, such as were available, were held in great reverence.

---

[10] As is indicated by the Pyu inscription on the 'Burma Rosetta Stone' for which see *infra*.

[11] See *The Glass Palace Chronicle*, pp. 6 ff.

[12] *Ibid*, p. 14.

[13] See *The Glass Palace Chronicle*, p. 87.

The Pyu language is Tibeto-Burman and several specimens of it have been obtained from stones on which it is found inscribed in South Indian script. Now a dead language of Burma, it has been completely deciphered by scholars with the aid of an inscription in four languages which is known as the 'Burma's Rosetta Stone'.

The 'Rosetta stone' was discovered in 1911 at a pagoda south of Pagan,—an epigraph by the Burmese king Alaungsithu, dated A.D. 1113, bearing the story of Kyanzittha's reign. The stone has four faces on which the same text appears in four languages,—Pyu, Mon, Burmese and Pali. The Pyu language seems to have survived the extinction of the Pyu at least for three to four centuries which can be the only explanation of its adoption on the 'Rosetta Stone'.

The original habitat of the Tibeto-Burman-speaking Pyu people is unknown, but if they hailed from India, their language bears no traces of it. How the influence of Indian culture and religious belief came to them is equally unknown, though it is supposed that they had relations of trade and commerce with South India. Yet the remains of both Hindu and Buddhist temples and images of Hindu deities and Buddha-images of Pyu workmanship, discovered in the course of archaeological exploration round Old Prome, testify to a strong current of Indian religious influence in Pyu civilization.

How Buddhism spread among them is unknown. It is of Theravāda provenance: no trace of Mahāyāna Buddhism is found in Pyu religious sculpture. A find of remarkable significance was made from the relic chamber of Khin Ba's mound at Hmawza: a few leaves of gold on which a portion of a Pāli scriptural text had been inscribed in South Indian Kadamba script of the 5th century A.D. How this text was obtained is a mystery, but it suggests the impact on the Pyu people of Theravāda Buddhism.

What is known about the Pyu leaves much unknown, especially about their exact relations with India and the penetration among them of Indian cultural influence. From the point of view of Buddhist history, however, it shows unmistakably that as early as in the 5th century,—about five centuries before Anawrahta,—there were Buddhists in Burma and the traditions of the Pyu Buddhist city of Śrīkshetra survived among the Burmans, incorporated later into their national chronicles.

The Mon and the Thai Mranma

Another people that merged in the Burmese population were the Mons of Lower Burma. The Mon, however, is not extinct, but under the name Talaing retains some distinction yet. The name, however, has a slight implication of inferior status.

'Talaing' has a verbal similarity to Telangana, a district of the Andhra-pradesh of India. The fact has prompted some scholars to seek for the origin of the Talaing people of Burma in this part of India, though in support of their Indian origin historical evidence is lacking.

Neither physically nor culturally is a Talaing of Burma different from a Burmese, but an educated Talaing still retains through his knowledge of the Mon language a sort of spiritual contact with the old Mon traditions of the country. These traditions go back to the 5th or the 6th century A.D.

The Mons and allied tribes have a wide distribution over southern Asia, representing precipitates in different lands of a primitive tribal movement southwards from a border of the Gobi desert, in search of more temperate climate and more arable land. The rice-and-bean-producing plains of Siam and Burma were a magnet to draw them on and some of these tribes settled along the banks of the Menam, the Mekong and the Irrawaddy.

To trace the social and cultural contacts of a tribal people wandering from land to land and the effects of such contacts on their evolution is hardly possible. But the Mons, when they settled in the southern countries, were by no means 'pre-cultural'. When they emerge into the ken of history, we find them in possession of all the rudiments of civilization. They live in separate States, follow the ways of civilized life and have developed social and religious institutions. They have also a prevailing sense of their ethnic unity.

The Mons, settled in Siam and in Lower Burma, called themselves *Rmen*. It is an old Mon word which we first find used as an ethnic name in Burma in an inscription of 1102, of the Burmese king Kyansittha's reign.[14] From its mediaeval form, *Ramen*, comes *Ramañña* and the name Ramañña-desha given by Arab geographers to 'the country of the Mons'. It connoted geographically a series of kingdoms or States, united culturally and racially, stretching from Lower Burma into Siam.

Buddhism of Theravāda variety was the prevailing religion in the Mon regions. From which quarter it spread here is unknown, but its source was certainly not in the north. We must look for it to the ancient Buddhist centres which sprang up in the south of the Malayan peninsula, Ligor and elsewhere, where there were Indian settlements and whence access was had across the Isthmus of Kra to Siam and farther north, to Lower Burma.

When they appear in history, the Mons have already imbibed Buddhism, and a literature in the Mon language has developed under that influence: it became the common heritage of all Ramañña-desha. Legends were its main stuff and staple—legends of Ramañña kings and their legendary genealogies (*Rajawan*), legends of the great pagodas (*Dhatuwan*) and moral episodes

[14] See *Epigraphia Birmanica*, vol. III, pt. I (*Mon Inscriptions* by Blagden, Inscription IX—Pagan). Also Hall's *History of South-east Asia*, p. 122.

from the lives of Ramañña kings (*Pun*).[15] From the 12th century on, under the influence of Ceylonese masters, this popular Mon literature was put into Pali.

The Mon legends, which at the beginning must have been just folk-literature passing from mouth to mouth, were pooled together by a Siamese monk of the 16th century in a work in Pali entitled *Nidāna-Ārambhakathā*. It has the distinction of being a work of national character. Based on old Mon legends it reflects strongly a sense of Mon individuality as a social and political unit. It purports to set down the genealogies of the rulers of Ramañña-desha in a narrative form, interspersed with accessory matters. These Mon kings bore at least three names: Sanskrit regnal names usually found in the inscriptions; the names by which they were generally known, and the names used in the formal genealogies. The narrative of kings centres mostly round the Mon sovereigns who ruled from their three capitals in Lower Burma,—Thaton, Martaban and Pegu.[16]

It was the uniformity of Mon culture and the existence of Mon States in a continuous land-block from which the concept of Ramañña-desha had stemmed. But these States were not militarily strong: they fell apart as soon as more sturdy and vigorous tribes from the north, the Thai and kindred tribes, penetrated into them and broke up their formal unity. Yet the concept of Ramañña-desha as a traditional geographical entity continued till the fifties of the 18th century when Alaungpaya (known as the 'Embryo Buddha') descended trom the north and swept away its last surviving remnants in Burma.

While the Mons, settled in their States in Lower Burma and Siam, were developing their own forms of culture, especially those associated with the practice of Buddhism, —their didactic literature, iconography, religious architecture and sculpture,—away to their north a people called the Thai were living in a kingdom of their own in a southern province named Nanchao of the Chinese empire.

Somehow the conditions of life in Nanchao became too hard for them to bear, and tribe by tribe they began to migrate southwards. This was probably sometime in the 8th century A.D. These migrant tribes were the distant forebears of those who in two after-centuries conquered both Siam and Burma. Prof. Luce says that "a map of Nanchao still shows about 50 Burma names".[17]

---

[15] See Hall's *Historians of South-East Asia* (Oxford University Press, 1962), p. 63.

[16] See *Ibid*, pp. 64 ff. (Article by H.D. Shorto on *A Mon Genealogy of Kings: Observations on the Nidana Arambhakatha*).

[17] See *Journal of Burma Research Society*, June 1959 (Prof. G.H. Luce's article on *Old Kyaukse and the coming of the Burmans*).

After long wanderings one Thai branch settled in Siam and another in the Shan States of Burma. The Thais of the Shan States are known in Siam as the 'elder Thai' (*Thai Yai*) and as Mranma in Burma. A majority of them left the Shan States and descended to the plains. Their first foothold on the plains was at Kyaukse, then known as 'the Eleven Villages', a hundred miles east of Pagan, inhabited by a settled Mon population.[18] The city of Pagan had been devastated by the invasion from Nanchao in 832 A.D. to which we have already referred, but it was afterwards repopulated by the Mons, not long before the descent of the Mranma from the hills of the Shan states.

In the wild and unsettled Shan regions, Buddhism was unknown: it never obtained a foothold there. "The Proto-Burman tribes of the Salween water-shed—the Maru, the Lashi and the Atasi of today,—are still non-Buddhist" —says Prof. Luce.[19]

But at Kyauske, the Mranma from the Shan States under their warrior-leader Anawrahta, came face to face for the first time with a Buddhist civilization and a culture far superior to their own. With their descent to the Kyauske plains, started a process of assimilation, intermingling of blood and acculturation of the incoming 'elder Thai', marking the inception of a Burmese nationality.

From Kyaukse Anawrahta proceeded to Pagan. It was the ancient capital town of the Mons called by that name since c. 617.[20] It is known from a Chinese source, dated 863 A.D., to what straits the city had been reduced by the Nanchao invasion of 832. "The descendants (of the victims of this invasion) are still there, subsisting on fish and insects. Such is the end of their people".[21]

But the end had not really come. In one of the legends in the chronicles, it is said that the walls of Pagan were built in 849.[22] Mon kings were on the throne for about a hundred and sixty years after the walls had been built in Pagan and there was a revival of Buddhism round 1000 A.D. under Caw Raham, called the 'Saint King' in the chronicle,—the first king of Pagan whose name appears in an inscription. He built a *Sīmā* (chapter-house) in Pagan. "Whether in old Thaton or Pegu, Kyaukse or Pagan", remarks Prof. Luce, "the triumph or revival of Buddhism is always marked by the building of a permanent 'thein' or Buddha-sīmā".[23]

---

[18] See *Ibid.*

[19] See *Ibid.*

[20] "It was not until the reign of king Narathihapate (ascended the throne in 617) that the town was known as Pagan"—*Glass Palace Chronicle*, p. 160.

[21] Cited by Prof. Luce in the article referred to in footnote (17).

[22] "Pagan, the Burmese capital, enters history in 849, the traditional date of the construction of its walls by Pyinpya"—Hall's *History of South-east Asia*, p. 122.

[23] See footnote 17 for the reference.

It was at Pagan, about a hundred miles from Kyaukse, that Anawrahta established amidst a Buddhist population the capital of his expansionist kingdom in 1020 A.D.

The kingdom gradually extended from Pagan to Thaton and farther across the Irrawaddy, spreading over the whole of Lower Burma down to the sea. It lasted from 1044 to 1287 A.D. and nearly the whole of the Burmese part of old Ramañña-desha was included in it. Upper Burma and Lower Burma were united under one rule.

Anawrahta and Burmese Buddhism

Anawrahta, the first Burmese king of Burma, is almost a semi-legendary figure in the chronicles. There is proof that he signed himself with a Sanskrit name, Aniruddha (The Resistless).

There is also no doubt that he was a pious Buddhist, though somewhat aggressive in his piety, for he brought to his capital by force, less often by persuasion, the sacred objects of Buddhism scattered in different parts of the kingdom. The biggest of his religious exploits was the sack of Thaton to be described later.

It is not known when Anawrahta became a convert to Buddhism. His own people before their settlement among the Mon population of Kyaukse had been worshippers of *Nāgas* (Serpents) and *Nats* (Guardian Spirits). Anawrahta himself, even after he had embraced Buddhism, does not seem to have discarded Nat-worship wholly, for he made provision for it in the great Shwejifon Pagoda, erected by him at Pagan. A large number of small terra-cotta images in soft clay have been discovered in the ruins of Pagan. They were Anawrahta's own handiwork as the inscriptions on them, which are in fairly correct Sanskrit, clearly show, e.g.:

> *Eshaḥ Lokanātha Mahārāja Śrī Aniruddha-devena kṛta vimuktyarthaṁ swahastenaiva hi.*
>
> (*Tr.* This Lokanātha image is made by Maharājā Śrī Aniruddha Deva with his own hand for his salvation).

The use of Sanskrit in the inscription and the mention of Lokanātha as the object of adoration leave no doubt that at the time when he made these images, he was not an adherent of Theravāda Buddhism. He subsequently embraced it under the influence and guidance of Shin Arahan.

The chronicles record the story of Shin Arahan, his first meeting with Anawrahta and his later activities in spreading Theravāda Buddhism in the kingdom. The following account is taken from the *Glass Palace Chronicle*, with accessory miraculous incidents left out:[24]

---

[24] See *Glass Palace Chronicle*, pp. 71 ff.

5

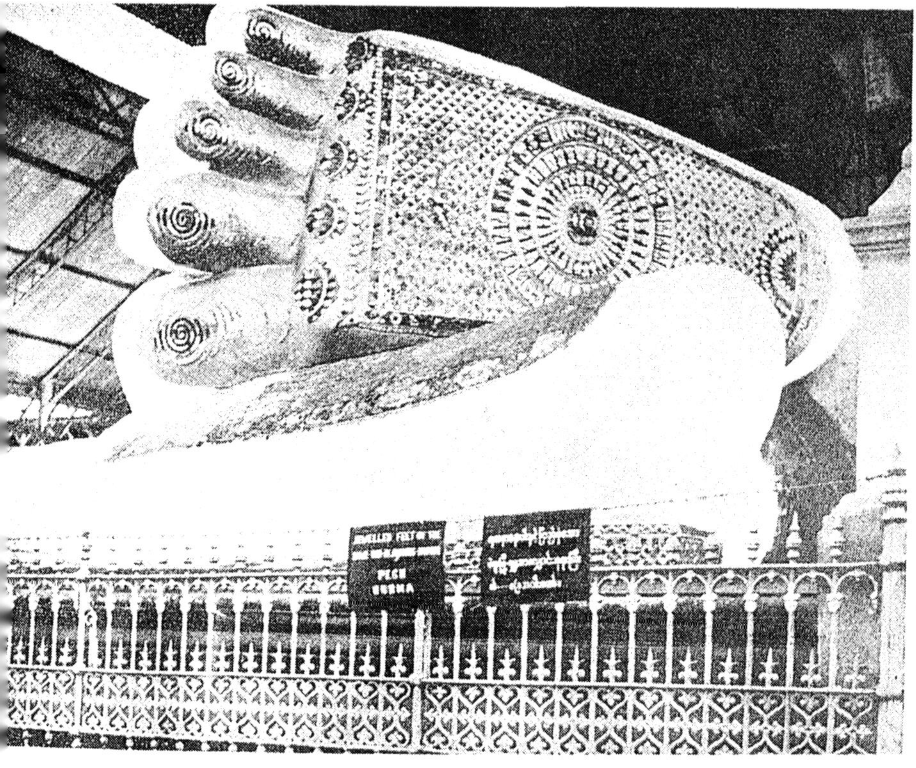

6

7. *Shwedagon Pagoda of Rangoon*

5. *The Great Mahamuni Pagoda at Mandalay (Built in 1870)*

6. *The Buddha foot in stone in Thun Nuljaunch Pagoda at Pegu (Burma); thickly studded with gems and jewels given as votive offerings to the Lord's foot.*

8. *Priests on a bamboo-scaffolding cleaning by inch a 48 foot Buddha statue (known loc as Shwethaly Aung) at Pegu (Burma); bra hazards for an act of piety.*

9. *A Siamese ritual dance (Bangkok, Thail*

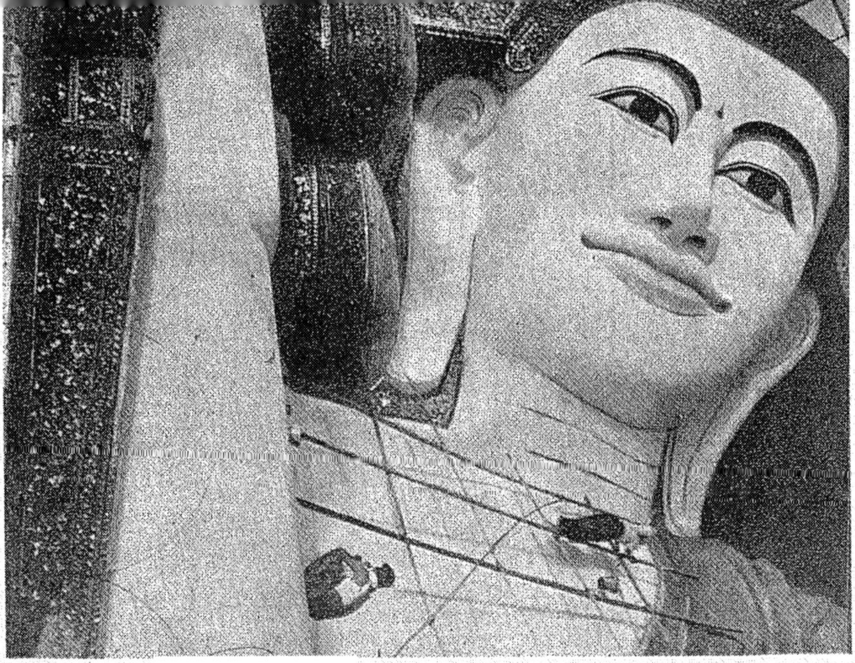

9

10. *The Emerald Buddha of Bangkok* (*Bangkok-Thailand*).

Roaming in the forest of Thaton, a huntsman came face to face with a wandering ascetic. Knowing that king Anawrahta was interested in men of this type, he escorted him to the king's presence at Pagan. He turned out to be a wandering Buddhist monk, Dhammādassa by name, but at the capital he was known as Shin Arahan (Venerable Arhat). The Burmese '*shin*' is equivalent to Ceylonese '*thera*',—an elderly monk of high standing,—and '*arhan*' is a variant of '*arhat*'. Perhaps it was a distinctive and honorific designation bestowed on him when his fame spread at Pagan.

The king, coming to know him and appreciate his worth, set him up in a dual capacity—as his own instructor in religion and as primate of the kingdom. So "the king and all the people forsook their own opinions and were established in the Good Law".[25]

Shin Arahan explained to the king that the religion of the Buddha consisted of three constituents,—(i) the Scripture, (ii) the study of the Scripture, and (iii) intuition. But the king had no scripture, and on enquiry as to where it could be found, Shin Arahan informed him that the holy texts as well as many sacred relics were available at Thaton. Anawrahta sent one of his ministers to Manuha, king of Thaton, asking for the scripture, but the latter insolently refused the request whereon Anawrahta set on foot an expedition against Thaton.

Manuha was captured and his thirty sets of *Pitakas* (Texts of the scripture) were carried away from Thaton to Pagan on 'thirty-two white elephants'. Anawrahta not only took Manuha to his own capital, but also all the skilled workmen of Thaton, both artisans and artists. A man of vision, his object was to transplant the Mon culture of Thaton in his own city. The defeated king was treated with exceptional generosity at Pagan and was allowed to build on his own whatever religious edifices he wanted to in the victor's city.

After the conquest of Thaton, Anawrahta led several expeditions to other places in Burma for the collection of sacred relics. At last he returned from these expeditions and undertook the building of the Swezigon Pagoda on a sand-bank, and, when it was completed, he entrusted Manuha and his family, with its maintenance. It is said that he also sent a deputation to Ceylon and obtained from the king of Ceylon a tooth-relic which had been miraculously reproduced from the original relic preserved in that island.

The *Pitakas* acquired from Thaton were in the Mon script. Anawrahta had all the thirty sets of *Pitakas* copied from Mon characters into Burmese.[26] He also had the texts 'arranged and collected and placed on a *pyatthad* (altar), richly fraught with gems, and caused them to be taught to the Noble Order (that is, to the monks)'. The *Glass Palace Chronicle* then records the many

---

[25] *Ibid*, p. 74.

[26] *Ibid*, p. 96.

pagodas and works of public utility,—dams, reservoirs, canals, etc.,—constructed by Anawrahta during his reign of approximately thirty-three years.

His end came unexpectedly: he was gored to death by a wild buffalo while hunting it from the back of an elephant. His obituary is recorded in these sombre phrases in the chronicle: "Thus this noble king, full of glory, might of arms and dominion, who for full thirty-three years of royal prosperity had advanced the welfare of the religion, his own welfare, and that of the generations of his sons, grandsons and great grandsons, died at the age of seventy-five....About the time of his death, bees clave to the throne-door of the palace; an ogre laughed from the top of the Tharaba Gate; the lustre of the royal sword faded; a vulture alighted on the palace. The *deinnatthe* (Day and Night) coincided with the *thingyan* (i.e. Sanskrit *Saṅkrānti*)".[27]

Shin Arahan survived Anawrahta and after the latter's death spent the remainder of his life in instructing the Burmese people in Buddhism. It is difficult to say whether the religion preached by him was exactly the Theravāda Buddhism of Ceylon. The Ceylonese influence had not reached Burma yet, and we may presume that it was the somewhat hybrid Mon-Thaton variety of Buddhism, combining in it the worship of Hindu deities and the practice of Hindu rituals.

Among the many beneficent acts of Anawrahta is mentioned his suppression of the Ari cult and its priesthood. It had a strong hold in Upper Burma. The Aris ministered a debased and nondescript cult compounded of magic, astrology, demonology, exorcism and the elements of *Nāga* (Serpent) and *Nat* (Tutelary Spirits) worship. Its filiation was to the *Tāntrika* cult that had bred from the corruption of Mahāyāna Buddhism in eastern India and was imported from there into Tibet where it was developed and dignified as a school of Buddhism.

The chronicle speaks of "thirty Ari lords and their sixty thousand disciples who practised it at Thamahti".[28] It was the name of a village a few miles south-east of Pagan. A king before Anawrahta, named Nyaung-u Sawrahan (ascended in 931) is said to have been a follower of Ari teachers and set up the figure of a *Nāga* for worship by the people. Some samples of Ari doctrines are given in the *Glass Palace Chronicle*: they are closely allied to *Tāntrika* doctrines: the 'Law of *Kamma*' has in it no place and sexual taboos are not recognised. The Chronicle mentions in particular the practice by the Ari priesthood of deflowering virgins on the night before marriage,—the custom known in anthropology as exercise of the 'right of the senior' (*Le droit de signeur*).

---

[27] *Glass Palace Chronicle*, pp. 99-100.

[28] *Ibid*, p. 71.

Anawrahta, under Shin Arahan's instruction, broke up this sinister Ari organisation, although the Ari cult itself, as it seems, was not quite extirpated.[29]

Ceylonese Theravāda Scripture in Burma

Shin Arahan had told Anawrahta that the scripture, its study and one's own intuitive understanding were the three essentials of Buddhism. On being asked by the king where the scripture was available, he had pointed to Thaton. When Anawrahta brought the scriptural texts from Thaton to Pagan "on the backs of 32 white elephants", they were preserved with great care and veneration at the capital. The question of some importance is—where did these texts come into Thaton from and when?

It is said in the chronicles that they were brought to Thaton from Ceylon by Buddhaghosa in the reign of the Ceylonese king Mahānāma. Buddhaghosa is said in the *Glass Palace Chronicle* to have crossed the sea from the Burmese port of Bassein to the 'middle country' (Magadha) in India and then gone from there to the island of Ceylon by sea.

The identity of this Buddhaghosa, the purveyor of the scripture from Ceylon to Burma, is a tantalizing question. In the minds of the writers of the Burmese chronicles, he seems to have got definitely identified with the famous Pali scholar, author of the *Visuddhimagga* and commentaries on the canon. He belonged to the end of the 4th century A.D. and the beginning of the 5th and most of his works were written in the Mahāvihāra of Anurādhapura in Ceylon during the reign of Mahānāma (409-413 A.D.).

The life-story of this eminent Pali scholar, writer and commentator appears in both Ceylonese and Burmese legends and the two versions are to some extent parallel, but then divergent. The Ceylonese legends recorded in the *Cuḷavaṁsa* appear substantially in a Pali work written in Burma, entitled *Buddhaghosuppatti* (The Advent of Buddhaghosa). But in these Ceylonese legends not a word is said about Buddhaghosa's connection with Burma nor of his presenting the works of Pali scripture to the king of Thaton, —an event colourfully described in the Burmese chronicles. In the Kalyani inscriptions of Dhammaceti of Pegu[30] which give a *resume* of the development of Buddhism in Burma, Buddhaghosa finds no mention at all, nor is the story of his presentation of books at Thaton referred to in the *Buddhaghosuppatti* which was written in Burma. The evidence is of a negative character, but it lends some colour to the plausible inference that the Pali Buddhist texts were brought to Thaton by some ancient monk of Burma, perhaps at a time when Buddhism was spreading among the Mons, and that this monk

[29] See May's *The Culture of South-east Asia*, p.p. 53, 162.

[30] See footnote 34 for the reference.

was a namesake of the more famous Buddhaghosa.[31] In any case the canonical texts had been received at Thaton at least a few centuries before Anawrahta came and carried them off to Pagan.

The arrival of the Buddhist books in Burma from Ceylon is thus described in the *Glass Palace Chronicle*: When the tidings spread that Buddhaghosa, (whatever his identity), was coming to Thaton with the books, "there was a general cry throughout all the kingdom of Ramañña, and king and queen, men and women, monks and lay-men, all welcomed them with diverse festivals, assemblies, celebrations, and almsgivings. As though the Lord Omniscient had appeared in their midst, they reverently raised the Pitakas, and, coming to the city-palace, they built a temple at a lovely place in front of the golden palace, and there they laid the treasures of the religion".[32]

We have no evidence that the works so reverently treasured in a temple at Thaton were open to study and investigation. When Anawrahta brought them to Pagan he found the texts in the Mon language. He had them rewritten in Burmese. But it was after his lifetime, in the reign of Kyanzittha (1084-1112), that these works became the subject of study and research by Burmese monk-scholars.

The capture of Thaton by Anawrahta was a key-event in early Burmese history. On a small scale, it was like a repetition of Europe's classical history of the Greeks capturing their Roman captors. Mon culture and civilization became dominant in the whole empire of which Pagan was the capital. Buddhism, as held and practised by the Mons, spread all over Burma, though it was not exactly the pure Theravāda Buddhism of Ceylon. Pali, the language of the Theravāda scripture, became Burma's 'classical' language. The Mon alphabet was adopted by the Burmese who wrote their own language in Mon script. With the influx of craftsmen from Thaton into Pagan began the era of temple-and-pagoda building which lasted for two after-centuries.

The Ceylonese scripture, since the time of Kyanzittha and under the primacy of Shin Arahan who survived Anawrahta and held the primacy, came in for critical study. The industry centred mainly on the comparison and collation of texts. It gave a fillip to scholarship in Pali and knowledge of the Ceylonese script. As Prof. Luce says: "Between the receipt of Sinhalese manuscripts (1070 A.D.) and the building of the Anand Pagoda (C. 1105), intensive scholarly work must have proceeded in Pagan".[33] The Burmese

---

[31] The Buddhaghosa problem is stated fully in Nihar Ranjan Ray's *Theravada Buddhism in Ceylon*, University of Calcutta, pp. 24 ff. See also The *Path of Purification* by Bhikku Nanamoli, R. Semaga, Colombo, 1956, p. xxvi.

[32] *Glass Palace Chronicle*, p. 48.

[33] See footnote 17 for the reference.

Tipitaka, based on the Ceylonese, was compiled. Between Burma and Ceylon, intercourse had been initiated by Anawrahta himself by advancing a loan to king Vijayabāhu of Ceylon, then engaged in restoring Ceylon's independence from Cola rulers and strengthening the depleted Buddhist Saṅgha of the island. This intercourse was sustained: and it led to the foundation in 1190 of a vigorous Ceylonese monk-organisation in Burma called the 'Siṁhala Saṅgha' which played later on a signal role in the diffusion of Ceylonese Theravāda Buddhism throughout South-east Asia.

The circumstances that led to the foundation of this body (Siṁhala Saṅgha) are described in the Kalyani inscriptions of Dhammaceti of Pegu.[34]

Accompanying one of Dhammaceti's missions to Ceylon was a Mon monk, born in the village of Chapata from which he took his name. He is described in the Kalyani inscriptions as 'a son of the people.' Chapata was not, however, the first monk from Burma to go to Ceylon. The primate Panthagu, Shin Arahan's successor to the primacy, had retired to Ceylon after the term of his office. Panthagu's successor, a Mon monk named Uttarajīva, also went to Ceylon in 1180 and on his return to Burma was invested with the title of the 'First Pilgrim to Ceylon'. Chapata was the 'Second Pilgrim'. He returned toBurma in 1180 after completing his studies there, and with him came four foreign monks from Ceylon, one of whom, Tamalinda, is believed to have been a son of Jayavarman VII of Cambodia.

Their first act on migration to Burma was to build a pagoda and a chapter house (*Sīmā*) at Nyaung-u for conferment of ordination on the pattern followed by the Mahāsaṅgha of Ceylon. It seems to have been different from the Mon-Buddhist pattern hitherto followed in Burma. It caused at the time a rift in the Burmese monk-community, one party standing by the old and existing rule of ordination, the other by that of the Ceylonese Mahāsaṅgha. The king was on the side of the reformers who carried on a vigorous propaganda in favour of the authentic character of Ceylonese Buddhism and the superiority of Ceylonese ordination. This controversy marked the beginning in Burma of the activities of the 'Siṁhala Saṅgha'.

Aside from its voluminous chronicles compiled in different centuries, the religious literature of Burma is characterised by its deliberate secondariness to the Ceylonese. It shows little originality. To the development of the philosophic side of the Theravāda,—its *Abhidhamma*, its doctrines and categories,—the contribution of Burmese monk-scholars has been by no means outstanding. To them Buddhism as presented in the Pali canon and expounded and amplified in the commentarial and original works in Pali became, since the early thirteenth century on, unquestionably definitive.

---

[34] See *Epigraphia Burmanica*, Vol. III, pts. 1 and 2; Mediaeval Mon Records—No. XII; *The Inscriptions of Kalyani Sima*, Pegu.

Religious Monuments of Burma

The faith of Burma has its peculiarly Burmese expression,—not so much in literary as in monumental form,—in its endless network over the country of religious edifices, great and small, old and modern.

These edifices are of two kinds—Pagodas (the name probably a corruption of Ceylonese *Dagoba*, from Sanskrit *Dhātugarbha*, i.e., holding holy relics in the womb, a reliquary Stūpa) and Temples for the installation of Buddha-images for worship. The Temple architecture, however, of which the finest specimen is the Anand Temple at Pagan built by Anawrahta's son and successor Kyanzittha, is not specially Burmese: the Pagoda decidedly is.

Throughout the Pagan period, down to 1287 when the city fell to Kubla Khan's grandson Prince Timur and Upper Burma passed into Mongol hands, the pious enterprise of building temples and pagodas was kept up by the kings of Pagan. Anawrahta, Kyanzittha, Alaungsittha and Narathihapata were all zealous builders of these religious edifices.

A class of labourers, 'Pagoda slaves', grew up in Burma, called *Purha kywan* in Burmese, consisting of men, sometimes even members of the Saṅgha, who dedicated themselves to the service of Pagodas. They were workmen as well as caretakers and enjoyed a special status, being forbidden to do any work in the villages.

For visitors Burma has been described as a 'land of pagodas': they dot all villages and towns and are by far the most noticeable feature of the landscape. From the first pagoda, the Swezigon, started by Anawrahta in 1054 and completed by his successor Kyanzittha, to the last one known as the Peace Pagoda built in 1957 under the direction of Prime Minister U Nu at Rangoon, the pagodas, great and small, old and new, are so numerous in Burma as almost to defy count.

It became a tradition of Burmese royalty to dedicate a pagoda. It was symbolical of the sovereign's adherence to the cause of Buddhism. When a pagoda became famous, it was usual to celebrate its history, legendary or authentic, in a *thamaing* (historical narrative), as it is termed. As late as in the eighties of the eighteenth century, king Bodawpaya built dozens of pagodas and ambitiously started to build an enormous one that should, if completed, be 500 feet high (Shwedagon at Rangoon being only 302 feet). Under the king's personal supervision, thousands of workmen laboured for seven years on its construction. But the work could not be finished, as time wore on to the eve of the first Anglo-Burmese war that resulted in the annexation of Burma to British India.[35]

[35] See Hall's *History of South-east Asia*, p. 504.

The pagoda is the Burmese form of a Stūpa,—an artificial mound, built supposedly over the body-relics of the Buddha or any of his sainted followers. But this strictly commemorative purpose of a Stūpa was later not insisted on,[36] and it became,—perhaps from the time of Emperor Asoka in the 3rd century B.C.—only a monumental emblem of the faith. As emblems of the faith, Stūpas were built in all the countries where Buddhism spread in its early (Hīnayāna) form. For these sacred mounds there did not exist any fixed architectural type. The unique distinction of the type that evolved in Burma was the replacement of the usual dome and overtopping *Harmika* (Stone-or-brick-built *Harmika*—umbrella) by a straight spire soaring flame-like towards sky. It is supposed to be in imitation of the spire of a Hindu temple. Whatever the fact, it strikes one immediately as the most impressive symbolical expression in achitecture of the soul's upward urge from the earth to the divine.

Rise of Pegu and Ceylonese Influence

When Pagan was captured by Timur in 1287, the Mon population of the city was driven further south. Slowly, in about two troublous centuries of foreign aggression and internal strife, a fresh centre of Mon life and culture was established at Pegu, to the south of Pagan. Pegu remained the capital of an independent kingdom till 1539.

Near Pegu was the small fishing village of Dagon. It had taken its name from the Shwedagon Pagoda that stood there, associated with the legend of Taphussa and Bhallika. In course of time the village became a famous place of pilgrimage and its pagoda attracted the attention of successive Burmese kings who contributed to its heightening and enlargement. Centuries later there grew up a township round this pagoda; its population increased, and it was named Rangoon in 1755, now the capital of Lower Burma.

Pegu continued as the capital of a Mon kingdom until the kingdom itself was wiped out in 1535. Enjoying a long spell of peace and prosperity, it throve as a famous commercial centre. But it was only in the fifteenth century that the kings of Pegu turned their attention to the need for stimulating and reviving Buddhism in the city. Of this revivalist movement, king Dhammaceti (1472-1492 A.D.) was the energetic leader.

A monk at the beginning of his life, he was chosen by Queen Shinsawbu (1453-1472 A.D.) to succeed to the throne. Forsaking the cloister at the Queen's instance for the hand of a princess, the erstwhile monk, now installed as a king, proved in his after-career to be a very wise and beneficent

[36] See Dutt's *Buddhist Monks and Monasteries of India*, pp. 184—186.

ruler. Led by his monkish predisposition, he turned his attention to ecclesiastical reform. For this he naturally looked towards Ceylon.

The prestige of Ceylon as the chosen home of Buddhism, where the religion was believed to be practised in its pristine purity, had gone up in the Buddhist countries of South-east Asia since the 12th century when Parakkamabāhu reformed the religion in Ceylon and re-organised the Saṅgha. It was not unusual for Burmese monks to go to Ceylon to receive a purer form of *Upasampadā* (Ordination) at the hands of Ceylonese *theras*. One such ordination ceremony had already been held on the Colombo lake where high dignitaries of the Ceylonese Saṅgha, like Vanaratana Saṅgharāja and Rāhula Mahāthera, had officiated. This had been twenty-six years before Dhammaceti made an organised attempt to give Burmese monks the benefit of a fresh ordination in Ceylon.

The attempt involved great preparatory labour and enormous expenditure,—the equipping of two ships to carry in each a party of 22 monks with an envoy bearing costly presents to the Ceylonese king. The voyage to Ceylon and back was also not uneventful: the vicissitudes that attended it are described in Dhammaceti's Kalyani inscriptions. The Ceylonese king Bhuvanaika-bāhu IV made arrangements for the ordination of these Burmese monks at Kalyani (now called Kelania) by the highest church dignitaries. When they were back at Pegu, the king, wishing perhaps to economise expenditure on such missions in future, set up a *sīmā* (consecrated area where the ordination ceremony of monks is held) in the neighbourhood of Pegu. Here Burmese monks were thereafter ordained during his reign. He gave it the commemorative name, *Kalyāni Sīmā*. He also put up here in marble slabs a long inscription, giving an account of the cultural and religious intercourse between Burma and Ceylon with a sort of preface purporting to be an historical *resume* of the growth of the Buddhist *sāsana* (regimen) in both countries.

Thus Ceylonese Theravāda Buddhism has become since Dhammaceti the established, state-recognised faith of the Burmese people.

The Cult of the Nats

An indigenous cult had been prevalent in Burma long before the introduction of Buddhism. Grudgingly allowed by Anawrahta, sought to be suppressed by later kings of Burma, it survived and survives still, sometimes under the protecting veil of Buddhism and sometimes without it. It is a folk cult known as *Nat-worship*.

A regional outgrowth of primitive animism, it evolved as an elaborate cult in Burma with attendant rites and ceremonies, priestly ministrations and its own legends and mythology. In form it was a kind of 'geniolatry'. It was the name given to it by an American writer, Louis Vossion, in a paper in the *Journal of American Folklore*, April-June, 1891, which was one of the earliest studies of Burmese Nat-worship. Stemming from a belief in the existence everywhere of guardian spirits with localised spheres of power and activity, it is in actual practice the propitiation of these spirits called *Nats* (a word of unknown derivation) equivalent to 'Lords'.

"At first the Nats that were worshipped were impersonal and local, as for example the Nats of the banyan tree, the hill, and the lake just outside the village, and the guardian Nat of the village itself. Later on thirty-six personal and national Nats came into being, who were distinct personages with their own life-histories, and who were worshipped all over the country. They did not replace the local Nats, but diminished their importance".[37] Out of the life-histories of these 'personal and national' Nats, the mythology of Nat worship was evolved.

Of the 36 Nats the most important was the Lord of the Great Mountain. His abode was on Mount Popa where he dwelt with his sister Lady Golden-Face. In the 9th century,—that is more than a century before the coming of Anawrahta,—they had become the guardian gods of the city of Pagan and its kings.

"There was an annual Nat feast on Mount Popa itself, at which hundreds of animals were offered in sacrifice to the Lord of the Great Mountain and Lady Golden-Face. People came from afar to take part in the feast, to get drunk with ecstasy and toddy wine, and to dance with abandon, believing themselves to have become possessed by the Nats. There were spirit-mediums in attendance at the Nat shrines, who provided wild music and the wilder dances. The Popa feast was held on a full-moon day in December, and on other full-moon days there were also feasts connected with other pre-Buddhistic cults".[38]

The figures of the Nats, conceived in anthropomorphic forms, were cast in images, installed in shrines and worshipped. Nat worship was closely allied with astrology and divination and the 'Nine Planets' had their place among the Nat Lords.

Though the number of Nats officially recognised is 37 (including Śakra, the divine protector of Buddhism called *Thagya* in Burmese, who was introduced into the pantheon by Anawrahta), the number was actually fluctuating and indeterminate. From time to time the official list of 37 Nats was drawn up by royal authority,——the final list was made in Burma under King Bodapaya whose kingdom fell in 1885. It was made by his minister Myawaddi.

[37] See Maung Htin Aung's article on "Folk Elements in Burmese Buddhism" in 'Perspective on Burma', *Atlantic Monthly Supplement* (9th in the series). Also Htin Aung's article on "The Thirtyseven Lords" in the *Journal of the Burma Research Society*, June, 1954.

[38] See *Ibid.*

The pictures of these Nats, in characteristic lineaments and postures as conceived in Nat mythology, may be consulted in R.C. Temple's *The Thirty-seven Nats*, — a book published in London in 1906 and now extremely rare, but available in the library of the International Institute of Advanced Buddhist Studies at the Peace Pagoda of Rangoon. They are mostly in human form, both male and female, but most often with multiple hands and legs, seated on different kinds of mounts, and distinguished by other marks of superhuman status.

How these 37 deities were congregated in the Nat pantheon is a problem on which Dr. Htin Aung has thrown some light.[39] They were taken from various sources. Old Nats yielded place to new Nats,—— the personalities of the latter being merged with those of the former; kings, queens and princes, apotheosized after death, became 'Lords'; the 'Nine Planets' were Lords, and among the remaining, some were drawn from imagination and some from Buddhist mythology. Among these Buddhist Nats is the Nat Mon. He stands for the Buddhist Māra and is a 'bad' Nat, with his three daughters *Tanhā*, *Rati* and *Arati* (Thirst, Attachment and Discontent).[40]

The making up of a pantheon with elements so heterogenous shows how inchoate the Nat cult is. In fact Nat worship is no unified system, but a bundle of astrological superstitions, concepts of magic and unmeaning rituals best designated by the term, 'proto-religion', used for cults of this primitive and amorphous character.

As the cult developed, a differentiation was adopted between 'Good Nats' and 'Bad Nats', i.e., those who exercised their powers for good and those for evil. In an old Burmese chronicle, it is said that Alaungpaya who led a campaign in the middle of the 18th century against the Mons of Burma had been 'inspired by the good Nats who observe religion.'[41] His own name meant 'Embryo Buddha'. We cannot be certain whether this differentiation between the good and the bad Nats had anything to do with Buddhist influence on Nat worship, but the 'Good Nats' came to be regarded as supporters of Buddhism and worshippers of the Buddha. Thus the folk-cult found a way to align itself with the cultured and state-sponsored religion.

Anawrahta, trying to introduce Buddhism among the people, came up sharply against the wide-spread native custom of Nat worship. It was not in his power to abolish it completely, but he tried to discourage it by assigning to it a position inferior to Buddhism,—even to give it a Buddhist colouring by raising Śakra, the divine protector of Buddhism, to the head

[39] See Dr. Htin's article on *The Thirtyseven Lords* in the *Journal of the Burma Research Society*, June, 1956.

[40] Sir R. C. Temple's *The Thirtyseven Nats*, London, 1906, p. 70.

[41] See Hall's *History of South-east Asia*, p. 343.

of the Nat pantheon. He collected the images of Nat deities from all the existing shrines. But, instead of destroying them, he put them all on an isolated platform in the Swezigon Pagoda built by him at Pagan. A Nat-worshipper would thus be compelled to come to the Buddhist place of worship and was expected to realise by comparison how far superior Buddhist worship was to the Nat Cult. One of the sayings, fathered on Anawrahta, about his collection of Nat images in the Swezigon pagoda is: 'Men will not come for the sake of the new faith. Let them come for their old gods and gradually they will be won over'.[42] Anawrahta tried also to cripple Nat worship by suppressing the Ari priesthood from which most of its ministrants came.

But Nat worship never ceased in Burma, in spite of the late efforts of king Bayinnaung (d. 1581) who aspired to be a model Buddhist king and issued edict after edict restricting Nat worship in the kingdom.

One way in which it managed to survive was by placing itself under the aegis of Buddhism. The 'Good Nats' were treated as Bodhisattvas attending on the Buddha and were assigned in Buddhist temples places as attendant gods. Even in the Shwedagon Pagoda of Rangoon, there are images of Nat deities, and one of them, *Yama*, god of death, is prominently placed. The observance of the worship of Nine Planetary gods was enlarged into a joint ceremony of the worship of the Buddha and eight Arhats along with the Nine Planets. The Nat gods in a Buddhist temple are usually shown in the attitude of worshipping the presiding Buddha-image with faces turned towards it. Many a Buddhist in Burma combines in this way Buddha-worship with Nat-worship.

The belief that the Nats are Burma's 'national' gods, functioning in times of national crisis on the side of the Burmese and partaking of the people's sorrows and sufferings in national calamities is deeply rooted in the minds of the populace. When the Tartar army invaded the country in 1277, men said that the Nat Lords fought side by side with the Burmese soldiers and some of the Nats were wounded by the Tartar's arms; the Lord of the White Horse and the Brothers Inferior Gold shared the sorrow and shame of the Burmese soldiers who retreated from the British in 1825; the gilded images of the Thirtyseven Lords at the king's palace shed human tears when Theebaw, the last king of Burma, was taken away as a prisoner by the British army in 1885; when great fires broke out in the city of Mandalay after an air-raid in April 1943, the Brothers Inferior Gold were seen fighting the fires shoulder to shoulder with the stricken people.[43]

---

[42] May's *The Culture of South-east Asia*, p. 54.

[43] See Htin Aung's article on *The Thirtyseven Lords* in the *Journal of Burma Research Society*, June, 1956.

These examples lend point and significance to the following observation made by Sir R.C. Temple:

"In order to understand the daily life and aspirations of the ordinary Burman, it is not sufficient to know that he is by professed religion a Buddhist and to understand what his Buddhism teaches. It is necessary to know also that he is a firm believer in Nats or spirits and to grasp how the superstitions connected with this faith affect him in his daily life and notions".[44]

Note on the Chronicles

As a number of references has been made to the Burmese chronicles, specially the *Glass Palace Chronicle*, a short note seems called for on this indigenous form of Burmese historiography.

The oldest chronicles of Burma go back to the 15th century. But few of these chronicles, written from the 15th century down to the end of the 17th, survive now. Among the survivals are the Taffgaung Chronicle, the Tharehkittara (Śrīkshetra) Chronicle, the Hngeppyittaung Chronicle and the Pagan Chronicle. These chronicles were written by monks, dealing with particular places or periods and embodying local legends. They were mainly intended to impart instruction in morals and religion. Products of monk-scholarship in Pali, drawing largely on works like the *Dīpavaṁsa* and the *Mahāvaṁsa* and their commentaries, these works were eked out with indigenous stories, some taken from existing local legends and some invented for didactic purpose.

It was in the 18th century that a voluminous chronicle, written not by a monk this time, but by a 'professional' chronicler, appeared. It was the Mahayazawin (The Great Chronicle) by U Kala (1724 A.D.). In compiling this work, U Kala consulted about 70 works from different sources, not the Pali chronicles and commentaries alone, but also local chronicles and old inscriptions. It was not of parochial range and interest, but pan-Burman in outlook and free from monkish moralizing. U Kala's monumental work set the standard for the later Burmese chronicles. There were other chronicles written in this century, but they were restricted in outlook, like the anonymous New Pagan Chronicle (1785) which conforms to the type of the old chronicles in being purely regional, confined to the dynasty of the Pagan kings, as well as in its moralizing tendency. Also, U. Kala's is a work of great literary merit. It was followed by another chronicle in 1798 written by an eminent scholar Mahasitthu and, in both this chronicle and the previous one, there is a marked growth of critical attitude towards the older chronicles and a greater reliance on the evidence of inscriptions.

---

[44] Sir R. C. Temple in Preface to *The Thirtyseven Nats*, London, 1906.

The 19th century was the age of official chronicles. Chronicle-writing passed from the hands of monks and came under the king's commission. King Bagyidaw in 1829 appointed a Committee of 'learned monks, Brāhmaṇas and ministers' to compile a revised and definitive official chronicle of the kings of Burma that should be "the standard—a balance, so to speak,—for all duties of the king, for all affairs of state, for all matters of religion and not a thing full of conflicting and false statements". The compilers had to revise and re-examine many of U Kala's observations in the opening parts of his work. The work of compilation in which the narrative was brought down to the year 1821 took about 4 years. This officially revised chronicle is known as the *Hmannan Yazawin* or the *Glass Palace Chronicle* after the name of the palace-hall where the authors used to assemble regularly for their labours.

Later in 1867 King Mindon appointed another committee and had a new chronicle compiled, taking up the narrative from the point where the *Glass Palace Chronicle* had ended. The industry of chronicle-writing under royal aegis continued in Burma till its annexation to British India in the eighties of the last century.

Except to those who are competent scholars in the Burmese language or are engaged in a special study of these chronicles, the best known and the most frequently cited one is the *Glass Palace Chronicle* (Hmannan Yazawin) of King Bagyidaw. Translated into English by Pe Maung Tin and G.H. Luce and published by the Burma Research Society, it went into a second printing in 1960 (Rangoon University Press, Rangoon, Burma). It is not, however, a translation of the whole of the original, but of the third, fourth and fifth parts which relate to Burma, carrying on the narrative from the foundation of the Taguang kingdom by the Sakiyan king Abhiraja to the fall of Pagan. The previous parts connect Burmese history through the legendary story of Buddhism to the Buddhist kings of ancient India. Maung Tin's learned introduction to this Translation is an able summing up of the history of Burmese chronicle-writing.

The chronicles (*Yazawin* in Burmese) are concerned mostly with legends of the royal dynasties and contemporary events. There is little information except what is incidental on the people's ethnic or cultural developments. So among modern Burmese writers on Burmese history a distinction is recognised between the *Yazawin* of the conventional type and the *Thamaing*, historical narrative proper, signifying a growing appreciation of history in its wider sense covering the economic, social and cultural life of the people.[45]

[45] See Tin Ohn's article on *Modern Historical Writing in Burmese* in Hall's *Historians of South-east Asia*, pp. 92-93.

For more detailed information on the Burmese Yazawin, the reader may consult: (i) Maung Tin's Introduction to the *Glass Palace Chronicle* (published by Burma Historical Society, Rangoon), (ii) U Tet Htoot's chapter on *The Nature of Burmese Chronicles* in Hall's *Historians of Southeast Asia* (Oxford University Press, 1961) and (iii) Tin Ohn's article in it on *Modern Historical Writings in Burmese*, from which we have quoted.

Chapter V

SIAM (including Laos)

SIAM since 1947 has adopted the official name of Thailand from the Thai. The Thai people, after whom it is now named, entered Siam from the hilly north, fanned out into the plains and became in ripeness of time rulers of the entire country. This was a couple of centuries after the appearance of the Thai in Burma. The original name Siam, however, is an ancient one; it occurs in Chinese annals, in Sanskrit literature and in Ceylonese chronicles,—in fact in all references to the country, ancient or modern, prior to 1947, —and is still preferred by Siamese scholars.

To a certain extent, there is a parallelism between the early history of Burma and that of Siam.

As geographical and political entities, both owe their origins to the great Thai tribal migrations from Nanchao in the 8th century, to which we have referred in the context of Burma; in both countries later generations of these Thai immigrants intermingled with the original Mon population; and in both, the conquering people from the beginning absorbed the superior culture of the conquered, including their Buddhist religion. *Ramaññadesha* was a sort of bridge connecting Siam with Lower Burma,——unifying and consolidating a common Mon culture in both.

Bounded by the Gulf of Siam on one side and the lands of Cambodia, Laos, Burma and Malay on the other, Siam in her irregular contour has a somewhat extraordinary look on the map,—'like the shadowy outline of the shrunken face and trunk of an elephant.'[1] All her contacts with countries on her borders had important political and cultural consequences in her history.

Early contacts with India and Cambodia: The coming of the Thai

The Mons were the original people of Siam. They had settled in ancient times in the valley of the Menam and along the lower reaches of its tributaries. This anciently Mon-occupied region is called Central Siam which comprises also the 'trunk of the elephant', extending along two-thirds of the Malay peninsula. The 'trunk' had some functional importance, as we shall see, in the making of the early history of Central Siam.

[1] Busch's *Thailand*, Asia Library, 1959.

The centre of Mon life and culture in this region was Lovo or Lopbury. To its south existed another Mon kingdom in the 7th century with its capital at Dvārāvati. It was a variant name of the holy city of Dwārakā in the Kathiwad peninsula of India. Mon Dvārāvati was known to both Hsüan-tsang and I-tsing, but little that is historical is known about it. Its reality seems to have dissolved in its legendary after-fame. The second capital of Siam was named Dvārāvati-Ayodhiā and in the *Ramakien* of king Rāma I (see *infra* under the *Chakri Dynasty*), it is said to have been the capital of Rāma, hero of the Indian epic, *Rāmāyana*.[2] Further to the south down below the 'trunk', is Malay extending to the sea-coast.

These Indian names of Mon localities indicate that a source of Indian contact was open during the 5th-6th centuries to the Mons of Central Siam. It was attained through its south-pointing peninsular extension.

Between India and the Malay peninsula, there were ancient trade relations. In consequence, a number of Indian settlements existed in those centuries in Malay. In several sites of Malay, archaeological relics of these ancient Indian settlements have been discovered,—some going back to the 5th century,—as Kinta, Perak, Wellesley, Parlio, the Marbok Estuary, etc. An upward route from the Malay sea-coast to Central Siam is indicated by the lie of these localities. In any case, some intercommunication between the Indian settlements of the south and the Mons of Central Siam is suggested by the finds in Malay of Mon iconographic samples. They are plain imitations of fifth-century Indian Gupta art.

How far this intercommunication was on a cultural level cannot be ascertained. But it was from the south that both Indian faiths,—Brāhmaṇism and Buddhism,—spread among the Mons. Buddhism seems to have been more popular and more wide-spread. In the two main accessory activities of these religions, viz., temple-building and image-making, the Mons developed an art of their own, so distinctive that it is recognised as the 'pre-Khmer art' of Siam.

In the reign of king Suryavarman of Angkor (1002-1050 A.D.), Central Siam came under Cambodian domination: it lasted for a little more than two centuries, though the Cambodians did not give up their possessions entirely for a century more. The Siamese in captivity is the subject of a piece of sculpture in a southern wall of the great Khmer temple of Angkor-wat at Siemreap. It is marked with the epigraph 'Syam' (Siamese) commemorating this early Cambodian domination. It spelt not merely political subjection, but cultural as well. Siamese art during the Khmer period shows, both in the style of temple-building and in the fashioning of Buddha-images, a remark-

[2] See Prince Dhaninivat's article on "The City of Thawarawadi Sri Ayudhya" *Journa[l] of the Siam Society*, Selected Articles, Vol. III, p. 230.

able deflection from its older norms and standards. Yet the tradition of 'pre-Khmer Mon' art re-asserted itself with the passing away of Angkor rule.

A century later the Thai people appeared on the scene and Central Siam passed from the hands of Angkor kings into those of the Thai.

The northern part of Siam, however, known till recently as Byab, where the well-known Siamese cities Lang-chang (ancient Luang-prabang) and Chiengmai are situated, was never reached by the expansionist Angkor kingdom. In Siam it is known as the 'Lanna country'. Here lived the aboriginal people of Siam. While in the other and Mon-inhabited parts of Siam, Buddhism prevailed, Lanna received Buddhism somewhat late,—only in the 8th century, through the missionary activities of Chāma Devi, of whom we shall speak later.

Into the pre-dominatingly Mon region, Central Siam, the Thai tribes from Nanchao came wandering through the mountains, foot-hills, jungles and hill-streams of the north. They found themselves in a country far different from their own,—among a people who had learnt the ways of civilization, established a stable agricultural economy, and professed a cultured and developed religion.

Over the 11th and the 12th centuries, the Thais spread themselves over the northern and north-eastern parts and were occupying also the central plains. Gradually consolidating their power, they overran the whole country, overflowing eastwards into Laos. While settling in the country, they went on absorbing by intermarriage the Mon element of the population, —yet not so thoroughly as it had been in Burma, for the Mon still exists in Siam distinct from the Thai. As there have been several Mon immigrations from Lower Burma into Siam in later times[3], it is somewhat difficult to distinguish Siamese Mons of older descent. But some of the Mon population in the country represent undoubtedly the remnants of what the Thai had left unassimilated.

In 1287, when Siam had been completely conquered by the Thai, three Thai chieftains got together and entered into an historic pact for division of the conquered territory. The two most important partners in this pact were Mangrai and Rama Khamheng. Under its terms, the regions along the Upper Menam were assigned to Mangrai, i.e., nearly the whole of northern Siam, and to Khamheng, the regions along the Lower Menam, i.e., central and southern Siam.

Both have gone down in the history of Siam as the main builders and organisers of Buddhism in the country.

---

[3] See *Journal of Siam Society* (Fiftieth Anniversary Commemoration Publication), Vol. I: Halliday's article on *Immigration of the Mons into Siam.*

Buddhism and the Thai Rulers of Siam

It is significant that in both Burma and Siam, where the Thai from Nanchao penetrated, the Thai rulers adopted and patronised the kind of Buddhism practised among their Mon subjects. It was different from Chinese Buddhism which their forbears must have known in Nanchao before their dispersal.

A Thai chief of Nanchao, after conquering some parts of Tibet and declaring independence of the Chinese emperor, set up in 766 a tablet at a spot in southern China. It records that the conqueror Ko-lo-feng has 'opened the door' to all the three religions of China,—Confucianism, Taoism and Buddhism.[4] The Thai tribesmen, before setting out on their long migrations from Nanchao, must have known the Chinese Mahāyānist type of Buddhism; their after-generations, coming to Burma and Siam, experienced a different kind of the same religion in practice among the Mons.

It was Hīnayāna Buddhism, which in its ethics put a premium on virtues that make for social peace and order, that was more helpful for the foundation of civilized life and more conducive to the stability of the body-politic. Thai rulers like Anawrahta in Burma, Rama Khamheng and Mangrai in Siam must have felt that the Hīnayāna Buddhism practised by the Mons could be made an ally of the state and a guarantee for its stability.

Mangrai and his successors in Lanna

When Mangrai began his reign in northern Siam (Lanna), Buddhism there was about five centuries old.

There are recorded legends about its first introduction there and later developments; they form the staple of two Siamese historical works in Pali—*Chāmadevī-vaṁsa* (The Lineage of Chāma Devī) and *Jinakāla-mālini* (The Garland of Buddhist times). They are late works,—the former written by a monk named Bodhiraśmi at Chiengmai or at Lampun about the beginning of the 15th century and the latter by a monk of the Ratnavihāra Monastery at Chiengmai in 1516. Some of the legends and traditions they record must have survived in the monasteries of Chiengmai and Lampun when these works were composed.

In both of them, Chāma Devī figures as the first messenger and propagator of Buddhism in Lanna. A princess of the Chāma royal house, she had been married to a Mon king of Lower Burma. Her mind, however, was set on higher objects and, having come to know that the people of northern Siam

---

[4] See May's *The Culture of South-east Asia*, p. 155 Also Carthew's article on *The History of the Thai in Yunnan* in the *Journal of the Siam Society*, Vol. III, p. 152: "The tablet of stone is probably the largest in South China......The local name for it is the *Tablet of the Southern Prince*"

had not had the benefit of Buddhist teaching yet, she came to the north from Lopbury, the ancient cultural centre of the Mons in southern Siam, to offer it to the people. She was the founder of the city of Haripunjiya and progenitor of a line of kings. She belonged probably to the 8th century. Founded by Chāma Devī, Buddhism had spread and throve in the Lanna country for about five hundred years before the Thai King Mangrai and his successors espoused its cause. Nearly one half of the *Jinakālamālini* is given to the story of Mangrai, his patronage of Buddhism, his fifty years of rule over Lanna and his royal dynasty.

Mangrai was the first Thai king of Lanna. He had already paid a visit to Pagan (in Burma) and was struck, like the Burmese king Anawrahta two centuries before him, with Mon Buddhist culture. At Pagan Mangrai studied specially the form of Buddhist temple architecture, and when he was back at his own capital Chiengmai, he built two temples,—one in the city and the other on the outskirts. The temple within the city was built in the style he had seen at Pagan and was the first religious foundation in that area. The other on the outskirts, known as the 'Seven-spire Temple', a grander and more spectacular one, was on the pattern of the Bodhgaya temple of India. This temple had been built by a Burmese king and Mangrai had the opportunity of seeing its blueprint at Pagan.

It was the achievement of king Kuna (1355-1385 A.D), the fourth king in the line of Mangrai, to introduce into this part of Siam the Theravāda Buddhism of Ceylon.

For this purpose, he invited to his kingdom a renowned Ceylonese monk named Sumana, then staying at Sukhotai, who propagated in Lanna the doctrines of the *Āraññaka* (Forest-dwelling) monks of Ceylon. The introduction of Ceylonese Buddhism in his reign gave a stimulus to Pali scholarship as well as to original literary activity. From the middle of the 14th century down to the 16th, Lanna produced a body of Buddhist literature in Pali of which *Chāmadevī-vaṁsa* and *Jinakālamālini* are outstanding examples.[5]

Rama Khamheng and his Stele

Rama Khamheng, the other Thai king who ruled over the central and southern parts of Siam, had his capital in the south, at Sukhotai which covered the twin cities of Sachanalai and Sukhotai.

He made it the lynch-pin of his policy to maintain friendly relations with the imperial court of China. 'The *Yuan History* records a whole series of missions from Sukhotai to the imperial court".[6] He himself paid two

[5] These two works will be found, with their original texts and a French translation, in Coedes's Documents on the Political and Religious History of West Laos in BEFEO, vol. xxv. The Pali texts with Siamese translations have also been published by the Sobhon Press, Bangkok, in 1909 and 1920.

[6] Hall's *History of South-east Asia*, p. 149.

visits to China, once in 1294 and again in 1300, and on the latter occasion he is said to have married a Chinese princess and brought back with him to his capital a number of ceramic workers from China. They were probably the pioneers of the ceramic art of Siam.[7] Remains of ancient pottery works are still to be seen in the neighbourhood of Khamheng's ruined capital.

The king must have had some previous knowledge of Buddhism as practised in China. But the Mon rites and ceremonies of the country, held in sylvan surroundings and with quiet, unostentatious piety, had evidently a deeper appeal for him. It appears clearly enough from the stele he has left. He and his court adopted this native Mon Buddhism, and the fact was declared to the people in the stele he has left which was discovered in 1833 by Prince (later king) Mongkut of Siam. Its text had been publicised by Khamheng himself in stone-inscriptions at different places.

It offers the earliest specimen of written Siamese. The script was of the king's invention. The opinion of modern scholarship is that it is based on a cursive form of Khmer writing.[8] The king declares in the inscriptions that, exercising his mind for some time past over the problem of putting the Thai language into writing, having long "sought and desired it in his heart", he was putting into use "these strokes of Siamese writing". To his Mon subjects, the Thai language in a script modified from cursive Khmer (which must have been well-known in this part where the Khmers for more than two centuries had held sway) was easily intelligible. Khamheng wanted his declaration on the stele to be widely known to his people. The king's script, known as 'Sukhodaya script', spread throughout the country and it influenced also the development of writing in the neighbouring state of Laos.

Nearly all our information about the early life and career of Khamheng and of the lay-out and landmarks of his capital Sukhotai is derived from the stele which is regarded with deep veneration to this day by the Siamese. Its original text is preserved in the Bangkok museum and a copy of it is posted for Siam's coming generations at the entrance to the second storey of the Chulalakorn University building at Bangkok. Like some of the edicts of Asoka, it is a self-revealing document.[9]

It begins with an autobiographical sketch telling of the king's parentage, his love for his brothers and his devotion to parents. It proceeds to speak of the military exploits of his youth and his inheritance of the entire realm,

---

[7] See Spink's article on *Siam and the Pottery Trade of Asia* in the *Journal of the Siam Society*, vol. III, pp. 254-256.

[8] See article by Burnay and Coedes on *The Origins of the Sukodaya Script* in the *Journal of the Siam Society*, vol. xvi, pt. ii.

[9] An English translation of the text of the stele will be found in Bradlay's article on "The Oldest Known Writing in Siamese" in the *Journal of the Siam Society*, Vol. VI, pt. I.

having been left the only heir after the decease of his brothers. Then it passes from autobiographical matter to a statement of the liberal principles adopted by him in the government of the state.

The king was a thorough believer in personal contact with his subjects. Access to him was made possible for every individual. At the palace-gate he had a bell hung up which any one aggrieved was allowed to ring to bring one's grievance to the king's notice. "Go, ring the bell which he has hung up there. Prince Rama Khamheng, lord of the realm, can hear the call. When he has made investigations, he will sift the case according to right". The king records that the city of Sukhotai has been rapidly prospering and he notices with approval the people's adherence to the religion of the Buddha, declaring that "Rama Khamheng, lord of this realm of Sukhotai, with matrons and nobles of the city, their retinues of servants and maidens, the gentry, both male and female and one and all, and the mass of common folk, have reverence for the teaching of the Buddha."

On the west of the city, was a monastery site secluded in the wood, called *Wat Araññika* ('Forest Monastery'). Here the king installed a learned 'Mahāthera' ('Great Priest') from 'Sithammarat'. This locality, mentioned in Buddhist works with as many as five variant names, viz., Sri-Dhammarāja-Nagara, Sri-Dhammarāja, Nakhon-Sri-Dhammarāja, Tambarattha and Tambralinga, is identified with modern Ligor. An ancient Buddhist settlement in Malaya, it lay at the time within Rama Khamheng's realm. The Mahāthera is described as 'the scholar who has studied the *Tipitaka* (Buddhist canon) unto its end'. He was named 'Head of the Order, the Archpriest above every other teacher in this realm'.

A temple, 'large, lofty and exceeding fair', was annexed to this forest-monastery. It held an eighteen-cubit Buddha-image standing erect. On the days of the New Moon and the Full Moon the king used to come here on elephant-back to worship. "He had the white elephant Ruchosi arrayed with trappings and housings, all of gold and ivory......and Prince Khamheng mounted and rode forth to worship the Buddha......and came back again".

There was a number of temples in the east of Sukhotai 'with venerable teachers in them'; to the north lay the inhabited country with villages, great and small, and beautiful groves of mango and tamarind trees, 'as lovely as though made only to be looked at'. The market-places, the villages and the royal palace were located in the south and everywhere there were monks' cells and temples. Sukhotai was thus laid out mainly as a Buddhist city with numerous facilities for the study and practice of Buddhism.

To complete all the amenities for Buddhists, he interred some sacred relics in the heart of the city of Sachanalai and built a great pagoda over them.

In the epilogue to the inscription, he makes the following proclamation:

"Rama Khamheng sought to be ruler and lord over all the Thai, to be preceptor and instructor to all the Thai, to know true virtue and righteousness. Among men that live in the realm of the Thai, for knowledge and insight, for bravery and daring, for energy and force, there cannot be found a man equal to him,—one able to subdue hosts of enemies, owning cities wide and elephants many".

——and then proceeds to define the boundaries of the realm over which he rules.

There is no doubt that Rama Khamheng was a devout Buddhist himself and tried his best to bring his people under the refining influence of Buddhism. But superstitions die hard and the king himself was not quite immune from them. While he inculcates Buddhism in his edicts, he draws at the same time the attention of people to a Demon-spirit who acts as the guardian deity of the realm:

"In yonder mountain is a Demon-spirit Phra Khaphung that is greater than any other spirit in this realm. If any prince ruling in this realm of Sukhotai reverences him well with proper offerings, this realm stands firm, the realm prospers. If the Spirit be not reverenced well, if the offerings be not right, the Spirit in the mountain does not protect, does not regard,—this realm perishes".

The superstition, so akin to Burmese 'geniolatry', does not seem to have yielded to Buddhist teachings. Right down to the time of Rama I of the Chakri dynasty, who, without suppressing the worship of spirits and demons, tried to subordinate it to Buddhist worship, the populace in Siam retained this superstitious demon-worship.

The traditional story is that Rama Khamheng (c. 1275-1317), after a long reign, found a watery grave, disappearing shortly before 1318 in the rapids of a river. His capital was evacuated as the result of a cholera epidemic and a new capital named Dvārāvati-Ayudhiā was founded on an island in the Mekong river by a new Thai prince of a different line. But to its last days Sukhodaya continued to be a centre of Buddhist learning and culture under the fostering care of Khamheng's successors.

Ceylon's Influence on Siamese Buddhism

There is an inscription by Khamheng's son and successor, Liddya, who ascended the Sukhotai throne in 1339, expatiating on the benefits and advantages of a visit to Ceylon.[10] Ceylon was regarded in that age by the countries of South-east Asia as the 'well of Buddhism undefiled'. Learned monks of Ceylon were therefore invited to Sukhotai, and one of them, Udambaragiri Saṅgharāja, is famous in the history of Siam for the alignment he gave to

[10] See *History of Ceylon*, vol. I, pt. II, p. 754.

Siamese Buddhism to the Sinhalese Theravāda form. The community of *āraññaka* (forest-dwelling) Bhikkhus of Ceylon were looked upon as the model in Siam and Udambaragiri belonged to that community. His arrival at Sukhotai was the occasion for a grand and well-organised ovation.[11]

> "At the time when the venerable monk had reached half of the way to the city from Nikon Pan, the king instructed builders to erect monastic quarters in the Mango Grove to the west of Sukhotai. Roads were levelled and strewn with sand and looked fine from all sides as if they had been constructed by Visvakarmā, the celestial artificer. Upon their arrival, fruits, floral offerings, candles, incense and 'plants of plenty' embellished their ways of approach".

Who this Saṅgharāja was is not exactly known; he was certainly a high-ranking Sinhalese *thera*, whom Dr. Paranavitana had tried to identify with Saṅgharāja Medhaṅkara, author of *Lokappadīpa-sāra*. In the colophon of that work he describes himself as the preceptor of the mother of the Burmese king, and also the *guru* (spiritual guide) of 'King Lidayya',[12] Khamheng's son and successor. It was *via* Ramaññadesha or Lower Burma that most of the Sinhalese monks used to come to Siam.

The visit of Medhaṅkara and other Sinhalese monks who followed him had the effect not only of bringing Buddhism in Sukhotai under a church government, but also of giving a great fillip to learning in Pali literature, both sacred and secular. One who became a master of this literature was Rama Khamheng's grandson, Lu Tai, who in due course came to the throne. He wrote an original treatise on Buddhist cosmology, entitled *Traibhūmika-kathā* (The Tale of the Three Worlds), an extant classic of Siamese literature.[13]

Upbuilding a Hierarchy in Siam

Buddhism had been growing up in its own way as a State-sponsored religion in Siam until the impact of Ceylonese Buddhism upon it was felt in the later years of Sukhotai. The idea of 'church government' being a function of the Saṅgha was central in Ceylonese Theravāda Buddhism, and this was impressed on Siamese Buddhism by instructors from Ceylon. The basis for a hierarchy had been laid in the Sukhotai era, though its superstructure was not built till in the next Ayodhian period.

---

[11] Coedes's *Recueil des Inscriptions du Siam*, vol. I, pp. 42-48, translated as above by Prince Dhaninivat in the brochure *A History of Buddhism in Siam*, p. 6.

[12] See *History of Ceylon*, vol. I, pt. II, p. 754.

[13] For a gist of this treatise, see Prince Dhaninivat's *A History of Buddhism in Siam*, pp. 9-11.

It may be presumed that the placing of religious matters under an ecclesiastical government was not an unwelcome idea to the kings of Ayodhiā who were increasingly burdened with political affairs.

At the end of Rama Khamheng's dynasty at Sukhotai and the establishment of Ayodhiā as the new capital, the Siamese kingdom had large territorial extensions. It became a powerful kingdom, controlling both the middle and the lower Menam valleys and a good part of Malay. A warfare also commenced between Siam and Cambodia lasting about a century from 1350 to the capture of Angkor by the Siamese in 1431.

There are several place-names in Cambodia with 'Siam' as one of the component words, e.g., Siem-reap, where the great temples (*Wats*) of the Angkor kings are located, and these place-names commemorate the fields of battle between the Siamese and the Cambodians in this hundred years' war. The Siamese capital remained at Ayodhiā till the catastrophe of a Burmese invasion in 1767. The invasion resulted in the shifting of the capital northwards to Bangkok. Ayodhiā had had a long lease of life: thirty-three Thai kings had ruled from that city.

The ecclesiastical system which had its beginnings in the Sukhotai period was established on the model of the Sinhalese *Saṅgha* and continued true to the model under the Ayodhian kings. Its background history was as follows:

Since Buddhism's early days in India,—that is, the time when Buddhist monks had developed a cenobitical life and organisation in the monasteries, —there had existed in the monkhood a class of monks who preferred an eremitical way of life to the cenobitism of the monasteries. They are referred to in the Pali canon as *Āraññaka* (forest-dwelling) monks. The two classes of monks,—forest-dwelling and convent-dwelling,—were formally distinguished in Ceylon: sometimes there were fierce disputes over points of Vinaya between the two which threatened to impair the Saṅgha's unity. In the reign of Vijayabāhu III of Ceylon (13th century), the king summoned a convocation to consider the points of dispute. This was followed by the publication by the king of what is known as *Kathikāvata* in Ceylonese history —a disciplinary ordinance for monks. To Vijayabāhu's convocation had come some of the great *theras* of the time, both classes of monks being represented, the *Gāmavāsi* (Town-dwelling) monks and the *Araññavāsi* (Forest-dwelling) monks, the latter led by Mahāthera Medhaṅkara.[14] This categorical distinction came to be recognised and accepted in Siam too. The Forest Monastery of Sukhotai in Khamheng's time was the resort of the *āraññakas* presided over by great Mahāthera from Thammarat who himself belonged to this category.

---

[14] See *History of Ceylon*, vol. I, pt. II, pp. 745-747. *Rahula's History of Buddhism in Ceylon*, p. 197, fn. 1. for the distinction in Ceylon between the Gamavasins and the Arannavasins.

But '*āraññaka*', monks who preferred life outside the monastery, were probably felt to be a misfit in an ecclesiastical organisation, and from the Sukhotai period to the Ayodhiā period, there was a slow transfer of authority in the monk-order from 'forest-dwelling' to 'town-dwelling' monks. The head of the 'town-dwelling' monks had in Siam the title of Phra Vanarat: it is in him that the duties of the Chief Executive of the Holy Order came to vest. An account of the Siamese ecclesiastical organisation, as it functions at present, is given in Busch's book on *Thailand* (Asia Library, 1957), which may be consulted for details. The organisation since its inception has not undergone any revolutionary change, though there have been reforms from time to time.

One effect, however, of giving the religion an official organisation may be noted. It certainly served to impair the spontaneous vitality of its prime,—what it had in the reign of Khamheng when no hierarchy existed. Religious art, as an expression and efflorescence of this vitality, suffered a decline. It is exemplified by the difference between the Buddha-images of the Sukhotai period and those of the Ayodhian. The fine idealism that inspired Siamese Buddha-images of the 13th and 14th centuries, when no clerical hierarchy existed, is never again re-captured in later iconographic art.

The Siamese kings being Buddhists themselves, there was no lack of royal patronage for the Saṅgha, but the kingdom had been growing in later periods to the size of an empire and the pressure of secular state duties on the kings grew inevitably more urgent. Monasteries and temples continued to be built, but the promotion of the cause of Buddhism among the people was by and large made the concern of the established hierarchy.

Three of the Ayudhian kings, however, concerned themselves with the affairs of the Saṅgha—Boromatrai Trilokanātha (1468-1488), Songdharm (Song'tom) (1610-1628), and Mahā Tammarāja II (1733-1758), known by the surname of 'His Majesty of the Sacred Urn'. Their contributions to the Buddhism of Siam were miscellaneous in character.

The first one of these three kings built the great temple, called Wat Culamani, at Pisunlok and decorated its precincts with works of sculpture. He is said to have embraced monastic life for a term of eight months.

The second was a scholarly king who was interested in safeguarding the purity of the canon. He made a royal version of the *Tipitaka* (Theravāda Buddhist canon) and also built a shrine to the footprints of the Buddha near Saraburi which, till recently, used to be visited by pious Siamese pilgrims.

In the reign of the third king, 'His Majesty of the Holy Urn', Buddhist culture seems to have received a new stimulus at Ayodhiā: it produced, before withering under the impact of the Burmese invasion of 1767, a splendid bloom, the fame of which reached Ceylon. The Sinhalese king Kittisiri sent three missions to Ayodhiā round 1750 to bring Siamese monks to his kingdom to give ordination to Ceylonese monks. Of these three missions, only the third was successful. It was warmly received by the king at Ayodhiā, and, in return for the courtesy, the Siamese king sent a delegation of monks to Ceylon under Phra Upāli. Its members remained in Ceylon for three years and ordained a large number of monks there. It was followed later by another delegation from Ayodhiā which also bestowed ordination on a number of monks in the island. These Siamese-ordained monks formed the nucleus of the body known as *Siyām Nikāya,* one of the three extant sects of the Sinhalese Saṅgha.

The Chakri Dynasty

After the fall of Ayodhiā in 1767 and the rise of Bangkok as the new capital, a new dynasty of kings, taking its name from Generalissimo Chaophya Chakri, who had rescued the kingdom from the Burmese, came to the throne. It is the present ruling dynasty of Siam (1782 -). In this dynasty till 1910 there have been six kings, each with the surname Rāma. The Chakri kings were actively interested in making Siam a full-fledged 'Buddhist State', guided by Buddhist principles.

The first sovereign, king Rāma I, was a 'warrior king', but there were other facets to his genius. He revised the Siamese law code and was also a poet of some distinction, being the author of *Ramakien,* a classical work in Siamese literature, written in verse in the form of recitatives for singing to the accompaniment of dance. It is the first systematic Siamese version of the story of Rāma, hero of the Sanskrit epic *Rāmāyana,* though it strays from it in many material respects.[15]

He was at the same time interested in producing a definitive edition of the scripture as well as in reforming the Saṅgha in Siam. He made a new and complete edition of the Buddhist canon which was written on palm-leaves. But, as the texts on which his work was based were not quite free from doubt, he summoned a council of the church to assist in the revision. The palm-leaf edition is known as the 'Great Gil Edition' and is piously preserved in the Royal Palace at Bangkok. The latest edition of the king's work was made in 1925-'28 and its magnitude is shown by the fact that it consists of 45 volumes, each of an average of 500 octavo pages. Rāma I was also keen on ensuring the purity of the Saṅgha and issued 10 royal decrees called in Siamese *Kotmai Phra Songh* to the monks of the realm. They are parallel to the *Kathikāvatas* of the Ceylonese kings which prescribe proper rules of conduct for monks under the king's imprimatur.

[15] See Prince Dhaninivat's article on *The Reconstruction of Rama I* in the *Journal of the Siam Society,* vol. IV, pp. 249-250.

He tried also to control prevalent superstitions among the people. The belief in the existence of tutelary spirits and in the need to propitiate them with offerings and worship was, as we have seen, the folk-religion of Burma which Buddhism could not eradicate. A like superstition, it seems, prevailed among folk in Siam too. It was un-Buddhistic, but so rooted in the mass mind that it could not be altogether cast out by Buddhist faith. Rama Khamheng, though a pious Buddhist himself, seems to have recommended the worship of at least the Great Mountain-spirit, supposed to be the tutelary deity of the realm. Rāma I followed the same principle in dealing with folk-superstition: without suppressing the worship of the Guardian Deity of the Realm (which Rama Khamheng had recommended), he decreed that it should be kept strictly subordinate to Buddhist faith. In one of his decrees, the king declares:[16]

"Men's mind must not go astray to other refuges .... such as spirits and geneii. A liberal man, even if he wished to honour such (non-Buddhist) agencies as the tutelary spirits, would do so by regarding them as benevolent ones which might ward off misfortunes, but they should never value them over and above the virtues of the Three Gems. A less informed man when faced with misfortune as a result of his own past misdeed, might come to think that the Three Gems were no longer able to give help and thus forsake them for superstition. He is thus rendered a headless trunk destined for perdition. It is therefore commended by His Majesty that henceforward, should there be altars of spirits of whatever species, even those of such a spirit as is known to be the Guardian of the Realm, it will be the duty of the officers of the administration to repair and honour them (as of yore by the people), but not to be held high to such a degree as to overstep the honour rendered to the Three Gems. And no sacrifice by killing of living animals is permitted".

The successors of Rama I went further in associating Buddhism with the State of Siam. Some of the kings of the dynasty tried to convert it into a completely Buddhist State by bringing its state-policies into line with the principles and precepts of Buddhism, i.e., by submitting state policies dictated by reasons of State to the sanction of spiritual authority. This was the purpose of the Siamese State documents which go under the name of *Royal Interrogations*. They are in the form of policy-problems formulated by the king to the clergy, for the latter's solution on the basis of Buddhist scripture.[17]

Thus during the First World War, the Supreme Patriarch of Siam gave, at the instance of the king, a call to the country to train a class of citizens

---

[16] Cited in Prince Dhaninivat's *A History of Buddhism in Siam*, p. 27.

[17] See Prince Dhaninivat's *A History of Buddhism in Siam* for these 'Royal Interrogations', pp. 29 ff.

whose duty would be to fight the country's enemies. It was based on a scriptural injunction which laid down that "war must be prepared for even in time of peace". The clerical verdict was in line,—and for this pontifical advice, ratification was found in a passage of the scripture which was quoted: "As towns on the borders of the state must be prepared inside and out, so be ye prepared likewise! Let not any opportunity escape you, for those who let opportunity pass by will be completely full of sorrow".

The Legend of the Sinhala Image

Siam abounds in Buddha images, mostly of metal, the work of different centuries executed by different schools of art.[18] But among all the images, the one that is the object of supreme veneration among the Siamese is now preserved in the Bangkok Museum. It is an image in bronze, 26 inches high, representing the Buddha seated on a lotus with palms in lap, disposed one upon the other. It is known as *P'ra Sihing* (the venerable Ceylonese image), believed to have been brought into Siam from Ceylon at some ancient time.

In the 13th century, when Ceylon was the source of Buddhism for all the south-east Asian countries, a Buddha-image from Ceylon would be regarded as an authentic one. The Bangkok image, however, is not the only 'Ceylon-image' (*Sihala-paṭimā*), —there is one at Chiengmai and another at Ligor (in Malay).

The legends that invest the Bangkok image with its supreme sanctity are given at length in the *Jinakālamālini.*

They centre round Rocharāja, a king of Sukhotai, of doubtful identity, who is said to have been in friendly alliance with the ruler of Dhammarat in Malay. The name of this king does not occur in the genealogy of Sukhotai kings and is surmised to be a variant name for Rama Khamheng himself. Dhammarat is identified with ancient Ligor (in Malay) which had become even before the foundation of Sukhotai a centre of Ceylonese Buddhism. It was from Ligor that Khamheng had brought the Ceylonese *Mahāthera* to preside over the Forest Monastery in his capital. Once on a visit by king 'Rocharāja' to Dhammarat, he heard from the Dhammarat king, his friend and ally, of the miraculous attributes and supernatural potencies of a certain image in Ceylon which both of them desired to possess. The image by a miracle came floating on the sea near Dhammarat. Its king made a gracious gift of it to 'Rocharāja' who brought it to Sukhotai.

---

[18] The following are the schools of art that developed in Siam in chronological succession: (a) Dvaravati (6th-11th century); (b) Ancient Hindu deity images (6th-8th); (c) Srivijai (7th-13th); (d) Lopbari (approximately 12th-13th); (e) Chiengsen (Circa. 12th-13th); (f) Sukhotai (13th-14th); (g) U-tong (12th or 13th-15th); (h) Ayudhia (14th-1767); (i) Bangkok (1782-20th).

The successors of 'Rocharāja' continued to worship the image, but, unluckily, its fame spread far and wide with the result that a number of local chiefs and potentates tried to gain possession of it. The image passed from hand to hand and place to place. "Suffice it to say", says May, summing up its after-history, "that it was taken successively to Chainet, Ayodhiā, Kampengpet, then to Tak (Raheng), thence to Chiengmai, Chiengrai, Chiengsen, back to Chiangrai, and finally came to rest at the end of the 14th century at Chiengmai in the temple named after it, *Wat P'ra Sihing*, It remained undisturbed until the capture of the town in 1662 A.D. by King Naraiyana who carried the image off to Ayodhiā. When Ayodhiā fell and was sacked by the Burmese in 1767 A.D., it was restored to Chiengmai, but in 1795 A.D. was brought to Bangkok where it has been ever since".[19]

This mysterious image, the holiest of all Siamese images and coveted trophy of many a fight and skirmish, has given rise among scholars to speculations on its origin. The question for instance has been raised whether the *P'ra Sihing* was actually made in Ceylon at all, as it has no pronounced characteristic of Ceylonese Buddha-images. A question more searching is whether the legends may not have fixed upon an image which represented in the legend-makers' eyes the very prototype of the fine idealistic Buddha-images of Sukhotai, and led them to invest it with the prestige of an authentic image from Ceylon miraculously received by 'Rocharāja' (Rama Khamheng) to be copied and reproduced by all artists of his kingdom.

BUDDHISM IN LAOS

From Siam, the Thais spread to Laos, but it was three years after the foundation of Ayodhiā in 1350 that Laos in the upper Mekong valley became a kingdom. It was through the coalescence of several small states, brought about by Fa Ngum, the most outstanding figure and accredited 'Hero' of Laotian history.

It is said that he had been brought up in his youth in the Angkor Court and married a Khmer princess, daughter of the Angkor king, Jayavarman Parameshvara (1327-'53?).

In Jayavarman's time, Cambodia had already come under the influence of Siamese monks: perhaps the king himself was a convert to Theravāda Buddhism. It is said that Jayavarman exhorted his son-in-law to rule his dominion according to Buddhist principles and sent to him, when the prince came to the throne, a party of monks bearing the Pali scripture and a Ceylonese statue of the Buddha which was afterwards installed by Fa Ngum at Luang Prabang, then in Laotian territory.

---

[19] *The Culture of South-east Asia*, p. 173.

Fa Ngum established Theravāda Buddhism as the officially sponsored religion of Laos and it is in this form that the religion is practised in Laos till today.

Side by side with Buddhism, there was in Laos the Siamese cult of Rāma. But it had neither in Siam nor in Laos any religious significance. A widespread cult in the southern parts of Asia, from Indonesia to Siam, it was just a source of inspiration in literature and a theme of some indigenous forms of art like mime and shadow-play. In Indonesia, it appears in the indigenous *Wayang* (Shadow-play) of Java; in Siam "traces of it abound in what is left of the art and culture of Ayodhiā, to say nothing of the Bangkok period; it is the theme of decoration in architecture, sculpture, woodwork, furniture and of course murals; it was a theme in literature (of which the outstanding example is the Siamese *Ramakien*); above all it dominated the theatre".[20] The Rāma cult in Laos inspired the voluminous Laotian semi-historical romance, *Rāma Jātaka*.[21]

But a considerable Buddhist literature also grew up in Laos of which the *Pannasa Jātaka* (a collection in Pali of fifty Jātaka tales) in three versions, the work of Laotian monk-scholars, is a monumental example. In Laos today there are many old monasteries and temples where Buddhism of the Ceylonese Theravāda school is both studied and practised. But the religion in Laos seems of late to have fallen on evil times on account of political troubles.

[20] See Prince Dhaninivat's article on "The Shadow-play as a possible origin of the Masked Play" in the *Journal of the Siam Society*, vol. xxxvii, pt. I.

[21] It is a history of Laos in the form of a *Jataka*. It has been summarised in English with annotations by Prince Dhaninivat in the ***Journal of the Siam Society***, vol. xxxvi, pt. I.

Chapter VI

CAMBODIA

Hindu Cambodia till 1431

UPON an area of seventy thousand square miles in the valley of the Mekong, Cambodia has a sparse population, of which the 'Khmers' make seventy per cent. Ethnically allied to the Mons and called 'Mon-Khmers' for the sake of distinction from Mons of other regions like Burma and Siam, they represent a special Mon type that originated and developed in Cambodia. These Mon-Khmers were the makers of Cambodian history. The present size and population of the country, however, are no index to its ancient past,—when Cambodia, with its sumptuous capital at Angkor was almost an empire in East Asia, covering large parts of Siam, Champa, Malay and other neighbouring states.

With the abandonment of Angkor in 1431, Cambodia seemed all at once released from its ties with the past; a new Cambodia began with a new faith and a new culture. Between the old and the new, no living tradition or formative influence remained. The cleavage was a complete, a phenomenal break in the historic evolution of its people.

A whole century's labour of French scholars and archaeologists was needed to exhume this dead and buried past of Cambodia,—nine long centuries of her history prior to 1431.

Cambodia is included in a large land-block of East Asia, called 'Greater India' by Indian historians and 'Exterior India' (*L'ind Exterieure*) by French. It is so called because in the early history of the countries comprising this block, it was Indian cultural influence that acted as the most sociologically dominant and formative force. Their social patterns and systems of government, their arts, religions and all higher culture were all derived from or modelled on the 'Hindu' culture-pattern that arose on Buddhist decline in India. The States within the block became, as Coedes describes them, 'Hindu States'.[1] Their kings bore Sanskrit names; government and administration were according to Hindu polity and Brāhmaṇical jurisprudence; society was stratified and governed by the Indian caste-system; the highest position was assigned to the Brāhmaṇas; Sanskrit learning

[1] Coedes's *Les Etats hindouises d'Extreme-Orient* (1944).

flourished, and the Indian religions, Brāhmaṇism and (Mahāyāna) Buddhism, were professed at least by the more respectable classes of society. Cambodia belonged, from the commencement of her history to the fall of Angkor in 1431, to this zone of Hinduised States.

This long period of Cambodian history is of purely modern reconstruction. The Mon-Khmers had no indigenous tradition of historiography and have left no chronicles like those of Ceylon or Burma. The only 'Cambodian Chronicle' in existence is a work of late origin, not earlier than the 15th century, A.D.—it gives only a list of kings whose places in genuine history are doubtful at best. Six centuries when Angkor was capital of Cambodia are, however, amply documented by a large number of inscriptions now available, published in instalments with French translation in six volumes by Coedes.[2]

When Burma and Siam came under Thai rule, Buddhism both as faith and culture existed in these countries. The Thai rulers took it from the conquered people; they raised Buddhism to the position of a State Religion, erecting temples, pagodas and convents to perpetuate the ministrations of the religion. But in Cambodia, the situation was different. What the religious beliefs and social customs among the Mon-Khmers of Cambodia had been before their conversion to Hinduism are not exactly known. Yet it is almost certain that Hinduism was to them an imposition from outside —a power that gained control and authority over the people, not because the people welcomed it, but through the dominating influence of kings, priests and men of high rank in society. The State and Society in Cambodia adopted the Hindu pattern, though Mahāyāna Buddhism had also a place in the pattern. Among the royalty and the aristocracy there were persons who preferred Mahāyānist Buddhism as then understood and practised in India. The civilization of ancient Cambodia evolved under these conditions but was discarded by the Cambodians outright when Theravāda Buddhism appeared in the country as an independent religion, not like Mahāyānism, a faith that subsisted under the franchise of Hinduism.

Ancient Cambodian Civilization

The story of the civilization that Cambodia discarded,—lighting new lamps for the old,—has been slowly unfolded to us since the discovery in 1861 of one splendid monument of it, the Temple of Angkor Wat, by a French zoologist named Henri Mahout. The temple had lain buried in thick tropical jungles and only a glimpse of it could be had in 1861. It served to set in train a century's archaeological exploration of the region followed by careful study

[2] Besides Coedes' six volumes, there is Dr. R. C. Majumdar's monograph on the *Inscriptions of Kambuja*, published by the Asiatic Society of Bengal in 1963. This work has been consulted in the following pages.

and decipherment of numerous inscriptions the exploration yielded. Little by little, out of the strangle-hold of giant trees and lianas, a lapsed civilization came back to life, unrolling the whole life-story of its growth, development, decay and downfall.

Cambodia in its heyday was an expansionist state. Its colonial possessions were a source of untold wealth and slave-labour. Its internal resource, however, was only an exiguous agricultural economy. But wealth exploited from abroad helped it to develop an opulent civilization,—prodigal and ostentatious chiefly in one direction,—in glorifying and maintaining at an incredibly high level the Brāhmaṇical religion with which the State was identified. For this, the state-exchequer was drawn upon without stint,—to build temples of fantastic proportions and maintain an enormous body of ministrants for ritual service to the gods, attended with pompous ceremonies and the upkeep on a large scale of seminaries of religious and sacerdotal learning. Among remains of this civilization, conspicuous by their absence are works of public benefit and utility like roads, aqueducts, water-reservoirs or irrigation canals. Obviously no attempt was made to extend and improve the State's agricultural economy, its only stand-by in the event of loss of outside territorial possessions.

As in all civilizations planned on the basis of caste and status, there was a cleft between the higher ranks of society and the proletariat. In the Cambodian inscriptions, there is no recognition of the latter. Yet they were not just 'hewers of wood and drawers of water'. If their services had been requisitioned in building the great temples and casting the magnificent images, they must be presumed to have had a well-developed sense of plastic art and a masterly knowledge of architecture. But the inscriptions high-light only the accomplishments of the great, of the kings who were magnificent builders, the priests who were profoundly learned in scriptural lore, and the scholars so steeped in Sanskrit literature that they could compose in immaculate forms of Sanskrit prosody long and fluent panegyrics on the kings and their court-chaplains. But not a window is opened on the life of the common people.

The Cult of the God-King (Deva-Rāja)

While all other ingredients of Cambodian civilization were derived from Hindu India, there was one for which the provenance was not India, but the island of Java. It was a cult on which kingship in Cambodia and a large part of its state-polity was based. Stemming from a peculiar concept of the king's divinity and his transmissible ego, it was formally introduced into the Cambodian State from Java by Jayavarman II (acceded in 802 ?), on the occasion of his assumption of the status of an independent 'overall king' (*Chakravartī Rājā*) over the whole of Cambodia.

It gave a sort of spiritual sanction for the divinity as well as the hereditary character of kingship. The person and status of a king were deemed to be divine and he was actually apotheosised after his decease. A temple, commensurate with his greatness, was built to preserve his 'ego', not extinguished with physical death. It was enshrined in the image of a deity. This deity was named after the deceased king and the royal ego residing within it could be made to descend on the lineal successor, evoked by priests of this mysterium with proper rites and ceremonies. The ego thus passed through the medium of the deity in line from king to king. Traces of this concept of a 'transmissible ego' are found in some of the ancient temples (*Menduts*) of Indonesia. It was in Indonesia that it seems to have developed into a cult, administered by a priestly coterie, specialising in its rituals.

Even before Angkor had become Cambodia's capital, the cult seems to have been known to Khmer kings. An inscription as old as 716 A.D. is claimed to be the first example in Cambodia of the practice of this cult. Pushkara, an early Khmer king, who ruled from the pre-Angkor capital Sambhupura, is the author of an inscription which reads: 'Pushkara had the god Pushkaresha erected by *munis* (sages) and the most eminent Brāhmaṇas'.[3] Pushkaresa (Lord Pushkara), bearing the king's name, was supposed to hold in deposit the king's sacred ego.

Jayavarman II, though not the founder of the Angkor, was the real founder of Angkor monarchy. He came to the throne near the beginning of the 9th century, and some facts of his reign (and also the reigns of some of his successors) are known from an 11th-century inscription.[4] It purports to relate the shifting fortunes of a priestly family and its branches over two centuries and a half (802-1052 A.D.) and gives incidentally some account of the kings whom the priestly family served from Jayavarman II to Udayādityavarman. The Sanskrit text is accompanied with a summary in the Khmer language.

In view of the importance of the Devarāja cult in Mon-Khmer civilization, its formal beginnings in Cambodia, as given in the Khmer version of the text, are worth reproducing here:

"His Majesty Parameshvara (Jayavarman II) installed the Royal God (*Devarāja*) in the town of Śrī Mahendra Parvata and established this family (i.e., the priestly family of which the history is given) there as permanent priests of the god. Here is the history of the branches of this family... His Majesty came from Java to reign in the city of Indrapura.

[3] See Hall's *History of South-east Asia*, p. 91.

[4] It appears on a stele called Sdok Kak Thom Stele (See Hall's *History*, p. 93). The Khmer text of the inscription is translated into English in Majumdar's *Inscriptions of Kambuja*, pp. 363-371, from which relevant extracts are given.

"Shiva-Kaivalya, venerable and learned *guru* (spiritual guide), was the royal priest of Parameshvara......His Majesty reigned then in the town of Hariharālaya. Shivā-Kaivalya was also established in the town...... His Majesty came thereafter to reign at Mahendra-parvata......Then a Brāhmaṇa came whose name was Hiraṇyadāma. He came from a *Janapada* (town) and was well-versed in magical science. His Majesty invited him to perform a ritual in order that Kambuja-desha (Cambodia) might no longer be dependent on Java and a Chakravartin (Over-all King) might rule in Kambuja. This Brāhmaṇa performed a ritual............and installed a Royal God (*Devarāja*). The Brāhmaṇa taught several *mantras* (incantations). He recited them from beginning to end in order that they might be written down and taught to Shiva-Kaivalya. He also directed Shiva-Kaivalya to perform the rituals of the Royal God. His Majesty Parameshvara and the Brāhmaṇa took solemn oaths that only the family of Shiva-Kaivalya and no one else should perform the worship of the Royal God. The priest Shiva-Kaivalya initiated all his relations into this worship. Then His Majesty returned to Hariharālaya to reign and the Royal God also was brought there......................... His Majesty Parameshvara died at Hariharālaya. The Royal God was there (i.e., where the king resided) and in all the capitals where successive kings took him as their protector".

By virtue of his possession of the 'royal ego', the Devarāja became the divine protector of the realm. A special priesthood was installed to minister his rites. These rites seem to have included certain elements of black magic: it is suggested by the incantations that the Brāhmaṇa taught Shiva-Kaivalya, the first arch-priest of Devarāja worship in Cambodia, *mantras* (incantations) described as *Vināśaka* (i.e., for destruction), *Sammohaka* (i.e., for stupefaction) and *Śirascheda* (i.e., for decapitation).[5] These acts represented the king's powers over his subjects as well as his enemies, and the incantations were passed on to the God-king and transmitted from him to his descendants.

There is indication in the inscription itself that the cult was brought by Jayavarman II from Java and was instituted to mark the installation of independent royalty in the realm. The Devarāja (image) was supposed to stand guarantee for the security and continuance of the kingdom. A hereditary priesthood was established to minister the rites of his worship.

Aristocracy followed the royal example by apotheosising ancestors. So numerous temples were erected embodying what Coedes terms, "personal cults".[6] In such a temple the enshrined deity does not bear the name assigned to it in the Brāhmaṇical *purāṇas*, but an approximate name reminiscent of

---

[5] See Majumdar's *Inscriptions of Kambuja*, p. 364.

[6] See Coedes's *Les Etats Hindois* in chapters dealing with the 'personal cult'.

the 'ego' of the ancestor incorporated with the deity. This transmutation of the name of the deity was the approved practice. Thus when Jayavarman VII, who was a Buddhist, set up an image of Lokeshvara (Buddha of the Mahāyānic pantheon), he made it in the likeness of his father and the image was known as Jayavarmeśvara (Deity of Jayavarman).[7]

From the time of Jayavarman II, over several centuries, it was deemed to be the duty of every Khmer king to raise a temple to a Royal God, who was supposed to protect the realm and guarantee continuance of the royal line.

Mahāyāna Buddhists among Angkor Kings

Were there Buddhists in this 'Hindu State' of Exterior India? There is evidence that there were.

In Funan, a purely Hindu state, out of which Cambodia, under its original name, Kambuja, emerged as an independent kingdom, there was not only a Buddhist population, but even Buddhists of high rank who held offices or commissions. We are told of one Buddhist priest Nāgasena who was deputed to the Chinese emperor by a king of Funan in the 8th century. The Chinese record of this deputation says that Nāgasena reported to the emperor that in Funan Brāhmaṇism and Buddhism were flourishing side by side.[8] Perhaps it was an overstatement motivated by the desire to please and placate the Buddhist emperor of China. But whether Buddhism was flourishing or not, the presence of Buddhists in the State is certainly indicated. Between Funan and Kambuja there existed, even after they had separated, a lively intercourse and, if there were Buddhists in Funan, there must have been in Kambuja also.

From the nature of the historical materials on which we have to rely for Cambodia's history, it is not possible to say what the incidence of Buddhism among the Khmers anciently was, nor the form in which it was practised. But in the succession list of kings, there are several who can be identified from their inscriptions as Mahāyānist Buddhists. The inscriptions also reveal that their Mahāyānism was of purely Indian brand, as it had finally developed in India in contact with Hinduism.

Since the 'Gupta Age' (300-550 A.D.) of Indian history, Buddhist Mahāyāna faith in India had been developing in its speculative philosophies and institutional forms a well-marked bent towards Hinduism, then gaining ground in the country. The earlier (Hīnāyāna) form of Buddhism had been trenchantly different from Brāhmaṇical religion. But the Mahāyāna in its metaphysical speculations followed the channels of Hindu philosophy and its forms of worship also came increasingly into the pattern of Brāhmaṇical

[7] See Majumdar's *Inscriptions of Kambuja*, p. 476.

[8] See May's *The Culture of South-east Asia*, p. 112.

worship. This assimilative process was consummated later by the acceptance of the Founder of Buddhism in the Hindu pantheon.[9]

One consequence of this rapprochement was a blurring of the distinction between developed Mahāyāna Buddhism and Hindu Brāhmaṇical religion. Some of the deities were interchangeable; the forms of worship were alike; the difference between the two seemed of no more consequence than a sectarian difference. Hence Mahāyāna Buddhism was easily accommodated within the system of Hindu culture that prevailed in these states of East Asia. Among the kings of Angkor, there were Buddhists like Dharaṇīdhara Varman II, Indravarman, Jayavarman VII and others, all of whom professed Mahāyāna Buddhism of the Indian form: they were not thereby recusants from the state's established religion.

These kings proclaim the Mahāyānist faith in the inscriptions, invoking the Buddha along with Brāhmaṇical deities; or only the Buddhist trinity,—the Buddha, the Dharma and the Saṅgha. They subscribe to the *Trikāya* doctrine, i.e., the concept of the Buddha functioning in three kinds of bodies, which is the fundamental doctrine of Mahāyānism. We may cite an inscription of Udayārka-varman, dated 989, as an example to show how the deities were syncretically treated. It records the restoration of a *liṅga* (Phallic Shiva Image) during the king's reign by one Saṁkarsha. He added to the *liṅga* three images, viz., those of Brahmā, Vishnu and Buddha and converted the whole group into a 'four-faced Shiva'—a factitious deity quite unknown to Hindu *purāṇas* where Brahmā alone is four-faced. The reason for it given in the inscription is that Shiva, though one and indivisible, is divided in his functions which the additional images are made to symbolise.[10]

The inscriptions in fact betray a total lack of awareness of any distinction between the divinities of Hinduism and those of Mahāyāna Buddhism. Their votaries were regarded not as belonging to two different religions, but representing two different sects. The custom of providing accommodation for Buddhists in the *āśramas* round the temples also indicates this attitude of mind.

The *āśramas* represent an interesting institution maintained by the Angkor kings in the vicinity of temples. There is no full-length description in any of the inscriptions, but there is no doubt that an *āśrama* was a seminary of learning where there were teachers and students of different religious sects. The teachers were mainly those who had forsaken the world and dedicated

---

9 See Dutt's *Buddhist Monks and Monasteries of India*, pp. 195-197.

10 See Majumdar's *Inscriptions of Kambuja*, p. 399:
"Shiva, although he is indivisible, is divided by the division of his functions. For this reason, I have established with joy and devotion this four-faced Shiva (*Caturmurti Siva*)". See Sloka 4, *Ibid.* The translation is mine.

themselves to the promotion of sacred learning in different sectarian schools. The kings mention these institutions with pride.

The *āśaramas* were principally seats of Sanskrit learning, and from them were drawn the great *panditas* (Sanskrit scholars) whose knowledge of the *Śāstras* and high proficiency in Sanskrit was drawn upon for the conduct of state-affairs and sacredotal concerns and also for writing panegyrics on kings and their genealogies which form the main subject-matter of the inscriptions.

It was the custom to provide accommodation in the *āśramas* sect-wise. The *Sougatas* were regarded as a sect and are thus described: "Those who do not change their sleeping places during the rains (i.e., those who observe the Buddhist custom of *Vassāvāsa*) and who live on one meal a day (a rule observed by Buddhist monks) and are able to perform the rites of their religion".[11] The reference to 'once-eaters' and 'observers of *Vassāvāsa*' is undoubtedly to Buddhist monks and the residence assigned to them is labelled as *Sougatāśrama*. *Sougata*, 'a follower of the Good Way', recalling the canonical description of the Buddhist religion as a *Magga* (Path) or *Jāna* (Way or Vehicle), was the name invented for a Buddhist when Buddhism was no longer the dominant faith in India. A *Sougatāśrama* was virtually a Buddhist monastery and among the inmates there were holders of stipends from the royal treasury. They are mentioned specifically as *Bhikṣus* and *Yatis*: "The *Bhikṣus* and *Yatis*, who are always engaged in studies, are to be given a (specified) amount of stipendary allowance every year".[12]

In another inscription the *Sougatas* (as described before, i.e., those who observe *Vassāvāsa* and take only one meal a day) are allotted to *Brāhmaṇāsrama* for residence.[13] A later king Suryavarman I (1002-1048 A.D.) recorded his donations to various āśramas including the *Sougatāśrama*.[14] Jayavarman VII (1181-1200 A.D.) who was a Buddhist, but a Mahāyānist Buddhist of the same type as other Angkor kings, was the famous builder of the Bayon temple where Vishnu and the Buddha are identified, though more usually the latter was identified with Shiva. At the end of one of his inscriptions, he refers to the āśramas built by him round a temple. Curiously enough, he refers to the temple as a *Vihāra*, i.e., in its developed meaning, as in Ceylon of a Buddhist sanctuary. An interesting thing we learn about Jayavarman VII from this inscription is that his wife and her elder sister were Buddhists and that the queen once celebrated her husband's return home after a spell of absence with a dramatic performance based on the *Jātakas* (Buddha's Birth-stories) and that when the king became a widower, he urged

[11] See *Ibid*, p. 131:
Sloka, 70. The translation is mine. See also on the same page *slokas*, 71 and 72.

[12] *Ibid*, *Sloka*, 72.

[13] In an inscription of Jasovarman. *Ibid*. p. 136: *Slokas* 72-73.

[14] *Ibid*, p. 330.

the elder sister of the deceased queen to preach the Buddhist doctrine in all Buddhist convents (*jinālaye*).[15] It points to the existence of Buddhist convents among the *āśramas* at Angkor.

Temples, Temple-worship and the Inscriptions

Though Purāṇic Hinduism was the state-religion of Cambodia, its pantheon was not composed solely of the deities of the *Purāṇas*. Shiva (in his phallic form) predominates; next comes Vishnu. But the *Purāṇic* source is eked out by a variety of divinities supplied by the Deva-rāja cult, the 'personal cults', and Mahāyānist Buddhism, besides local deities named after their places of worship. Buddha, Lokeśvara, Trailokyanātha, Prajnāpāramitā (goddess), etc. represent the Mahāyānist faith. The Angkor pantheon was in fact a mixed one of deities, both Hindu and Buddhist and deified persons.

Till the end of the 14th century, the temples and the inscriptions form the groundwork of Cambodian history. Thereafter the temples ceased to be built and the high-flown Sanskrit inscriptions to be written, and the country passed the cross-roads into a different way of life.

The temples high-light the architectural achievements of the 'classic period' of Cambodian civilization. They struck the world with wonder when French archaeologists exhumed them bit by bit from their jungle-burial of five forgetful centuries. Their architectural proportions are breathtaking, unmatched in India or perhaps in any other part of the world; their wealth of sculpture almost unlimited. The Angkor Wat at Siam-reap for example represents one whole square mile of construction with a broad moat running on all sides. The grandest temples of Cambodia are three—(i) Pra Vihāra (now regained by Cambodia from Siam by a judgement of the Hague International Court), (ii) Angkor Wat and (iii) the Bayon.[16] Their designs were indigenous; the engineering skill was of native provenance; the masonic work and sculpture the output of local talent. Yet how high is the level of artistic excellence attained! Contesse Coral-Remusat has traced the development over five centuries of this remarkable architecture and art, from primitive one-roomed shrines to the vast architectural complex of Angkor Wat.[17]

But the sad irony of fate is that the construction and maintenance of these temples, especially those of royal foundation or dedicated to the Royal God, proved disastrous to the kingdom in the end.

---

[15] See *Ibid, The Phimanaka Inscription of Jayavarman VII*, pp. 515 ff.

[16] For descriptions of these temples, see May's *Culture of South-east Asia* Ch. VIII; Malcolm MacDonald's *Angkor*, Jonathan and Cape, London, 1958; Coral Remusat's *L'art Khmer*, Paris, 1940.

[17] Coral-Remusat's *L'art Khmer*,

To conduct the daily and occasional functions of religion at these temples, a numerous priesthood, maintained at State expense, was required. There are references in some inscriptions to the performance of one-hundred-thousand *Homas* (offering of burnt sacrifices) and ten-million *Homas*.[18] These were long-drawn sacrificial ceremonies, dragging on from year's end to year's end and calling for the co-operation of an immense number of *Hotās* (Offerers) and *Yājakas* (Performers of Rituals). Their fees and perquisites were on a lavish scale. We are told of a *hotā* named Śivāchārya who acted as the chief of sacrificial priests for four successive kings, one of whom appointed him as High-Priest over 88,000 priests,—the number presumably functioning in the kingdom at that time.[19]

For these sacerdotal activities the drain on the state resources was enormous. The details of state expenditure on them are given in two inscriptions of Jayavarman VII.[20]

Being a devout Buddhist king, he built the temple known as Pra Khan, setting up in the main sanctuary an image of Lokeśvara in the semblance of his father Dharanindra-varman II, to which we have already referred. The temple was evidently a Devarāja temple: the monument at its centre is mentioned as *Rājyaśrī* (Kingdom's Glory). In the dedicatory inscription, "reference is made to the images of deities, 20400 in number, made of gold, silver, bronze and stone; 208,532 slaves and a quantity of precious metals and 514 separate temples and 2,066 minor or accessory constructions.[21] The king proceeds to list the total endowments made for the upkeep of this vast temple,—13,500 villages; 306,372 male and female slaves brought from Champa, Yavana (Yava), Pukam (i.e. Pagan in Burma) and Rvan (Mon country); and 400,126 *Kharis* of rice.[22] The king's successors are exhorted to maintain this gigantic foundation.

In the reign of Jayavarman VII (1181-c.1220 A.D.) the Cambodian state was expanding, and there were resources enough in the royal treasury to keep up in magnificent condition the Devarāja temple built by him. But the king was not content with finishing this one establishment, but was carrying into effect at the same time new building projects on a vast scale, the construction of Angkor Thom and the Bayon. Dr. Hall sums up thus the results of this insensate and ruinous state-policy: "Thousands of villages were assigned for the upkeep of the great temples, while tens of thousands of officiants

---

18 Mentioned in an inscription of Suryavarman. The king is said to have performed *Laksa-homa* and *Koti-homa* (Majumdar's *Inscriptions of Kambuja*, p. 431).

19 *Ibid*, pp. 326-327.

20 Inscriptions No. 177 (*Ibid*), p. 459 and No. 178 (*Ibid*, p. 475).

21 *Ibid*, pp. 476-477.

22 *Ibid*, p. 477.

and hundreds of dancers were employed in their service, not to mention the army of labourers, masons, sculptors and decorators required for the constructional work. Jayavarman VII may have been the greatest of Khmer monarchs, and it may be claimed that his reign represented the apogee of Cambodia, but he impoverished the people with heavy taxation and insatiable demands for forced labour and military service".[23] Significantly enough, he was the last great builder among the Angkor kings.

The inscriptions pertaining to the temples which profusely document Cambodian history, recording genealogies of Angkor kings, along with those of their court-chaplains, their achievements in war and peace and their royal munificence to temples and *āśramas*, are mostly bilingual,—in classical Sanskrit and in vernacular Khmer. The Sanskrit portion is the main one,—the subsidiary Khmer being concerned chiefly with various prescriptions for the foundations, inventories of their assets and requirements and lists of slaves and dancing girls assigned to each, sometimes with mention of their names, and sundry other matters of practical and operative importance. Evidently the Khmer text was meant for the information of ordinary people, while the Sanskrit for study and appreciation by the learned. Couched in elegant Sanskrit verse in different meters of Sanskrit prosody, the style is high-flown, erudite, decorated with scholarly allusions to Sanskrit classics and Indian mythology. They are elaborate literary compositions in which one may detect the Roman hand of *pandits* and scholars who received training at the *āśramas*.

The object and purport of these inscriptions is the eulogy and glorification of the kings, their ancestors and the eminent ecclesiasts who served under them. There is hardly anything else of historical importance,—no reference to the people or the condition of society and not a word to indicate the people's attitude towards the throne and the pampered priesthood. It seems tacitly taken for granted that the king, being a god-king, is beyond criticism by the people, and the overgrown priestly corporation a necessity to keep up regular temple-worship, supposed to ensure welfare of the realm. The skill, labour and resources of the subject people were freely drawn upon in this king-centred State in the absorbing industry of temple-building. That did not, however, avail to raise the status of the people above hewers of wood and drawers of water. A great distance separated the summit of society from the bottom.

Discontent, born of social injustice, went on breeding at the bottom. There were ominous spells of inaction and violent outbreaks in the state and no broad-based stability was achieved for the body politic.

---

[23] Hall's *A History of South-east Asia*, p. 111.

During the 'classic' period of Angkor, there were two serious revolts and Suryavarman II (1113-1150 A.D.), builder of Angkor Wat, had so impoverished the people by his stupendous constructional activities that a period (1150-1181 A.D.) ensued when no temples were built nor inscriptions written. It was also a period of internal troubles. In later inscriptions, short and casual references occur to two serious revolts—one of the *Rahus* which was certainly a 'peasants' revolt' and the other led by a chief, named Tribhuvanāditya, who killed Yasovarman and occupied the throne for some time.[24] The king of Champa, taking advantage of the unsettled condition of the State, started in 1167 a series of incursions into Cambodia, though in the long run the tables were turned and Champa itself became a vassal state of Cambodia.

Influx of Theravāda Buddhism

Suddenly we see a new factor introduced into the social life of this caste-ridden, priest-dominated country in the form of a new faith. Nobody could suspect at the time its revolutionary potentialities. It started among the by-passed inconsequential commonalty, while royalty and nobility clung to the State's venerable old traditions. But the very foundations of these traditions were being sapped as, one by one and group by group, the people began to welcome and embrace the incoming faith.

The exact commencement of Cambodia's conversion to Theravāda Buddhism is not known, but it first manifests itself in an inscription in a private temple, the date of which is conjecturally put at 1230 A.D. in the reign of Indravarman II, who was a Buddhist king.[25]

The inscription is not in Sanskrit, but partly in Pali and partly in Khmer. After invocation to the *Triratna* (i.e. three gems, viz., the Buddha, the Dhamma and the Saṅgha), it mentions the regnant king Siri-indavamma (Srī Indravarman), who gave permission to a lady, a lay devotee (*upāsikā*), to build a *vihāra* (image-house or temple) at the spot and instal a Buddha-image. The king donated four villages to the shrine and eight plots of land to the priests. The Khmer text, apparently trying to bring the foundation into line with the *Deva-rāja* cult, gives to the image the name 'Srī Srī Indra Mahādeva'. But it was not a Shiva or Mahādeva temple at all. The great significance of the inscription lies in the fact that it is written in the sacred language of Theravāda Buddhism and its text proclaims that the temple is intended for Buddha-worship (*Buddha-pūjā*—See v. 9). Evidently Theravāda Buddhism had arrived in Cambodia.

Its initial progress in the country is obscure. The interesting questions,—Who were its pioneers? How was it propagated? How could it march

---

[24] See *Ibid*, p. 106.

[25] See inscription No. 188 of Indravarman (Majumdar's *Inscriptions of Kambuja*, pp. 533-535).

in only a century's time from poor men's cottages to the exalted throne of Angkor kings? What were its first reactions on a society governed for centuries in the traditional Brāhmaṇical system?—can be met only with speculative answers. But the religion once introduced must have made vigorous headway among the common folk of Cambodia.

King Jayavarman Parameśvara came to the throne in 1327,—little less than a century from the first Pali epigraphic record of the foundation, with permission and subsidy from the Buddhist king Indravarman, of a Buddha-temple undoubtedly of Hīnayāna (Theravāda) worship. The religion got so well established in a century's time that king Jayavarman Parameśvara, in spite of his upbringing in the traditional faith and ideology of Angkor monarchy, chose to embrace this new religion of the people. His acceptance of Theravāda Buddhism is indicated by his advice to his son-in-law Fa Ngun of Laos to govern according to Buddhist principles and his gift to him of a codex of Pali scripture. Any way, we find Sanskrit inscriptions gone out of use in the reign of Jayavarman Parameśvara; Pali becomes the official language, and though at Angkor itself the royal patronage of Sanskrit learning was retained, it was hardly with any zest or real purpose.

At the end of the 14th century, Chinese envoys came to Angkor to ask, comforming to the use and wont of the old emperors of China, for tribute or presents from the new king of Cambodia Indravarman III. The leader of this embassy was Chou Ta-Kuan. He lived for some time at Angkor and wrote a work entitled 'Memoirs on the customs of Cambodia'. Everybody at Angkor, says Ta-Kuan in this work, worships the Buddha and he mentions men of religion to be seen here who 'shave the head, wear yellow clothing, and leave the right shoulder uncovered' and are called 'Chu-ku', a Chinese expression interpreted to mean 'reverend sir'.[26] The reference is usually taken to be Siamese Buddhist monks.

Were monks from Siam the pioneers in Cambodia of Theravāda Buddhism?—The question does not admit of an off-hand answer out of Ta-Kuan's remark. We cannot be sure that the monks referred to by him were really Siamese monks. The Cambodian monks whom I met on my visit to Phnom-penh in September 1962 were somewhat reluctant to give Siam the credit for introducing Theravāda Buddhism into their country. The question, however, cannot be dismissed at that.

Siam's Part in Cambodian Buddhism

There are at present two sects of Theravāda Buddhism in Cambodia, differing not in doctrines, but in certain forms of Vinaya observance. The older and more numerous of these two sects is called the *Mahānikāya* and the

---

[26] Hall's *A History of South-east Asia*, p. 115.

other *Dhammayutt*. Both sects regard some Siamese texts as fundamental.

Outstanding among these texts is a work entitled *Mangalattha-dīpinī*. It has been published about a decade now by the government of Cambodia. We know the authorship and the place of origin of the work from its colophon: "This work was written by Siri Mangala, a venerable monk well-versed in the three *pitakas* and also a solitary meditator (*vivekavirata*), living in a solitary place at Navapura (Chiengmai, formerly in Laos, now a town in northern Siam) and was written in 886th Buddhist year (i.e. 1469)". The work deals with Buddhist ethics under themes like the following: 'What is goodness? What is auspicious (*maṅgala*)? etc; then it goes on to describe 38 kinds of *Maṅgala*. In the context of Tu-Kuan's report about the presence of Siamese monks (if they were really Siamese) at Angkor at the end of the 13th century, the prestige to which this work rose among the Buddhists of Cambodia bespeaks continuing Siamese influence.

About the Siamese origin round the middle of the 18th century of the Dhammayutt sect, definite facts are known. It was founded by king Mongkut of Siam, 'one of the most remarkable personalities that ever occupied the Siamese throne'—one who was called to the throne from a monastic cloister and returned thither at the end of his kingly career. During his reign thousands of Mon refugees from Lower Burma were living in Siam, and it is said that he met a Mon monk by chance and came under his influence. King Mongkut himself was well-read in western lore and the doubt sometimes crossed his mind whether monastic life as it was in Siam could justify its existence in the modern world....The Mon monk is said to have dispelled his doubts and the king set himself on return from throne to monastery to the work of reforming Siamese monachism. The result was the foundation of a new sect of monks called Dhammayutika in 1833. Some years afterwards it spread to Cambodia and Laos. The foundation of this sect and propagation of its tenets was one of the great events of Mongkut's tenure of the throne.[27]

On the other hand, the monks of Cambodia deny Siamese influence on Cambodian Buddhism and their arguments are briefly as follows:

(i) Chou Ta-Kuan's reference is to Cambodian monks, who fit the description given by him;

(ii) The *Mangalattha-dīpinī* was written at Chiengmai when it was in Laos and not in Siam and may be properly regarded as a Laotian rather than as a Siamese work;

(iii) A few old inscriptions of Cambodia testify to the existence of Theravāda Buddhism in the country long before 1230 A.D.

---

[27] See Prince Dhaninivat's brochure, *A History of Buddhism in Siam*, 1960, pp. 32-38 (on 'King Mongkut's Monastic Reform').

Fall of the Old Faith and Old Regime

In 1431, Angkor with its numerous gods, and their statues and images, its vast temples and untold works of art, —the nerve-centre of Khmer civilization,—lay paralysed under the threat of a Siamese invasion. Siam had been the old rival and enemy of Cambodia, and it was not for the first time that the two countries stood face to face for a showdown. Cambodia had never been afraid to meet Siam on the battle-field and many fights had taken place on the Cambodian soil itself. Yet at the testing time when the capital itself was invaded, the behaviour of the Cambodians was strange and abnormal. They seemed to sulk and freeze; they quickly evacuated; they left the capital city as though it were a worn-out shell. Not a hand was lifted to save the city and its hoarded monumental treasures, as though the city and its religious monuments were not theirs at all.

The only plausible explanation of this strange attitude of the people can be that they thought the city not worth saving. It stood for a scheme of life and system of faith on which the outlook of the Khmers had completely changed meanwhile. The change had been brought about by the teachings of Theravāda Buddhism: in 1431 the Khmers were all Buddhists of that school.

The new faith had no alliance with the old regime and its traditions. It had come independently to the people and stayed in its own right,—unlike the Mahāyāna Buddhism which had existed only under the franchise and allowance of the Brāhmaṇical State-religion. The new faith struck at the roots of caste, priesthood and the cult of the divinity of kingship by its simple message of the power of *Karma* (Deeds), unheard before by the Khmers, viz.,

"None is by birth a Brāhmaṇa; none
By birth non-Brāhmaṇa; by deeds is one
A Brāhmaṇa, by deeds non-Brāhmaṇa.
By deeds one is a farmer and by deeds
An artisan; by deeds a trader too;
By deeds one is a servant or a thief,—
By deeds a soldier or a celebrant,
And so a rājāh (king) is by deeds".[28]

The teaching that the value of a man from the highest rank to the lowest in society accrues from his deeds, not from the accident of birth or social status, made nought of the Deva-raja cult, the pretensions of priesthood and

---

[28] *Sutta-nipata*, vv. 650-655. The translation is taken from *The Living Thoughts of Gotama the Buddha* by Coomarswamy and Horner (published by Cassel and Co. London, 1948).

aristocracy, and the privileged position of the Brāhmaāas. The civilization based on these concepts appeared to be a mockery of true religion, a sham and delusion. The works of art and architecture, the seminaries of Sanskrit learning, the temples and images at Angkor,—all these appurtenances of Khmer civilization raised no emotional response in the people's minds. At the earliest opportunity, they fled away from them like the early Christian converts fleeing from the pomps, shows and vanities of pagan civilization.

Theravāda Buddhism was a message of liberation for those who were conditioned to look upon their kings as gods, to rely for individual and collective welfare on the ministrations of Brāhmaṇa priests and to accept as God-given the caste-ridden society and the milieau of life it created. It emphasized the worth of man as man, laid stress on *Bhāvanā* (Becoming), that is, the process of an 'individual's growing through self-culture and self-knowledge from more to more', and, for refuge in life's trials and tribulations, substituted for the old stone-hewn gods the holy trinity of the Buddha, the Dhamma and the Saṅgha.

The monk preachers of the new religion were also of a different breed from the high-brow priests from whom they used to learn the sanctions and injunctions of religion. The monks did not speak to them *ex cathedra*, but as men to men. They were simple and lowly, intimate with common people, sympathetic and helpful, and naturally more after their hearts.

Finally, Theravāda Buddhism released them from the service of the 'greedy gods' whose yoke had so long been so crushing a burden.

The builder of Angkor Thom and the Bayon, Jayavarman VII (1181-c. 1220 A.D.) was the last great king to inherit the traditions of Angkor royalty. "After the fierce and brilliant sunset of Jayavarman's reign, the kingdom was drained of light. Dusk fell upon the scene, a twilight gentle and reposeful, but ominously still and quiet, a prelude to a dark and stormy night".[29]

After the Khmers had left Angkor to its doom, the tropical jungle slowly stepped in and covered from sight all its old monuments. So they would have remained to this day but for a century's Herculean labours of French archaeologists and scholars.

And the civilization never, since the fall of Angkor, had any continuation in Cambodia. It withered to the very roots.

Cambodia as a Buddhist country is the youngest one in south-east Asia. Its activities in the cause of Buddhism do not go back far in time. Officially they are now represented by the functions of the Ministry of Cults and the institutions run by the Mahānikāya sect, the High School named Vidyālaya Preah Suramarit and the Buddhist Mahāvidyālaya (University), built by Prince Sihanouk and named after him.

---

[29] Malcolm MacDonald's *Angkor*, 1958, p. 61.

Chapter VII

VIETNAM

Buddhism in Vietnam

VIETNAM forms the easternmost limit of the land-block comprising the countries of south-east Asia. It is a slender coastal strip of plains and small deltas, variegated by hilly regions in the north and the centre, the whole territory measuring about 700 miles north to south, touching China on the north and the Gulf of Siam on the south. It resembles in shape a capital 'S' with the lower arc in a slight bulge.

The country was populated by migrations of people from the north into the south over nearly 800 years of Vietnam's early history.

The Viets, after whom the country is named, migrated at first from Central China to the valley of the Red River where an emigrant colony was formed. The Viets were not ethnically related to the Chinese and, although their colony was called Nam Viet after them, it was known as Giaochi in China after its conquest by the Han emperor, Wu-ti, in the first century B.C.—the name by which it is referred to in the old Chinese annals. Regarded as a border-district of China, it came completely, both culturally and politically, under Chinese domination. "During the first few centuries of the Christian era, there was intense effort to introduce Chinese civilization into Vietnam by scholars, diplomats and the Chinese official agency."[1] Buddhism in that era formed no part of Chinese civilization; it did become so much later, not till the 5th or 6th century A.D. It was Confucianism and Taoism that spread under the cultural drive from China into the Red River Valley, but they touched only the upper classes of society, while the lower classes, the peasant population, stuck to their old cults of ancestor worship and animistic religion.

It was not till 1803 that the country acquired its present name Vietnam. It was conferred by the Chinese emperor Kia-king, who received in that year envoys from the Vietnamese king, Nguyen Anh, who, after his investiture at Hue, took the name Gia-Long. The Chinese had in that year no right to or interest in Vietnam as they had given up their rule in that country so far back as in 939. But the Chinese emperor saw in

---

[1]Buttinger's *The Smaller Dragon*, p. 77

Gia-Long's despatch an opportunity to annex the territory as a tributary State to his empire. The annexation was solely on the strength of a courteous clause in the Vietnamese king's despatch describing his country as a 'little vassal of your empire'. The Chinese emperor, taking him at his word, sent him the seal of a satellite ruler containing the picture of a camel, the symbol of vassalage. An imperial decree was issued on the occasion in which Vietnam was invested with its modern name which has stuck to it since and has uniformly appeared in maps and dictionaries published after 1946.[2]

Chinese culture, diffused in Vietnam during its early centuries of Chinese rule, was mainly the teaching of Confucian philosophy and Taoist doctrines. Buddhism had not become yet part and parcel of Chinese culture and was not officially propagated. But it infiltrated into Vietnam from both China and other sources. There is, however, no legend or history to pinpoint the first introduction of Buddhism into the country.

Amongst the pioneers of Buddhism from China, we know the names of two Indian monks, Mahājīvaka and Kalyāṇaruchi, one Tibetan monk Kang-seng-houci, and one Chinese monk, Meou Po. They all came from China by sea to what was then known as 'Giaochi' (*i.e.*, North Vietnam), then regarded by the Chinese as an outlying district of China.

Later came the famous Indian monk Vinītaruchi, illustrious in the history of Vietnamese Buddhism. Not much is known about his personal life. He is said to have come to Changan from India in 593, stayed for six years at Konnang Teheon where he engaged himself in translating a number of Buddhist works into Chinese and then proceeded to 'Giaochi' where he was nominated the Chief monk of the Phapvan Temple in Luy Lan and spent fifteen years in the country before passing away. He belonged to the Chinese Cha'an school of Buddhism founded in China by Bodhidharma, and Vinītaruchi's Vietnamese disciple Phap Hien is regarded as its first patriarch in Vietnam. The school is prevalent to this day mostly in North Vietnam.

Vinītaruchi left behind him a long line of famous monks and teachers of this school,—Phap Hien (626 A.D.), Do Phap Hian (990 A.D.), Van Hanh (1018 A.D.), Tu Dao Hanh (1122 A.D.) and others.

It is likely that other Indian monks, on their voyage from India to China during the periods of Tang and Sung in China, broke their long and arduous journey at some Vietnamese port before proceeding to their destination and their teachings spread among the common people of the locality. They were, as we may presume, exponents not of Chinese, but of Indian Buddhism, Mahāyānist or Sarvāstivāda.

---

[2] *Ibid*, p. 52.

Chapter VIII

'CHINESE TURKESTAN' AND THE OASIS STATES

BETWEEN India and China,—joining Kashmir and ancient Gandhara (now merged in Afghanistan) with China's westernmost province, Kansu,—is a country which used till recently to be known as Eastern Turkestan. No longer known by that name, it is covered now by a state called Sinkiang. Whether Sinkiang's boundaries coincide with those of old Turkestan cannot be ascertained, for in desert regions boundary-marks have a knack of shifting unpredictably. In the midst of this area is Taklamakan, a vast extension of the Gobi desert extending from the border of Mongolia to near the basin of the Tarim river.

An arid desiccated region, it might have been merely an expanse of waste-land, but for the merciful ministrations of a few hill-streams carrying moisture from the mountains to the thirsty plains. They have created patches of oasis-lands in their valleys before being choked up in desert-sands. The southern rim of the Taklamakan is a little more hospitable: it is in the basin of a river called Tarim which, rising in the Pamirs to the west and catching the currents of two confluent streams, flows a long way down the desert's southern rim, losing itself in the desert near Tun-huang like all the hill-streams of this area.

There are indications that the country round Taklamakan was anciently better populated and more habitable. It presents now for the most part a typical desert landscape,—bare hills looking moth-eaten and wind-eroded and sand-dunes shifted about by desert-wind, all under a haze of wind-blown far-flung drifts of gritty biting sand. Its aridity has perhaps increased with passing years, for there are signs here and there, like bamboo-poles oddly sticking out of some sand-dunes, of human habitations long abandoned to the mercy of the desert. There is a sparse population in this area yet. It consists of a few, hardy tribes of diverse ethnic origins,—Turkis, Uighars, Khazaks, Uzbegs, Tajiks, etc., all Moslem by religion and agriculturists or herdsmen by occupation except where they live in communes under the Soviet Union and where they can find employment as farmers or factory-hands. The present inhabitants are completely innocent of the past of this region, and when they chance upon some remnant of a temple or a stūpa they readily mistake it as a memorial to some Moslem saint of yore.

domination. A Chinese-created upper class came into existence in Vietnam. "It had a Chinese culture and was constantly replenished by Chinese appointees: refugee intellectuals, mainly those who arrived in great numbers before and after the fall of the second branch of the Han dynasty in 220 A.D."[4] Statecraft passed into the hands of these 'mandarins' after 187 A.D. and their position remained entrenched till the eighteenth century when the country came under French colonial power. The mandarin class, with its proud badge of Chinese culture, was most actively influential in stabilizing Confucianism for long centuries in Vietnam and also in spreading Taoism, which took many perverted forms among the people.

This was the milieu in which Buddhism was first introduced into Vietnam and it spread among ordinary folk obviously because the mandarins and their Confucian creed were unpopular and Taoism had degenerated into unintelligible rituals and magical practices.

The Confucianist mandarin is referred to here and there in Vietnamese folk-literature, but only to poke fun at him as a dandy and do-nothing fellow. There is a love-song in which a Vietnamese peasant warns his love against taking a Mandarin for a husband: 'Never marry a literate man (i.e. a mandarin). He has a long back which he likes to cover with beautiful materials; he keeps combing his hair and lets his nails grow and he leaves his table only to go to bed'.[5]

While Chinese Confucianism did not make much headway among common people, in spite of the mandarins' great power and prestige and control of economics and statecraft, we find the doctrines of Buddhism like the law of *Karma*, rebirth, suffering and the laws of causation and impermanence seep slowly into the people's mind. The main idea of the story of the great epic *Kimvan Kiem* by the Vietnamese poet Nguyen (1765-1821) is to show how 'Nhan Qua' (*Karma*) works out in the lives of individuals. Without being a professedly Buddhist poem with a didactic aim, it illustrates extensively and on a truly epic scale the Buddhist *Karma* doctrine.[6] It must have been assimilated by the Vietnamese mind from Buddhist teachings long centuries before the poet Nguyen could think of using it for the purpose of epic story-telling.

---

[4] *The Smaller Dragon*, p. 102.

[5] *Ibid*. See p. 409.

[6] *Kim Van Kiem* is the most considerable epic in the native literature of Vietnam. It is considered by Vietnamese scholars to be a classic of the highest merit. An analysis of the poem accompanied with critical comments will be found in Thai Van Kiem's book on *Vietnam, Past and Present*, published in 1957 under the auspices of the Vietnamese Department of National Education and the National Commission for the UNESCO.

It is significant that within a century of the withdrawal of Chinese rule in 939 A.D. there was an upsurge of Buddhism in Vietnam under Vietnamese kings. After a period of unsettlement and internal troubles, Vietnam came into her own with the establishment of the native Ly dynasty in 1010. The urge of Vietnamese nationalism not only brought its own monarchy to the throne, but it was accompanied also perhaps by a revulsion against the superimposed Chinese culture which had served to suppress largely the indigenous culture of the land. Not only was the exclusive right of the Mandarins to all posts under the State rejected after China's renunciation of suzerainty, but it seems that Confucianism itself, of Chinese origin and breed, was dethroned from its superior position. It was no longer necessary for officials to be Confucian scholars. Buddhism, however, had been spontaneous in its growth in the country and during the Ly dynasty which lasted for 215 years and the dynasties that followed, the Tran and the later Le, covering altogether more than seven centuries of Vietnamese history, high official posts were filled by Buddhists.

How many of the kings of these dynasties were professed Buddhists, it is not possible to say. The kings of the Ly dynasty seem, according to the legends related about them, to have been Buddhists. About the others there is no reliable indication, though there is no doubt of their having been active patrons of Buddhism. Their patronage of the religion generally took the form of building Buddhist temples and pagodas, besides appointing Buddhists in foreign service and in the educational cadre. The Ly kings ordered Buddhist text-books to be written and used the elite of the Buddhist clergy as leaders in education and sometimes as encumbents of higher administrative and diplomatic posts.

The country under native rulers was prospering economically; the royal treasuries were flush[7] and the kings built temples and pagodas and decorated them with a liberal hand and in such profusion that king Thank Tong (1459-1497) of the later Le dynasty decreed that no new ones should be added.[8]

The most spectacular monuments of Buddhism in Vietnam are the pagodas, built mostly in Chinese style, on extensive grounds and surrounded by lawns and flowering trees. Under the Ly dynasty the pagodas were given large domains, mostly through royal grants. Pagoda-building was specially favoured by the earlier Ly rulers and some of the later Tran. The rulers of the Tran dynasty (1225-1398) also restored several Buddhist pagodas as places of pilgrimage. It is interesting to note that not all the pagodas built by the Vietnamese kings were dedicated to the Buddha as the custom is in all other countries of south-east Asia. Several of them are purely commemorative,

---

[7] See *The Smaller Dragon*, p. 44.

[8] *Ibid*, p. 148.

enshrining memories of some illustrious figures of Vietnamese history. Thus there were Buddhist pagodas built to the memory of Tran Hung Dao, the Vietnamese hero who beat back the invading Mongolian hordes under Kubla Khan in 1287. The practice did not detract from the sacred character of the pagoda: in the Buddhist canon a *stūpa* (a sacred mound, of which the pagoda is a form) is allowed to be built not to the memory of the Buddha alone, but also to commemorate pre-eminent worthies whose memories are held sacred.[9] Pagoda-building did not come to a close with the edict of Thank Tong, for the magnificent pagoda of Thien Mu, west of Hue, was built in 1601 by one of the rulers of the last Vietnamese dynasty of Hue.

After its heyday in Vietnam under the Ly, the Tran and the late Le dynasties, Buddhism did not till the present century have a history of uninterrupted progress. There were occasional revivals of Confucianism and the rise of rulers partial to Chinese culture and not friendly to Buddhism. The last Vietnamese ruling dynasty of Hue, the Nguyen, however, was with a few exceptions almost consistently pro-Buddhist. The dynasty covered four centuries from 1513 to 1925.

When, after the lapse of about nine hundred years of independence, Vietnam came under French colonial dominion, the Christian missionaries were at large in the country, giving to Buddhism little room to flourish. The Vietnamese were opposed to their efforts though some of them rendered the country great service. But their independence having gone, the people had little initiative in action.

In other countries of south-east Asia, as we have seen, Buddhism attracted kings, who endowed it with royal munificence and aided its growth and propagation as a system of culture approved by the state. The monks formed organisations and lent themselves to the systematisation and consolidation of this culture. But such was not the state of things in Vietnamese Buddhism. It never clung to any canon nor evolved one of its own nor did it ever attain a footing from which it could wield shaping influence on society or over affairs of state.

The want of canonical directive was often the cause of rituals and ceremonies, popular in Vietnam, in which Buddhism was mixed up with concepts alien to it. An outstanding example is the ceremony held on the 15th day of every 7th lunar month for the benefit of 'wandering souls' (*Co Hon*). It is a national ceremony thus described by a Vietnamese writer:

---

[9] See *Mahaparinibbana, Suttata* V. 27.
Four classes of beings are enumerated as deserving of *Stupa* commemoration. To the Vietnamese who counted patriotism as a great virtue, those who had saved the country or laid down their lives for it were as deserving of commemoration by *Stupa* as men of religion.

"Every village has a cemetery, although wealthy families often have their own family plots. Near the common cemetery stands the Am Chung Sinh (temple), the purpose of which is to care for the Co Han, watched over by a temple-keeper. Offerings to the Co Hon are made most often in summer when disasters such as cholera, epidemics and floods sometimes cause death in mass. But the most important event is the Wandering Soul's Day when prayers are said for the salvation of the dead in general and the Co Hon in particular.

(*Note*—The *Co Hon* are those departed souls who have left none on earth to provide them with the wherewithal for living in after-life).

"The ceremony called Dan Chay may last up to several days and begins with a procession around the cemetery to invite the dead into the Am Chung Sinh for the ceremony. Amid dirges, a monk heads the procession followed by a line of women who chant prayers and carry religious flags.

"Finishing the circuit of the cemetery, the procession stops before an altar set up in front of the Am Chun Sinh. The altar has two levels, the higher used to honour the Buddha with incense and offerings of fruits and rice, and the lower used for offerings to the dead. Rice-soup, fruit and meat are most common, but it is best if they include the 'Tan Sinh' (three living creatures), fish, meat and shrimp and the 'Ngu Qua', five kinds of fruit.

"Monks and women pray to heaven to forgive the souls languishing in hell. Then birds are released from cages and food is offered to the Co Hon.

"The Hell in the ceremony is made of paper and bamboo. After suitable prayers have been said, the 'Paper Hell' is torn up so that the condemned souls can get out. The general belief is that the dead continue to lead a life not very different from our own. Their society is about the same as ours. They can be poor and unhappy or rich and happy. And it is obvious that souls who have no descendents to care for them are needy and unhappy. So it is the living who have the responsibility of helping them".

It is a Buddhist ceremony peculiar to Vietnam, but it is easy to see how it grew out of primitive eschatological notions, which form no part of Buddhism, under the impact of the Buddhist doctrine of Compassion.

The two countries which most contributed to the propagation and spread of Buddhism in Vietnam were China and India. Buddhism in the country, as we have said, was distinguished by having two forms—the Religion of the North and the Religion of the South. There were obvious historical reasons for the Chinese provenance,—the contact of a thousand years between the two countries, the migrations of Chinese Buddhists into North Vietnam

[10] See *Vietnam*, News Magazine, No. 3, published from Saigon, p. 30. Also *The Disposition of Buddhist Temples in Vietnam* (published by the Review Horizons, 1956, Saigon), pp. 13-15.

in the early Christian centuries, the comparatively easy access from China to the Red River Valley which had been the original Vietnamese colony, etc. But India was far off and the contacts were few. Those few contacts, however, were both commercial and cultural. As Cady says: "Early Vietnamese contacts with India were in part commercial and in part religious because of Buddhist pilgrims' journeys in both directions. Sea-borne missions from India stopped in Vietnam en route to China proper, and Vietnamese pilgrims subsequently obtained copies of the sacred Buddhist texts from cultural centres in south Sumatra. But for various reasons Chinese culture took precedence over Indian in Vietnam."[11]

Hanoi became the capital of Vietnam under the Ly kings. It soon rose to be a Buddhist centre, the Ly kings being Buddhist rulers. Near Hanoi was a sea-port for voyages from India and back. It must have been used by Buddhist monks from India on the sea-way to China during China's Tang and Sung dynasties. Probably in Vietnam there were also some small Indian colonies of mercantile origin. In the history of Buddhism in Vietnam, no Indian names stand out except Mahajīvaka, Katyāyan-śrī and Vinītaruchi. But Indian influence is traceable in the art, culture and religion of its people. It lends point to the observation of the Vietnamese scholar Duenig Quam Ham: "Thanks to Chinese monks, and especially to Indian monks, Buddhism has gradually spread over the country,—yet with no organization". Nearly 80 per cent of the Vietnamese over North and South Vietnam are now Buddhist, though the *Saṅgha* (monk fraternity) is not organised as in other parts of south-east Asia.

In the last century and in the present, Buddhism in the south has had a new spurt of life under the influence of missions from Ceylon and a Buddhist university, Van-hahn, is now functioning at Saigon.

Unlike the other States of south-east Asia, Vietnam is politically divided. By 1954 it had been split up into two parts with a communist Viet Minh government in the north and the government of the French-sponsored 'associated State of Vietnam' in the south. The division between the north and the south was formally acknowledged in a Cease-fire Agreement reached by the United Nations at Geneva in July 1954. Next year South Vietnam was declared to be an independent republic, but North Vietnam remained a separate communist State.[12]

It was nearly eight years ago that the antagonism in political ideology and practice between the two parts of Vietnam reached the point of militancy and since North Vietnam's thrust into the south with the

[11] *South-east Asia: Its historical development*, p. 17.

[12] See Brian Harrison's *South-east Asia* (published by MacMillan and Co., 1963), p. 255 (Second edition).

Vietcong guerilla forces, armed hostility between the two parts began. Since this outbreak, the U.S.A. has been taking active part with the South Vietnamese, carrying on large-scale bombing operations. Vietnam has thus shot into the spotlight and became newsworthy in the world's press. But it had little pull before this in international affairs and its history over two thousand years had little interest for eastern or western historians, except in the comparatively brief context of western colonialism. The colonial history of Vietnam began as late as in the 17th century and ended in 1955, —only a chapter of her national history.

There are only two complete histories of Vietnam, one by a communist Vietnamese scholar and the other by an American, viz., (i) Le Thanh Khoi's *Le Vietnam, Historie et Civilisation* (published in Paris in 1955) and (ii) Joseph Buttinger's *The Smaller Dragon* (published by Frederick Praeger, New York, in 1958). From these books, however, as well as many others dealing with Vietnam in the colonial context, not much can be gathered about the Buddhism of the country. Saigon is at present its Buddhist centre with its Buddhist Van Hahn university which is interested in collecting, editing and publishing Buddhist works written in the Vietnamese language.

typical Vietnamese Pagoda (Xa-Loi, South Vietna

ietnamese Buddhists at the gate of a temple
ia Dinh Town in Saigon suburb)

Chapter VIII

'CHINESE TURKESTAN' AND THE OASIS STATES

BETWEEN India and China,—joining Kashmir and ancient Gandhara (now merged in Afghanistan) with China's westernmost province, Kansu,—is a country which used till recently to be known as Eastern Turkestan. No longer known by that name, it is covered now by a state called Sinkiang. Whether Sinkiang's boundaries coincide with those of old Turkestan cannot be ascertained, for in desert regions boundary-marks have a knack of shifting unpredictably. In the midst of this area is Taklamakan, a vast extension of the Gobi desert extending from the border of Mongolia to near the basin of the Tarim river.

An arid desiccated region, it might have been merely an expanse of waste-land, but for the merciful ministrations of a few hill-streams carrying moisture from the mountains to the thirsty plains. They have created patches of oasis-lands in their valleys before being choked up in desert-sands. The southern rim of the Taklamakan is a little more hospitable: it is in the basin of a river called Tarim which, rising in the Pamirs to the west and catching the currents of two confluent streams, flows a long way down the desert's southern rim, losing itself in the desert near Tun-huang like all the hill-streams of this area.

There are indications that the country round Taklamakan was anciently better populated and more habitable. It presents now for the most part a typical desert landscape,—bare hills looking moth-eaten and wind-eroded and sand-dunes shifted about by desert-wind, all under a haze of wind-blown far-flung drifts of gritty biting sand. Its aridity has perhaps increased with passing years, for there are signs here and there, like bamboo-poles oddly sticking out of some sand-dunes, of human habitations long abandoned to the mercy of the desert. There is a sparse population in this area yet. It consists of a few, hardy tribes of diverse ethnic origins,—Turkis, Uighars, Khazaks, Uzbegs, Tajiks, etc., all Moslem by religion and agriculturists or herdsmen by occupation except where they live in communes under the Soviet Union and where they can find employment as farmers or factory-hands. The present inhabitants are completely innocent of the past of this region, and when they chance upon some remnant of a temple or a stūpa they readily mistake it as a memorial to some Moslem saint of yore.

But the ancient Chinese Buddhists knew it as a Buddhist country. In fact its conversion to Islam was not before the tenth century.

A series of oasis-states existed in Central Asia from Kapisa, on India's extreme north-west, to Yarkand in West Asia and some of them were round the 'Chinese Turkestan' region. Counted in clockwise direction, they were—(i) Kapisa, (ii) Bamyan, (iii) Bactria, (iv) Sogdiana (Samarkand), (v) Khashgar, (vi) Turfan, (vii) Kucha, (viii) Kharsarh, (ix) Lulan, (x) Tun-huang, (xi) Muran, (xii) Charchan, (xiii) Niya, (xiv) Khotan, and (xv) Yarkand. In most of these oasis-states there were small cells of Buddhism and two of them within 'Chinese Turkestan' rose to be once famous seats of Buddhism and Buddhist culture, viz., Kucha and Khotan.

The story of the exploration of this part of Asia and recovery of documentary evidence that Buddhism once flourished here goes back to the seventies of the last century.

The Explorations and Discoveries

That such a dessicated part of the continent had an historic past and a tale of civilization, whose material relics lay buried in sand, came to the knowledge of western archaeologists only in 1879. Some time previously a Russian botanist had come to Turfan (on the north of Taklamakan) and he reported on his return on the richness of historical remains lying scattered round the locality. It presently roused the curiosity of European archaeologists, and archaeological expeditions to the site were undertaken by different European countries.

It put in train a series of explorations, opening an ever-widening vista of research in different fields. Remains of once residential houses and cave-monasteries, along with sundry artifacts, came to view at widely scattered places round the Taklamakan desert. The most interesting finds were from the contents of refuge pits and basement-rooms among the ruins, where people before deserting their homesteads had dumped their unwanted papers. A huge collection of them was made. It stirred European philologists to a great spurt of activity. These recovered documents were distributed to scholars at different seats of learning in Europe to decipher and interpret. Among them was a number of Buddhist manuscripts, written in Indian scripts,—*Kharoṣṭhī*, *Brāhmī* or slanting *Gupta* characters,—composed in different languages then current in the area.

The most systematic and most rewarding were the three explorations by Aurel Stein, sponsored by the Government of India in 1900-1901, 1906-1908 and 1913-1916.

Stein amassed a huge quantity of artifacts as well as papers and manuscripts which were later offered to eminent European scholars to work on. The most important of the manuscripts have not only been deciphered, but edited, translated and published,—the outstanding publication being Dr. Hoernle's *Manuscript Literature found in Eastern Turkestan* in two volumes (Clarendon Press, Oxford—Vol. I published in 1916). This work, besides cataloguing, editing and translating all the manuscripts in Indian *Brāhmī* script, introduces us to two languages of Mid-Asia, Tokharian and Khotanese. The former was spoken in the region to the north of the Tarim basin,—in Kucha and Turfan. The discovery of this language was an event in the history of Indo-European philology. It made short work of the hitherto accepted classification of Indo-European languages according to the shibboleth that the European languages were of 'centum' type and the Asiatic 'Śatam'. But in Tokharian, spoken in the heart of Asia, the word for 'hundred' was 'cante', almost the same as in Latin.

The artifacts collected by Stein were of a miscellaneous kind. Among them were found small slabs of sculpture, Buddhist paintings, both mural and in rolls of cloth or silk, and Buddha and Bodhisattva images, big and small. The biggest collection made by Aural Stein was not exactly in Mid-Asia, but in the Chinese caravan-town of Tun-huang on the border of China outside the Great Wall.

This town had been a sort of gateway: the flux of mid-Asian trade, along with some of mid-Asian Buddhist culture, passed through it into the 'Celestial Empire'. In the early history (Changan period) of Chinese Buddhism, Mid-Asia was a sort of hinterland from where the Chinese used to bring Buddhist texts and Buddhist teachers into their country. Its history will be related later.

Chinese pilgrims of 5th-7th Centuries in Oasis-States

As we have already seen, a number of oasis-states existed round Taklamakan which have shifted their sites or entirely disappeared.

The history of their foundation is unknown: perhaps they came into being as precipitates from long-range tribal migrations that passed over this region in primitive times. Most of these migrations date probably back to the first or second century, B.C. The tribes that drifted into Mid-Asia from north and west were not all of one race, but round Taklamakan the Homo Alpinus strain was prominent. We know for example from a Chinese source that Kucha, oasis-state on the north of Taklamakan, was under a dynasty of kings significantly described in the 18th century A.D., as 'white' (*po*) by the Chinese.[1]

Chinese Buddhist pilgrims to India, from Fa-hsien (c.400 A.D.) to those of the mid-seventh century, used to pass into India through the oasis-states, sojourning for a period in their capital cities for rest and recoupment.

---

[1] See Hoernle's *Manuscript Literature*, etc., vol. I, p. 218.

Most of our knowledge about the social and cultural conditions of these states in these centuries is gleaned from their travel-records.

Fa-hsien started on his passage to India from some point in the oasis of Charchan. Following northwestward the course of the Tarim river, he came to Kharsarh and proceeded thence to an oasis named Korla. From there, he made a bee-line southwards across the lower spread of Taklamakan and, crossing the Tarim and the Khotan rivers, reached Khotan in a month and five days. He stopped for three months at Khotan to witness the forthcoming 'procession of images', which was a regular Buddhist festival of the locality. Leaving Khotan, he trekked on to Kapisa and was right on the Indian border. For pilgrims from the east in those times, Kapisa was the gateway to India.

After Fa-hsien, Sung-Yen (c. 518 A.D.) went from Tun-huang to Khotan, along the trans-Taklamakan route negotiated by Fa-hsien. From Khotan he passed through Udyana to Peshawar and Nagarhar returning to China in 521 A.D.

Next went Hsüan-tsang (629 A.D.) on his pilgrimage to India, making the longest tour through Mid-Asia. Avoiding the shorter desert-crossing through Taklamakan, he took perhaps for reasons of his own the longer route along the north-west right up to the Pamirs and came to Khotan through Tashkan and Kashgar. He followed practically the same circuitous route on his return journey to China.

The oasis-towns where the pilgrims halted or sojourned were mere intermediate stopping places for them, with the history or antiquities of which they were scarcely concerned. Only of Kucha and Khotan they spoke at some length because they were places of which the fame had reached them in China. The historical materials, however, brought to light by Aurel Stein and others, have greatly extended the scope of our information about the oasis-states. They confirm the following conclusions:

(i) Some of these states were undoubtedly of ancient origin, even going back to the B.C. centuries and had probably been founded by peoples of an Indo-European stock. There were legends among them of their ancient origin connecting their kingly dynasties with either the Sakya clan to which the Buddha belonged or with some descendant of Emperor Asoka. But these legends were probably faked ones,—invented and made current by monks who wanted to show that these states were Buddhist from their beginnings.

(ii) When they emerge into the ken of history in the early A.D. centuries, Buddhism is seen to be their prevailing religion. All the remains discovered in them are of temples, monasteries and stūpas; among art-relics, Buddha-images and pieces of Buddhist sculpture and painting; and material traces of Buddhist rites and ceremonies. There are no visible marks of any other religion except in Turfan and some neighbouring states, where papers and manuscripts have been discovered relating to other faiths, e.g., Manichaeism and Nestorian Christianity.

(iii) The prevalent style of sculpture and painting follows generally the Graeco-Buddhist school that developed in Gandhara and Kashmir in the early A.D. centuries. But here and there, though rarely, it is modified by the introduction of some racial characteristics, though the models and patterns, generally speaking, are of pure Indian provenance, e.g., the attirement of the Bodhisattvas, the poses and *mudrās* (disposition of fingers) in the female figures, the current symbols of the religion and the painted Buddha-life episodes.

(iv) In the monk community there was undoubtedly a number of Indian monks, emigrés like Kumarāyāna, father of Kumārajīva, from India's north-west and they were settled in some of these oasis-states. The Mahāyāna Buddhism and the Hīnayāna Sarvāstivāda, which in the early A.D. centuries had their strong-hold in Gandhara and Kashmir, must have been propagated by Indian monks.

(v) There were monk-scholars in the monasteries who, wishful to introduce the scripture to lay people, translated their Sanskrit texts into regional languages, but these languages having no script of their own, one of the three Indian scripts, probably well-known there, viz., *Brāhmī*, *Kharoṣṭhī* or the 'slanting' *Gupta* script was used. The *sūtras* translated were all from Indian sources and no trace of 'Chinese Buddhism' is evident in any of them.

(vi) There were caravan-routes across the deserts and along the mountain gorges for trade, connecting the States of Mid-Asia with India's northwest frontier. These routes were available to those who wished to pass on to somewhere in Mid-Asia from the Indian border.

(vii) The routes to Mid-Asia could not have been altogether unknown to Indian inhabitants of the north-western provinces, for during the early A.D. centuries this part of India was under Kushan rule. The Kushans themselves had probably come by these routes from Mid-Asia into India.

Kucha and Khotan

Kucha on the north and Khotan on the south of Taklamakan seem to have been materially most prosperous and culturally most advanced among the oasis-states. Both these states were probably founded by people of Indo-European stock.

Kucha emerges into history as early as the 2nd century, B.C. when it came in contact with the Chinese empire. It is mentioned by Chinese annalists. Under a dynasty of kings which in the 1st century A.D. had the Chinese name *Po* (white), it became a flourishing and highly cultured state. Here the Buddhist religion had come early and enjoyed a particularly flourishing period in the 4th century, A.D. "The state and its 'white' dynasty lasted down towards the end of the 8th century, A.D., when both utterly disappeared from history ".[2]

Kucha, as already mentioned, had a language of its own which was spoken also in the state of Karshar. The manuscripts recovered from Kucha, mostly translations into the Kuchan language of scriptural texts in Sanskrit, show the native language to have been well-developed about the middle of the 7th century A.D. An Indo-European language spoken in the centre of Asia, it had the crucial characteristic of the European branch of the family retaining, as already noted, the 'K' sound which is aspirated in the Asian. But it had no script of its own and the script of the Kuchan translations from Sanskrit is either Indian *Brāhmī* or *Kharoṣṭhī*, or the slanting *Gupta*. Hsüan-tsang remarks that "the style of writing is Indian, with some difference".

The geographical position of Kucha was such as to keep it open to both Indian and Iranian influences, though the mode of living of the people was more Iranian than Indian. "Kucha", says Grousset, "from the literary and religious points of view formed an integral part of Outer India; from the point of view of material civilization, it was at the same time a province of Outer Iran".[3] It is said that when the Kashmirian scholar, Kumārāyana, father of Kumārajīva, came from Kashmir to settle at a township in the Kucha state, he retained his Indian style of living in preference to the current Iranian style of Kucha.

Sometime in 629-630 A.D., Hsüan-tsang on his pilgrimage to India crossed the Tsunling Mountain through Kucha and he has left a glowing account of Kucha's material prosperity and Buddhist culture.

It seems that at that time the Buddhism that prevailed in Kucha was of the Hīnayāna Sarvāstivāda school.

"There are about one hundred convents (*sanghārāmas*) in this country with five thousand and more disciples. These belong to the Little Vehicle of the school of Sarvāstivāda. Their doctrines (i.e., teaching of *sutras* and rules of dicipline, *Vinaya*) are like those of India and those who read them use the same (originals) ... They live purely, and provoke others (by their conduct) to a religious life".

Like the Khotanese, the people of Kucha delighted in holding 'image-processions'. They were a popular festival, grand and spectacular, and Fa-hsien stayed for three months in Khotan for an opportunity to witness it. But the Kuchans had other accomplishments too. They were famous as musicians. "In their skill in playing on the lute and the pipe", says Hsüan-tsang "they excel all other countries".

[2] *Ibid*, Vol. I, p. 218.

[3] Grousset's *In the Footsteps of the Buddha*, George Routledge and Sons, London, 1932, p. 57.

Two very striking personalities erupted from Kucha into the early history of Buddhism in China—Śrīmitra (early 4th century) and Kumārajīva (early 5th century). Both had drifted into China under exceptional circumstances, settled at Changan, distinguished themselves as Buddhist teachers and died at a ripe old age at the capital city, deeply venerated and honoured by Chinese Buddhists. But they were two sharply contrasted personalities.

According to one legend, Śrīmitra was a Kuchan prince, who had given up the throne and embraced monkhood and entered China with Chinese refugees in 307-312 A.D. He was an ascetic, an adept in *Dhāraṇis* (Tāntric incantations) and was introduced into the inner circle of the metropolitan aristocracy by Wan Tao who had 'discovered' him. Here he made a great impression by his spells and magical formulae, though the Chinese gentry looked upon him as only a 'venerable curiosum'. He did not speak Chinese, but amazed people by anticipating the sense of their words by 'silent understanding'. Yet he is said to have translated three collections of spells. There is no doubt that he was a pioneer of Tāntric Buddhism in China and the high regard in which he stood among the Changan gentry of his time was marked by Emperor Ch'eng's building a *chaitya* at the place where he died.[4]

Kumārajīva on the other hand was a highly accomplished scholar, exegete and Mahāyānist teacher, not an ascetic or Tāntric like Śrīmitra. He was born in Kucha and it is said that the name given to him was a combination of the names of his Indian father Kumārāyana and Kuchan mother Jīvā.

Kumārāyana, his father, was a Buddhist *pandita* of Kashmir. He had emigrated to a town in the Kucha state named Kiue-tsa near the foot of Tsunling mountain. The family, however, did not lose touch with Kashmir and, after the death of Kumārāyana, Kumārajīva's mother took the boy back to Kashmir where he proved to be a scholar of great promise. Both mother and son came back to Kucha after staying for some time at Kashgar where the son's studies were continued. It is said that as a result of these studies he became a convert to Mahāyāna Buddhism and won great fame as a scholar. His fame in Kucha as a scholar of Mahāyāna Buddhism spread even to China. When Kucha was conquered by China in 384, Lü Kuang, the Chinese general, captured Kumārajīva and, a few years later, brought him to Changan which had become a great centre of Buddhist studies. He was appointed there as head of an organisation which had been functioning like the White Horse Monastery of Loyang to produce translations of Buddhist texts.

Kumārajīva made a great impression on the emperor who put him at the head of the imperial translation bureau with an army of assistants and

[4] For this account of Srimitra, see Zürcher's *The Buddhist Conquest of China* (published by E.J. Brill, Leiden, 1959), pp. 103-104.

clerks under him. "Early in 402, on arrival at Changan, he became the *Purohita* (High Priest) of the Later Ch'in, excessively venerated by members of the royal family, and leader of several thousands of disciples from all quarters of the empire".[5] One of these Later Ch'in emperors, as the story goes, tempted him to marry and for that purpose sent him from his court ten glamorous ladies to choose a bride from. It is said that Kumārajīva was overcome by the charms of one, doffed his monk's robe and settled down to worldly life after marrying her. He soon came, however, to repent of his lapse. It is reported that thereafter he always used to begin his sermons with the apologetic exordium: 'Follow my work, but not my life which is far from ideal. But the lotus grows out of mud. Love the lotus; do not love the mud'. When he died at Changan in some year after 412 A.D., his body was cremated according to Indian custom, as the Chinese knew that he was Indian on the father's side.[6]

At Kucha Hīnayāna Buddhism of the Sarvāstivāda school prevailed; but Khotan, the most advanced State in the south, was a stronghold of Mahāyāna Buddhism.

Like Kucha, Khotan also claimed an ancient origin. Hsüan-tsang records a local legend about the foundation of Khotan. It tells that Asoka's son Kunāla blinded at Taxila by a cruel step-mother left the country with a number of followers and adherents and settled at Khotan. The kings of Khotan, it is said, were his descendents. The legend is reproduced also in Tibetan histories of Buddhism, but has no historical confirmation.

The fame of Khotan as a seat of Mahāyāna Buddhism was known in China long before Fa-hsien's visit. A Chinese monk named Chu Shih-hsing, desiring to collect Mahāyānist Buddhist texts, had undertaken in 260 A.D. a difficult and arduous journey from distant Loyang to Khotan where he died. Later we find a Khotanese scholar Mokṣala translating at Changan the *Prajnāpāramitā* of 25,000 verses brought from Khotan in 291 A.D. A number of Mahāyānist texts came into Changan from Khotan.[7]

Fa-hsien remarks that "the country is prosperous and happy and the people are very wealthy". About Buddhism in Khotan, he says: "The body of priests number several myriads, principally belonging to the Great Vehicle. They all have food provided for them". There were fourteen great monasteries in the State, of which the chief one was called Gomatī Vihāra where Fa-hsien and his companions were lodged. "The Gomatī priests, as they belong to the Mahāyāna, are principally honoured by the

---

[5] *Ibid*, *p. 226.*

[6] For life-sketch of Kumarajiva, see Dutt's *Buddhist Monks and Monasteries of India*, Allen and Unwin, London, 1962, pp, 303-306.

[7] See Zürcher's *The Buddhist Conquest of China*, pp. 61-62.

king". Another monastery, located outside the city, had the name 'New-king Vihāra". It was a magnificent edifice, with carvings and inlay work, covered with gold and silver and adorned with jewels, "elegant and splendid beyond the power of description". Religious music was customary and the principal Buddhist festival in the country was the 'Image-procession'. In this festival, an image of the Buddha with attendant gods and Bodhisattvas was placed in a car and pulled with great eclat through the city's streets.

Hsüan-tsang visited Khotan about a couple of centuries after Fa-hsien. Some changes during the intervening period seem to have taken place in the Buddhist institutions. Hsüan-tsang speaks of about a hundred *sanghārāmas* with some 5,000 inmates who all study "the doctrines of the Great Vehicle". But he does not make particular mention of the Gomatī Vihāra nor of the 'New-king Vihāra' which was the most splendid of the monasteries of Khotan in Fa-hsien's time.

Of the Khotanese, he speaks admiringly: "They have a knowledge of politeness and justice. They are naturally quiet and respectful. They love to study literature and the arts in which they have made considerable advance". The advancement of the Khotanese in the arts is borne out by the finds of Aurel Stein in Khotan's sand-buried ruins.

They consist of stucco relievos and mural paintings, besides a number of manuscripts in Khotanese. The relievos and paintings, as Stein remarks, are "undoubtedly derived from that Graeco-Buddhist art which flourished during the early centuries after Christ in the extreme north-west of India".[8] Yet some of them betray strikingly incongruous intrusions of Iranian influence. The most noticeable is the conception of 'Persian Bodhisattvas' which appear on a wooden panel from Khotan.[9] The divinity of each Bodhisattva figure is indicated by its four arms; the figure itself is that of a powerful male, "wholly Persian in physical appearance and style of dress". "The long ruddy face, surrounded by a heavy black beard, is a feature never seen on any sacred Buddhist figure. The large curling moustache and the bushy black eye-brows add to the martial look of the face. Over the head with its long back locks rises a high golden tiara closely resembling the headdress of the Sasanian kings of Persia".

The contents of Khotanese manuscripts recovered are collected in Hoernle's *Manuscript Literature of Eastern Turkestan*. They are partly in Sanskrit and partly in Khotanese versions, the script for both being a variety of Indian script. "The writing as well as the shape and arrangement of these manuscripts are of course derived from India". The 'old' Khotanese language in which they are written is of Iranian derivation. In its

[8] Stein's *On Central Asian Tracks* (Chinese Reprint), p. 62.

[9] *Ibid*, pp. 64-65. See illustration of a 'Persian Bodhisattva' between the pages.

development through the centuries the Khotanese language seems to have passed through two stages. In its earlier stage it is found in the Buddhist literature; in its later, in the official documents of the 8th century.

Ancient Khotan lasted down to the end of that century. In its palmiest days it was a centre of Buddhist culture and scholarship, so well-developed that at times it supplied Buddhist texts and teachers to the Chinese capital.

The most famous Khotanese scholar and teacher in China was Sikṣānanda. He was invited under imperial authority to proceed to China and take part in the State-sponsored industry of translating Buddhist Sanskrit texts into Chinese. Having settled in Changan in 605 A.D., he translated with the help of an Indian monk named Bodhiruchi and the Chinese scholar I-tsing the *Avataṁsa Sūtra* into Chinese. After ten years' work in China, he returned to Khotan, intending to produce other translations of the *sūtras.* Again he was invited to the Chinese capital where he was received with great honours. But he never returned to his native town and breathed his last at Changan.

Tun-huang

Since Han times (early Christian centuries), the Chinese had made several advances into Mid-Asia, mostly by fits and starts and from stage to stage. Remains of ancient Chinese *limes* (military roads from a base of operation) have been found in Mid-Asia demarcating the limit of each advance.[10] By the 8th Century A.D., a large number of mid-Asian States passed under Chinese suzerainty and *Ambams* (local Chinese governors) were posted at their capitals. The most strategic approach by the Chinese to mid-Asia was through the border town of Tun-huang outside the Great Wall.

Round 102 B.C., a Chinese general Li Kuang-li had proceeded on a punitive expedition along the Tarim river to Ferangana with a huge army. Small states in the basin of the river fell to Chinese power and came under Chinese suzerainty.[11] The outward route-march of Kuang-li's army was through Tun-huang, then a small agricultural-military settlement. This ancient Han expedition blasted the way for advance from China into the Tarim basin; the route remained serviceable down to the close of the 8th century when China lost her suzerainty over the Tarim States. But this one-time highway of military advance became afterwards a way of more peaceful approach, facilitating intercourse between foreign monks and Chinese and trade communications between Mid-Asia and China.

One of the landmarks of Tun-huang was a range of hills to the south-west with a narrow stream running through the foothills and smothered quickly

---

[10] See *Ibid*, pp. 178-179.

[11] *Ibld*, p. 22.

in desert-sands. Some grottos of these hills were preferred by monks for solitary meditation and perhaps for this reason the hill-range became a centre of attraction to Chinese Buddhists.

It was sometime during the Changan period (4th-5th centuries) that the idea was conceived by imperial authorities at Changan to convert the hill-range with its caves into a Buddhist centre. About five hundred caves were taken in hand and as many as three hundred of them were decorated with sculpture and mural paintings. They wher then known to the Chinese as 'Chi'an-fo-tung', i.e., Caves of a Thousand Buddhas. Monks coming from Mid-Asia into China used to break journey here and sojourn for some time for rest and refreshment. The incoming monks were provided with quarters for their stay before going into the interior. The place was kept by the Chinese Buddhists.

From a mere *serai* (wayside resting place) for travelling monks, it developed into a permanent centre for study and discussions. Monks brought their books and holy souvenirs and left them here for safe-keeping. So at Tun-huang a huge wealth of deposited manuscripts and painted scrolls slowly accumulated.

From Tun-huang an Indian (or Indo-Scythian) monk-scholar, Dharmarakṣa, came in 266 A.D., to Changan, which had then become the country's new capital after the fall of Loyang. He died here at the ripe old age of eighty-seven,—in 308 or 317 A.D. At the time when Dharmarakṣa appeared at Changan, the city was simmering with Buddhist activity, specially with the industry of translating Sanskrit *sūtras* into Chinese. This absorbed the new-comer and he became "the greatest Buddhist translator before Kumārajīva". His first translation was of a piece from the *Prajnāpāramitā Sūtra of 25,000 verses* and his later translations were of 175 texts of which 90 have found place in the Chinese *Tripitaka.* His several tours from Changan into mid-Asia were rewarded by the find of a number of Buddhist manuscripts which he brought into China.[12]

The immense wealth of literary and artistic materials, accumulated through the centuries at Tun-huang, had, at some time of trouble and disorder, been stowed away for safety in a hidden crypt. In 1907 when Aurel Stein visited the place, it was in the keeping of a Taoist priest. Being thrown open, the crypt revealed an immense collection of Buddhist manuscripts, rolls of sacred painting and objects of art. All these were of Mid-Asian, Chinese and Tibetan provenance. Among the paintings, the most interesting were figures drawn in the style of Indian Ajanta murals. A complete account of Stein's discoveries is given in Chapters XII-XIV of his book *On Ancient Central-Asian Tracks.*

[12] See Zürcher's *The Buddhist Conquest of China,* pp. 65-67.

Chinese Suzerainty and Indian Culture in Mid-Asia

Chinese control over the Tarim basin came to an end about 791 A.D., after which for nearly a century the Tibetans ruled in this part.

On the nature and extent of Chinese control over the oasis-states, a good deal of light is thrown by the mass of documents that have been picked up from the rubbish-deposits. Thrown away as waste-paper when people left these towns, they are found to relate purely to administrative acts and orders or private transactions between parties. It seems from them that the Chinese were content only to exercise administrative authority and sustain political suzerainty over the people of these states.

There is almost no evidence of any cultural impact. In the manuscripts of religious texts discovered, there is nowhere any trace of Confucianism, Taoism or Chinese Buddhism. Buddhism (Indian Mahāyāna or Saravāstivāda) on the other hand is the staple theme in them except, as we have noted, in a few manuscripts discovered at Turfan and neighbouring oasis-states, which contain texts of Persian Manichaeism and Nestorian Christianity.

The cultural influence of Gandhara and Kashmir makes the leading feature of their culture and corporate religious life. This influence took deep root in the soil; it was unshaken by Chinese political suzerainty or later Tibetan rule. The face of Mid-Asia was set towards north-western India. On the Indian culture of that region it drew for all the needs of physical, intellectual and spiritual welfare.

As an example of this, we may take the science of medicine. The Chinese had their own medicine and system of healing. But it was the Indian *Ayurveda* that seems to have been accepted in Mid-Asia. One of the early finds at Kucha was a bundle of manuscripts in Sanskrit and in Kuchan translation. Colonel Bower, their discoverer so far back as in 1890, handed them over to the Asiatic Society of Bengal and, after being edited by Hoernle, they have been published by the Society and are known as the 'Bower Manuscripts'. Explorations made later have also brought to light several fragments of the *Ayurveda* which will be found included in Hoernle's work, *Manuscript Literature from Eastern Turkestan.*

It is again not improbable that through contacts between Mid-Asia and the Indian border-provinces, some spoken Indian dialects of those parts of India were known round Taklamakan. The scripts of the oasis-states were all of them Indian of different varieties. At a site near Khotan a manuscript in Kharoṣṭhī script was discovered in 1892 which contained a large portion of the *Dhammapada* of the Theravāda canon.[13] But the language of the Khotanese version is not Pali, the sacred language of

[13] See H.W. Bailey's article on *The Khotan Dhammapada* in the *Bulletin of Oriental and African Studies,* vol. xi (1943-1946), pp. 488 ff.

Theravāda Buddhism, but a variety of Prākrit, formerly spoken in India's north-western provinces. It is not, however, known whether this 'Khotanese *Dhammapada*' was actually used by the Khotanese monks or was in the private possession of some Indian monk at Khotan.

The life and culture of the oasis-states before their complete destruction by the Moslem onslaught of the 9th-10th centuries is necessarily known to us only in shreds and patches. But archaeology has spot-lighted a few significant facts,—the currency of the Indian Ayurvedic system of medicine, possible knowledge of some north-Indian dialects, contents of Buddhist manuscripts written in Indian scripts, which represent only the Mahāyāna and Sarvāstivāda Buddhism as they were prevalent in Gandhara and Kashmir (uninfluenced by Chinese Mahāyāna Buddhism), the adoption in painting and sculpture of Indo-Hellenistic art-modes as developed in Gandhara and Kashmir and, negatively, the absence of any trace of Chinese cultural influence. They sum up to the conclusion that the Mid-Asian oasis-town civilization had its only source in India and neither in China nor in Iran.

Even before commencement of the Christian era there were trade-routes from India's north-western border far into Mid-Asia in several directions. Perhaps the people of Mid-Asia first came to know of India and her civilization from traders and merchants. They brought to them Indian manufactures among which were probably small and artistic Indo-Hellenistic Buddha-images or Buddhist symbols wrought in Gandhara or Kashmir. These objects must have roused their curiosity and interest, specially when they were told that they were holy objects worshipped in India. In the Kushan era (early A.D. centuries), the routes into Mid-Asia from India must have been to some extent known to Indians of the border provinces where the Kushans ruled.

The urge to propagate Buddhism in regions where it was unknown was, as we have seen, a primitive urge in Buddhism. It impelled monks to wander far and wide, regardless of all hardships and privations, and we may suppose that Mid-Asia was in their orbit. Though there are very few names on record of early Indian missionaries in this part of Asia, we happen to know of two from a Chinese source.

In the Chinese *Tripitaka*, there is a collected series of lives, entitled *Kao-seng-chuan* ('Biographies of Eminent Monks'), composed under different imperial dynasties.[14] They include the 'biographies' of two Indian monks who left India and went to China making the round of the mid-Asian oasis-states. They were Jinagupta and Dharmagupta.

Jinagupta, according to the Chinese account, was born in 522 A.D. in a Kshatriya family in Peshawar (ancient Purushapura) and his father is said to

[14] All the three series of *Kao-seng-chuan* are included in vol. 50 of the Taisho Edition of the Chinese *Tripitaka*.

have been a minister in Gandhara. Jinagupta became at an early age a convert to Buddhism and, after completing his preliminary studies, left the country with nine monk-companions to propagate the religion of the Buddha abroad. He passed through Kapisa and entered the 'country of the White Huns' which included Badashkan and Wakan. From there he proceeded to 'Tashkurgan' in the Pamirs and reached Khotan, crossing the great snowy mountains. Having stayed for some time in Khotan, he left for China.

Some time after Jinagupta, another Indian monk Dharmagupta went to China through Mid-Asia. He was a native of Sourāshtra (in India) and became a monk at the age of twenty-three and studied Buddhist scripture at a monastery called *Kaumudīsaṅghārāma* in Kanouj. He then left with his teacher on wanderings abroad. Having spent five years in the 'Takka province' (northern Punjab which had its capital at Sakala, modern Sialkot) in a monastery named Deva-vihāra, they crossed the north-western border of the country. From Kapisa, they trekked to different countries till, crossing the Pamirs, they reached Khashgar. Having spent a couple of years there, Dharmagupta proceeded to Kucha where he spent two more years. He sojourned also at different monasteries at Karashar and Turfan before entering China.

Between the 3rd and the 8th centuries, A.D., there had been comings and goings of Buddhist monks between China and India. It made for the promotion of a sustained cultural intercourse between the two countries that sprang from Buddhism, then a common ground of intellectual and spiritual interest for both.[15] It drew a number of scholarly monks from China to India and *vice versa*. There were two known routes overland between the countries through Mid-Asia,—the longer one *via* the Pamirs on the west and the shorter across Taklamakan to Khotan.

The fact that in the Mid-Asian States Chinese Buddhism has left no trace and the current faiths were only the Buddhism of Indian Mahāyāna form (with its Indo-Hellenistic art) and the Hīnayāna Buddhism of the Sarvāstivāda school, both first developed in India's north-western border provinces, points to the work of Indian monks from that quarter. But few among them are known and their names are only in Chinese records.

[15] See Dutt's *Buddhist Monks and Monasteries of India*, pp. 294 ff.

Chapter IX

CHINA

Buddhism in the Han Period

CIVILIZATION in China was already old when Buddhism first appeared in the country in the early part of the Han period (B.C. 206—A.D. 210). The 'celestial empire' was then confined to northern China, and here had developed a pattern of state and society rooted in the teachings of Confucius as interpreted by the intellectuals, the so-called 'scholar gentry' of the age. Loyang was then the imperial capital, and into Loyang came some strange manuscripts, whole or in fragments, from countries regarded by the Chinese as 'barbarian'. They were brought by merchants along with their merchandise and were taken up in the little cells of Buddhism coming into existence in the city's foreign quarters. Wandering monks who also had manuscripts in their possession were about this time drifting into the city from outside the Great Wall.

This was the first uneventful introduction of Buddhism into China in the form of manuscripts. Yet it seems to have set the whole course of its development in the country. Its main reliance was on books and, after Buddhism had made a little headway in China, the quest for books on Buddhism went on from century to century.

The manuscripts that came so casually into China were at first of no use to the Chinese. They could not be read, being in foreign script and foreign language, unintelligible except to a polyglot Chinese scholar. But in the little Buddhist cells that had started to spring up in the capital, they were regarded as of especial value, being scriptural texts, fragmentary or complete. Yet, as curiosities, some of them found place in private collections and even in the great imperial library at Loyang.

Some of these Buddhist cells of the early Han period developed afterwards into 'ssu', i.e., Buddhist establishments or monasteries, and the one that became famous in later history was the 'White Horse Monastery' at Loyang commemorating in its name the Chinese legend of the first coming of Buddhism into China. The legend is that on a certain night in 64 A.D., the emperor Ming-ti of the Han dynasty saw in a dream a divine figure with a halo round its head. It was the figure of the Buddha come to meet the emperor,—and as though in fulfilment of the dream there appeared next morning at his palace gate two Indian monks on white horses, Kāśyapa-mātaṅga and Dharmaratna (or Dharmāraṇya). Now discredited by sober historians the legend, which has slightly different versions, is recalled by the name of the monastery, Paī-ma-ssu (White-Horse Monastery). There were other monasteries bearing the same name at Changan and Hopei.[1] But the Paī-ma-ssu of Loyang, though the name originated probably much later than its establishment, became the first seat of an industry that constitutes a special feature of the history of Buddhism in China—the translation and issue of Buddhist texts from available manuscripts.

Buddhism obtained no recognition among the Chinese literati nor spread among the people till the Han State began to break up in the 2nd century A.D. The life and culture of the old Han State was so conditioned that it would in any case have been difficult for a new system of thought or belief such as Buddhism presented to find within it a recognised place.

The Han was an expansionist state in the north, —hardly an empire yet. The vast southern part of China beyond the Yangtse river was *terra incognita*, out of bounds till the time the Han State began to dissolve. Here lived people untouched by Chinese civilization; the Chinese of the north called them 'barbarians'. North China, conterminous with what was known as the Han empire, was the 'Central Country' (*Chung-yuan*) or 'Central Kingdom' (*Chung-kuo*). It had been the cradle of Chinese civilization more than a millennium and a half before Han rule. Its capital Loyang had been founded by an emperor of a pre-Han dynasty in c. 1020 B.C. The system of social life and intellectual culture that prevailed in this 'Central Country' had crystallised round two schools of thought, Confucianism and Taoism, founded respectively by Confucius and 'Lao-tze',—the latter a somewhat doubtful personality,—both of the 6th century, B.C.

Confucianism was definitely 'this-worldly' in its outlook and in that sense not exactly a religion. It had a cosmology of its own and a theory of cultured civic life and it aimed to fit into its ideal pattern the order of society and system of government. The teachings of Confucius and Lao-tze had been conserved in a number of texts regarded traditionally by the Chinese as classics of their culture, foundation-stones of their civilization. Writing, since remote antiquity, had been in vogue in China.

The Confucian metaphysics, cosmology, ethics and politics supplied the *rationale* of Han social and political system. The intellectuals believed that the prevailing social and political structure under which they lived was the concrete materialization of what Confucianism contemplated, that its alignment was with cosmic principles: hence impregnable and everlasting. This

[1] See Zürcher's *The Buddhist Conquest of China*, E. J. Brill, Leiden, 1959, p. 31-31 (Text) and p. 330 (Notes), item 71.

was the belief of the cultured and educated section of Chinese society of that age, known by the blanket name, scholar-gentry or the *literati*. The members of this section of society hailed from respectable families, received culture and education from Chinese, specially Confucian, classics, filled the state offices, and were looked up to as setters of the tone of society. There was no middle class. Below the scholar-gentry or the *literati* were the illiterate masses,—the vast peasant population of China. Society under the early Hans was in these two tiers.

The existence of a *third* school of thought, besides Confucianism and Taoism, one of 'barbarian' origin, among the foreign immigrant population of Loyang took at least a century to come to the knowledge of the scholar-gentry. In the meantime, however, little cells of Buddhism continued to function in Loyang and possibly elsewhere in the north. The Buddhists were supposed to be Taoists of a sort, and a number of Chinese joined their congregation probably under the impression that their religion was a new kind of Taoist worship.

But while the scholar-gentry took no notice of Buddhism, it was making headway in the Han State from the small Buddhist establishments by the propagation of Buddhist literature in Chinese versions. This literature was patronised and financed by a few wealthy Chinese of Loyang who had felt attracted to this new religion and its ethical teachings.

First Renderings of Buddhist Texts

Legend has it that the work of supplying Buddhist texts in Chinese was started by the two Indian Buddhist missionaries, said to have come to the Han emperor Ming-ti's palace at Loyang in 64 A.D.

One of these texts in Chinese, attributed to the Indian missionaries of the legend, is known as the *Sūtra of Forty-two Sections*.[2] Its actual authorship is ascribed to Dharmaratna (or Dharmāraṇya). It has been piously preserved by the Chinese as the 'first ray of the Law in China'. It is not exactly a translation, but a summary of Buddhist teachings according to the Hīnayāna school, 'specially compiled for the benefit of a *Sramana* (Buddhist monk)'. The work has an introduction, most probably a later addition to the work,—containing a version of Ming-ti's dream and the miraculous appearance of Kāśyapa-mātaṅga and his companion at Loyang.

Along the ancient silk-ways of China connecting Loyang over hundreds of miles across hills and deserts with Parthia and other parts of western

---

[2] This *Sutra* will be found in translation in Beal's *Catena of Buddhist Scripture*, Kegan Paul, London, 1871 and in summary in Wieger's *A History of Religious Beliefs and Philosophical Opinions in China*, translated from French into English by Werner, Hsien-hsien Press, Peking, 1927. A modern translation is Chu Chan's *The Sutra of 42 Sections*, Buddhist Society, London, 1947.

Asia, and through the Tun-huang pass in the south connecting China with Mid-Asia, came into Loyang complete manuscripts or fragmentary leaves till they rose to a considerable heap. They were mostly in Sanskrit,—texts either of the Hīnayāna Sarvāstivāda School or of the Mahāyāna. The texts were translated indiscriminately in the Chinese Buddhist establishments,—their originals could be read only by a few who had sufficient linguistic training and ability among the motley company of monks from India, Central Asia, Sogdonia, Iran and Parthia who lived in the foreign quarters of Loyang. But besides these foreign monks there was also a few polyglot Chinese scholars who knew the 'barbarian' languages and who, on reading some of these strange manuscripts, were attracted by the doctrines set forth in them and wanted to impart them to their countrymen.

A pioneer among the polyglot Chinese scholars was Chih Ch'ien. He belonged to the early part of the 3rd century. He started in 222 A.D. to collect either at Loyang or at Chien-yeh, capital of the Wu Kingdom, these imported Buddhist manuscripts and to translate them into Chinese. The number of translations made by him is variously estimated from 27 to 129. His biographer says: "He realised that, although the Buddhist doctrine was practised (in China), yet the scripture was mostly (available) in barbarian language which nobody could understand, and since he (Chih Ch'ien) was well-versed in both Chinese and barbarian languages, he collected all (these) texts and translated them into Chinese". In a later edition of the biography the word 'Indian', meaning 'Sanskrit', was substituted for 'barbarian'.[3] The number of translations, however, made during the Han period and later in the 'Three kingdoms' was small, in comparison with the vast number that followed.

But even before Chih Ch'ien had launched on his work, a systematic organisation for rendering Buddhist texts in Chinese had come into existence at Loyang between the middle of the second or in the first decade of the third century. A number of Buddhist teachers and translators of diverse nationalities had been active in this direction at Loyang. They made a remarkably heterogenous group,—of Parthians, three Yue-chis, two Sogdonians and three Indians[4]—but they formed an energetic, if not too efficient a team for the translation work.

The Nestor among them was An Shih-kao, a Parthian of a royal family, who had embraced monkhood and settled at Loyang in 148 A.D. He spent more than twenty years in that city and was at the head of this team of translators. Their translations were selective and they betray no Mahāyānist influence: on the other hand they lean to Taoism in their elaboration

---

[3] See Zürcher's *The Buddhist Conquest of China*, E. J. Brill, Leiden, 1959, p. 24 (Text).

[4] *Ibid*, p. 32.

of Buddhist *Dhyāna* (Meditation) including some of Taoist respiratory practices. The bias in favour of Chinese Taoist concepts is all too evident in their work.[5]

From the inception of this translation work, the attempt to make the Chinese versions of Buddhism acceptable to the Chinese mind is perceptible. It was not fidelity to the original texts, but their intelligibility to the Chinese that was principally aimed at.

When translation work was placed on a systematic basis at Loyang, it used to be carried on in the following fashion.[6]

The Master or *Ācārya* (who was a Sanskrit knowing scholar) had before him a manuscript of the original text or he recited it from memory. If he had enough knowledge of Chinese, which was seldom the case, he would give an oral translation. It was then 'transmitted' by a 'bilingual intermediary'. Chinese assistants,—monks as well as lay men,—noted down the translation, after which the text of it was subjected to a final revision. During the process and perhaps also on other occasions, the Master gave oral explanations of the contents of the scripture under translation. These often crept into the text. (Translated 'notes' figure in most Chinese versions and at least one of the Han-time translations forms an inextricable mixture of text and explanatory notes,—says Zürcher. Many early Buddhist commentaries were wholly or mainly based upon these oral explanations).

The material funds for the work came at first from lay Chinese citizens, sympathetic to Buddhism, who 'encouraged and helped'. Zürcher names two such Chinese donors (c. 179 A.D.) whose names have been preserved in a colophon. First started at Loyang, this remained in outline the normal method of translating Buddhist scripture.

It is obvious that in this process the 'bilingual intermediary',—a Chinese who himself was not an adept in Buddhism,—would try to convey the Master Translator's meaning in approximate terms of Chinese philosophy, thus imparting to purely Buddhist concepts the nuances of Confucian and Taoist terms. Thus *Tao* was the expression used for Buddhist *Dharma*, *Bodhi* or *Yoga*; *Chenjen* (immortal) for *Arhat*, *Wu-wei* (non-action) for *Nirvāṇa*; *Hsiao-hsun* (filial submission and obedience) for *Śīla*.

It was the unconscious inchoate beginning of the *Ko-i* system which will be described later.

The first imperfect renderings of Buddhist scripture by the Shih-kao group seem to have strengthened the impression in Chinese mind that the new 'barbarian' religion was nothing but a variety of Taoism. "The few Chinese who became interested in the foreign religion were attracted by its novel

---

[5] See *Ibid*, p. 33.

[6] See *Ibid*, p. 31.

formulae for attainment of supernatural powers, immortality or salvation and not by its ideas. This early Buddhism (in China) was generally regarded as a sect of Taoism".[7] The idea persisted long: it gave rise to many novel theories aiming to establish the oneness of Taoism and Buddhism. The process of discriminating and separating Taoism from Buddhism was started long afterwards by Tao-on (312-385). He was a precursor of Kamārajīva, the foremost Buddhist teacher in China in the early fifth century, in whose hands the work started by Tao-on reached its completion. Buddhism was rarely mistaken for Taoism after Kumārajīva.

In fact it was not till the Confucian scholar-gentry of China turned to the interpretation of Buddhism as a system of thought and doctrine and to its evaluation in the light of Confucian traditions that the Chinese mind entered into its component ideas and doctrines. The propaganda of Buddhism through Chinese translations, the proliferation of centres of Buddhist teaching, its spread among the populace through the influence of eminent Chinese and foreign monks, and lastly, its official recognition from time to time,—these factors gave the 'barbarian' religion a status in China that the scholar-gentry could not ignore.

Inclination to 'Dark Learning'

But there were deeper reasons, social and political, that prompted and impelled them to investigate the philosophic contents of the 'barbarian' religion.

The Han social and political order was based on the analogy of Cosmic Order as it had been conceived and set forth in Confucian philosophy.[8] The analogy between the two was a mere construct in speculation, but the scholar-gentry, who were pillars of the Han order, believed solemnly in its pragmatic reality. It led them to the utterly unreal assumption that the Han order and its institutions were bound to last for ever even like the Cosmic Order itself. But unfortunately for the theorists, the Han order began soon to fall and go into chaos,—and when the event occurred, the trust in Confucian cosmology itself was shaken to its very roots.

The Han throne had in fact been decaying ever since the middle of the 2nd century B.C.; a new social order had been intruding itself into the old; a struggle ensued among the four groups of which the emergent social order was composed,—the entrenched aristocratic families, the eunuchs (personal servitors of the ruler), the *nouveaux riches* and the intelligentsia. It broke into violence in 166 A.D.,—and, to cap it all, the growth of political organisation among the Taoist population climaxed in the Taoist Yellow Turban rebellions of 184 A.D. in the east and 189 A.D. in the west. The

[7] Wright's *Buddhism in Chinese History*, pp. 32-33.

[8] It is elaborated by Wright in *Buddhism in Chinese History*, pp. 11-17.

scene was that of a 'civilization in crisis' or 'an age of confusion'. In the second half of the second century A.D., the Han order started definitely to collapse and on its ruins rose the 'Three Kingdoms'.

Though Confucianism continued to be accepted by the literati as the only valid school of social and political thought, its metaphysics and cosmology on which the now dissolving order had been patterned, were beset with doubts. The philosophy seemed unreal,—unadjusted to the realities of 'this world', the only world Confucianism contemplated.

What troubled the minds of the scholar-gentry, concerned with problems of social stabilization and harmony, was the poignant question—why the Han order, so well-geared to cosmic principles, should go so quickly into chaos? Could these principles, judged by the results, be regarded as eternal verities? There was a groping of mind for a fresh world-view,—for a new learning so far unexplored. This unexplored learning came to be called by the name, 'Dark Learning' (*Hsuan-Hsueh*).[9]

Hsuan-Hsueh was the leading way of thought till the end of the 4th century among the Confucian scholar-gentry. They pursued it in their salons as a form of speculative discussion called *Ching-tan.* The term means 'Pure Conversation' and denotes a special type of rhetorical discussion on philosophical and other subjects. It had been much in vogue among the cultured upper classes since the 3rd century A.D. There are specimens in Chinese literature, cast in dialogue form, of these *Ching-tan* discussions. Buddhist ontology and metaphysics came within their scope and among occasional participants were cultured Buddhist monks. Those who carried on *Ching-tan* were retired or leisured Chinese scholars who had picked up some acquaintance with Buddhist Mahāyānist works through Chinese translations. By that time, the series of five Mahāyānist scriptures,—*Prajnāpāramitā*, *Śūraṅgamasamādhi Sūtra*, *Vimalakīrti-nirdeśa*, *Saddharma-puṇḍarīka* and *Sukhāvatīvyūha*, had their Chinese versions. Topics like Non-being or Emptiness (*Śūnyatā*) and the true nature of the phenomenal world became favourite topics of *Ching-tan* from the early 4th century on. The Buddhist clergy of that era counted among them some brilliant *literati* like Chih Tun (314-366).

Since the beginning of disruption of Han State and society, Buddhism had been entering into the thought of the scholar-gentry of China who were groping confusedly for some new learning, some way of escape from the hide-bound concepts and the rigid world-view of Confucianism. Among them were some who, desiring to avoid the service of the falling State and all the risks of a political career, went for retirement into a monastery. There

[9] See Zürcher's *Buddhist Conquest of China,* p. 46 (Text). The 'Dark Learning' prevailed till the fifth century among the scholar-gentry of China.

they came in contact with men learned in Buddhist lore. The practice of *Ching-tan* and the pursuit of 'Dark Learning' which was being identified more and more with Mahāyānist Buddhism attracted them deeply. Soon among these retired scholar-gentry appeared a few Buddhists and teachers of Buddhism whose presentation of Buddhist ideas and doctrines was usually in two forms—their *Koi* system of teaching and their 'apologetic' writings.

Sinification of Buddhism

They accepted Buddhism and accorded it recognition as a religion of the country,—but strictly from their own standpoint. The *Koi* and the apologetics were elaborate attempts at an acculturation of Buddhism,—studied efforts to make the 'barbarian' religion one with China's traditional culture. The Buddhist texts also were taken selectively and syncretically and were so rendered in Chinese as to satisfy the people's intellectual and spiritual needs. The commentarial and exegetic portions of them were also so framed as to be intelligible to and acceptable to the Chinese mind. Finally when schools of Buddhism (*tsung*) arose in China during the 5th-8th centuries, they did not become replicas of Indian schools of Buddhism, but independent ones in which the cleavage between the Hīnayāna and the Mahāyāna, so pronounced in early Mahāyānist works, was hardly insisted on. Buddhism went on developing in China in the trends of the Chinese mind and became a 'sinified' Buddhism.

The process of 'sinification' had already begun tentatively and unobtrusively in the employment of Confucian and Taoist terminology for Buddhist concepts in the early renderings: it developed systematically in *Ko-i* teaching.

Ko-i was a specialised method of teaching Buddhism to men from the *literati* or gentry class who come to its study equipped with the knowledge of Confucian and Taoist classics. Its inventor was the distinguished Buddhist preacher Tao-an (312-385) who himself came from an eminent Confucian family. He became famous, however, as a teacher of Buddhism. We are told that he invented *Ko-i* to meet the needs of those who knew the doctrinal terminologies of Confucianism and Taoism, but not the Buddhist terminology. It was primarily meant for 'scholars of distinguished families.'[10]

In the 4th century, its vogue in China was great. Its essence was the 'matching of meanings',—that is, the matching of Buddhist concepts with Confucian and Taoist or the collating of categories, plausibly analogous, from Confucianism and Taoism alongside Buddhist doctrinal categories. It led to equations which were not quite exact. Thus the fine normative virtues of Confucianism (*Wu-Ch'ang*) were equated with the five Buddhist

[10] *Ibid*, p. 12 (Text).

Śilas, the four Buddhist *Mahābhūtas* with the Chinese five Elements (*Wu-hsing*), viz., metal, wood, water, fire and earth" and so on.[11]

The following is a sample of *Ko-i* teaching:

Chu-Fa-ya was a scholarly Chinese of the first half of the 4th century A.D. who became a convert to Buddhism. He hailed from Hopei. It is said in his biography that "young members of gentry families all adhered to him for information and instruction". "Since at that time the disciples who followed him were all well-versed in the secular canons (i.e., Chinese classics) but had not yet become conversant with the principles of Buddhism, Fa-ya, together with K'ang Fa-lang and others, took (with them) the numerical categories of the *Sūtras* and matched these with (terms from) secular literature, as a method to make them understand; this was called 'matching meanings' (*Ko-i*). (Thus he alternately explained the secular canons and the Buddhist scriptures; "together with Tao-an and Fa-t'ai he used to explain the doubtful points which they had assembled, and together they exhaustively (studied) the essentials of the *Sūtras*".[12]

But Tao-an himself gave up *Ko-i* when he realised the defects of this rough-and-ready mode of instruction, and a disciple of Kumārajīva, Hui-yui, condemned the method in these terms: "At the end of the Han and the beginning of Wu......worthies who sought the essence of Buddhist ideas had for the first time lecturing places. They inflated their lectures with *Ko-i* and distorted them with paired explanations".[13]

While many among the scholar-gentry became advocates of Buddhism and even preferred to live in the monasteries and preach the religion in their own fashion, there were others of this class who condemned the customs and practices of the Buddhist *Saṅgha* as well as the tenets of the religion. When the party of opposition became strong, there were official persecutions, mainly directed against monkhood. The Buddhist advocates sought to meet the arguments of the opponents in a mass of writings which are captioned as 'Buddhist apologetics'.

These works purport to evaluate the 'barbarian' religion. They extol its merits and point to its consistency with the indigenous values inculcated by Confucianism and Taoism. Finally, they stress its fundamental oneness with traditional Chinese culture.

One of the earliest works of Buddhist apologetics is one entitled *Mou-tze* written in the last years of the 2nd century, A.D., by a Chinese official named

---

[11] See Tang Yung-tung's article *On Ko-yi in Radhakrishnan: Comparative Studies In Philosophy presented in Honour of his Sixtieth Birthday*, New York, 1950; Wright's *Buddhism in Chinese History* pp. 36-38; Zürcher's *Buddhist Conquest of China*, pp. 12, 184 (Text).

[12] See Zürcher's *Buddist Couquest of China*, p. 187 (Text).

[13] Wright's *Buddhism in Chinese History*, p. 38.

Mou.[14] It is a voluminous work,—a kind of 'cyclopaedia of the points at which Buddhism has to be reconciled with or adapted to Chinese traditions'. It surveys all the points at which Buddhism differs from them and comes at the end to the conclusion that the Buddhist religion, though a 'barbarian' one, is decidedly equal, if not superior to, indigenous Chinese systems. There are 38 sections in it in dialogue form, containing interchanges between the author and the imaginary interlocutor.

At the time when this work was written, knowledge of Buddhism had not spread appreciably among the scholar-gentry. Mou 'reaches into the varied texts of Confucianism and Taoism to find passages which appear to sanction a Buddhist belief or practice'. The interlocutor in one of the dialogues asks why he quotes only Chinese texts instead of Buddhist *Sūtras* in support of his arguments. Mou's answer is that he does so because they understand only the Chinese classics, and to explain the doctrines of Buddhism to them out of the *sūtras* would be like 'speaking about the five colours to the blind or playing the five tones to the deaf'.

The attempt of the apologetics was to graft the 'barbarian' religion to native roots,—to make the alien system appear in both doctrine and practice as a continuation of China's traditional philosophies,—also to rehabilitate the Buddhist monkhood in the eyes of Confucian gentry. In doing this, however, they went too far afield. They propounded theories which had no relation to history, like the conversion of China to Buddhism by the Indian Buddhist emperor Asoka, the meeting of the Buddha and Confucius and the latter accepting the former's discipleship, Lao-tsu having preached Taoism among the 'barbarians' and those teachings having come back to China under the name of Buddhism, etc. These were fantastic attempts to naturalise the foreign religion in China.

The pseudo-historical arguments were never very convincing, but they indicated, first, a widening of the mental horizon of the scholar-gentry, so long reluctant to seek for anything good outside Confucianism; secondly, the growth of a belief that Buddhism, despite its differences, was a school of thought consonant with the cultural traditions of China,—perhaps a complementary one; and thirdly, the possibility of its development on the Chinese soil to meet Chinese needs. The apologetics in fact had been all along quoting from or referring to ancient Confucian or Taoist works to define, support or emphasize Buddhist metaphysical or ethical concepts.

The two passages cited below[15] show clearly enough how in the latter

---

[14] For an outline sketch of this work, see Wieger's *A History of the Religious Beliefs and Philosophical Opinions in China*, pp. 370-372. Also Zürcher's *Buddhist Conquest of China*, pp. 12-13, and Wright's *Buddhism in Chinese History*, pp. 38-39.

[15] Taken from Zürcher's *Buddhist Conquest of China*, pp. 137 and 1333 (Text).

half of the fourth century the distinction made between Chinese culture and Buddhism ceased to be insisted upon and Buddhism came to be regarded as part and parcel of China's indigenous culture:

(i) Chu Tao-ch'en (286-374) was a renowned Chinese Buddhist scholar with a large number of disciples. He lived in a mountain-retreat in Chekiang and delivered discourses on Buddhism to monks and lay men. "Sometimes he expounded the *Vaipulya Sūtras*, (i.e., the *Prajñāpāramitā*); sometimes he explained Lao-tze and Chuang-tzu, so that for all those who followed him and revered him, the inner and outer teachings (i.e., those of Buddhism and those of Chinese secular philosophy) were combined and harmonized."

(ii) Sun Ch'o (c. 300-380) was a famous literateur of his time and wrote an exposé of Buddhism, in which he stated his main conclusions in these terms: "(The Duke of) Chou and Confucius are identical......(The difference in) names merely denoted the inner and outer (teachings)". According to Sun Ch'o, 'the doctrines of the Confucian sages and the Buddha diverge on account of the different circumstances under which they were revealed and to which they were adapted. But the inner nature of these saints, the source and motive power of their teachings, is one and the same: the inner nature is the fact of "being awakened" (i.e. becoming the Buddha)'.

Buddhism had been preached in China at first by foreign monks, very few of whom knew Chinese, and propagandised to the literate Chinese through translated texts. These translations were crude in expression and uncongenial to Chinese taste. The texts were manuals, commentaries and versions of Buddhist *sūtras*, such as were available. Some of these works that enjoyed an exceptional popularity were afterwards revised and rewritten to suit Chinese literary taste. An outstanding example of it is the Chinese *Dharmapada*, a work by Dharmatrāta translated by Vighna, an Indian monk who arrived in China round 224 A.D. It became a most popular work, but not before it had been polished to suit Chinese taste, in spite of Vighna's protests, by his Chinese collaborators.[16]

Between 290 and 320, an intellectual clerical *elite* had arisen in the Buddhist Church. It consisted of both naturalised foreign monks and Chinese scholars. They were not propagators of Budhism in mere extracts, passages and categories, but of a *complete* Buddhism,—an entire doctrinal system in which were also integrated some of the *hsuan-hsueh* speculations as well as the moralistic-ritualistic trends of Confucian thought. A classic specimen of work of this type is *Feng-fa Yao*, written by Hsi Ch'ao (336-377), one of the scholar-gentry, brought up in a Taoist family. It is translated by Zürcher in Appendix B to Chapter III of his book, *The Buddhist Conquest of China.* It presents the ethical side of Buddhism, but selectively

[16] See *Ibid*, pp. 47-48 (text)

under such topics as were calculated to interest the Chinese mind.

The passing of Buddhism into Chinese ways of thought and expression, its recognition as an integral part of Chinese culture, its acceptance as a school of thought which filled the vacuum created by the decline of belief among scholar-gentry in Confucian metaphysics and cosmology,—were the factors that led to the dawn of a new era in the Buddhist history of China.

In this new era, Buddhism has finally taken hold of all strata of Chinese society, 'from the imperial devotees of the Liu-Sung dynasty and their Buddhist courtiers down to the literate masses of the population.' It has developed through its critical as well as exegetic treatment in the hands of the scholar-gentry into as integral a part of Chinese culture as Confucianism and Taoism. At the same time in the field of doctrinal studies the ancient Chinese concepts have lost much of their force,—'a period of specialised studies and better translations, of more knowledge and less phantasy'.[17]

The dawn of this new era was in the early years of the fifth century at Changan. Here Buddhism was under the fostering care of a State ruled at the time by a Tibetan Governor. Changan quickly became the most prominent centre of Buddhism in north China under the impact of two dynamic personalities, Tao-an and Kumārajīva.[18]

Buddhism in the 'Three Kingdoms'

The Han empire was brought to a close by a sanguinary orgy of war-lordism out of which three somewhat short-lived kingdoms emerged,—the *Wei* in the north (220-265), the *Shu* (Han) in the West (221-263) and the *Wu* in the south-east across the Yangtse (220-280). Of these, it was the south-eastern kingdom of Wu that kept up Buddhist learning and teaching at several centres. Its capital was Chien-Yeh (modern Nanking) and it seems that here Buddhism was protected by the court.[19] At Loyang also, the cradle of Chinese Buddhism, then in the kingdom of Wei, it did not cease to be cultivated.

Under the Han Empire China had a large extension in her external relations. Most important for the development of Buddhism were her relations with Mid-Asia. The oasis-states had come under Chinese suzerainty with a Chinese embassy in each capital town. There was an increase and acceleration of trade and traffic through Tun-huang between China and Mid-Asia.

---

[17] See *Ibid*, p. 239 (Text).

[18] Among their many contributions to Buddhist development was a new and improved mode of translation and Kumarajiva himself produced a large number of translations in this improved mode.

[19] Zürcher says : "If the traditional accounts of the activities of Chih Chien and Kang Senghui contain at least a nucleus of truth, we must assume that in the region Chien-Yeh and the Court of Wu", *Buddhist Conquest of China*, p. 74.

Tun-huang grew into an entrepot as well as a regular way of access from China to Mid-Asia. For Buddhism in China which had to depend so largely on the availability of Buddhist texts, this extension of China's contact with Mid-Asia was decidedly favourable. It was in the post-Han period that Chinese Buddhist monks first started going into Mid-Asia in search of Buddhist texts.

Khotan was a stronghold of Mahāyāna Buddhism, and a learned Chinese monk, Chun-Shih-hsing, went in c. 260 all the way from Loyang to Khotan with the express purpose of collecting the texts. The *Pāramitā* works were already known in China, but the greatest work of the category, the *Prajñāpāramitā of 25,000 verses* was discovered at Khotan by this illustrious Chinese monk. He was not, however, allowed to take it to China, but in the teeth of local opposition, could only copy portions of it.[20] It was translated into Chinese by a Khotanese disciple of the Chinese monk, named Mokṣala, with the help of an Indian assistant in 291. The text under the name of *Fangkuang Chin* ('The Scripture of the Emission of Rays') became one of the fundamental texts of Chinese Buddhism. It is said that "it was widely circulated at Loyang and hosts of retired scholar-gentry made copies of it. People were sent to Tsang-yuan to have it copied on pieces of silk. When the copy was brought back to Chung-shan (modern Tinghsien in Central Hopei), the king and all the monks welcomed the *sūtra*...with a display of pennants and streamers".[21] The purveyor of this illustrious work died at Khotan at the age of 79.

The episode illustrates with what eager expectancy the Buddhists of China used to await the arrival of every new Buddhist manuscript in their country from abroad.

Another monk of Indo-Scythian origin, who hailed from Tun-huang and travelled extensively in Mid-Asia for the collection of texts, was Dharmarakṣa. He returned from his Mid-Asian tours to China with a large number of texts which he himself did into Chinese. He was at Changan from 266 to 317, and his work and influence in the city helped it to rise to a major Buddhist centre in China. He was not only a great translator, but an intinerant preacher, organiser and supervisor of Budhist establishments in different cities.

During the 'Three Kingdom' period, "the places from which Buddhist activities are reported are all main cities situated along the eastern extension of the continental highways—Tun-huang, Chiu-chuan, Changan, Loyang and Chenlien". Buddhism was a more or less urban phenomenon. Foreigners who congregated in the cities were the main donors and devotees. The rise

[20] *Ibid*, pp. 62-63.
[21] *Ibid*, p. 64.

of Tun-huang, as a great Buddhist establishment, with the caves of a Hundred Buddhas, officially affiliated to and patronised by the Buddhist congregation at Changan, has already been described.

The scholar-gentry of Northern China, since the outbreak of the fierce struggle of war-lords, had been migrating south-eastwards into the more settled kingdom of Wu. Some Buddhist scholars among them set up little centres of Buddhism in the capital city or near it, on mountain-sides or at beauty-spots. They devoted themselves to the study of Buddhism and cultivation of *Hsuan-hsueh* (Dark Learning).

Two most prominent figures of this category in the kingdom of Wu were Chih Chien, an Indo-Scythian lay man, and Kang Senh-hui, a Sogdian monk and translator. Both of them were accomplished scholars,—naturalised *literati* trained in Confucian and Taoist classics. But they were unlike the masters of the old Han times 'who tried to expound the principles of a barbarian creed in a world of strangers'. for Buddhism by that time had become part of current philosophical learning in China. They were joined by two Indian masters later on,—Vighna and 'Chu Chiang-Yen', whose Indian name is unknown. The former has gone down in the history of Chinese Buddhism as the author of the most popular Chinese version, we have already referred to, of the Buddhist classic *Dhammapada*. It is not a mere translation of its Indian original, but a compendious work in polished Chinese style,—a sort of 'Buddhism for Chinese readers'.[22]

Sometime after the Three Kingdoms had petered out with the extinction of their ruling dynasties, North China was subjected to a large-scale invasion by barbarians from steppe-lands beyond the Great Wall. The Wall made the northern Han frontier. The steppe-landers, however, had been known to the Chinese since very ancient times under the blanket name of Hun;[23] they had made several incursions in past times across the Great Wall and were always a thorn in the side of the empire. But in the early years of the 4th century, A.D., their organised full-scale invasion was comparable in the range and magnitude of its effects with the Hun invasion of Rome.

Its immediate consequence was the fall of the two great cities of the empire, the nerve-centres of its political and cultural life. Loyang the capital fell in 311 and Changan, the next chief city, in 316.

The condition to which they were reduced is known from contemporary evidence. Loyang had been beseiged and "the last emperor fled because of

---

[22] *Ibid*, pp. 47-48.

[23] See Hirth's *Ancient History of China* (Columbia University Press, New York, 1911) p, 67——"The various names under which those northern and western neighbours of the Chinese are mentioned during the earlier periods of history appear to be variants of the same name, Hun or Hunnu".

famine and his fortified residence was burnt down and the town destroyed". Changan sank to the condition of a deserted village: where "there were not more than one hundred families; weeds and thorns grew thickly as if in a forest; only four carts could be found in the city".[24] The barbarians largely displaced the old Chinese population and wreaked terrible vengeance on the scholar-gentry, pillars of the Hun State. At Loyang, it is said, 3,0000 members of the metropolitan gentry were massacred at the time of its fall.[25]

The composition of society in North China was almost completely changed by the Hun influx. The upper tier of it vanished completely. There was a mass exodus of the gentry-class into the south, till then an unsettled part of China, with ill-developed agriculture and means of communication, inhabited chiefly by people whom the northerners called 'barbarians.' Very few of the scholar-gentry were left in the Hun-occupied north. It did not, however, mean the total extinction of Chinese culture. Its tradition was kept up to some extent by leading men among the invaders themselves. The leaders among them had come in touch with Chinese civilization and were more or less outwardly sinicised,—the founder for example of the expansionist Hanshu kingdom in the West, who, though not a Chinese, claimed descent from the old Han emperors. The Hun settlers inter-marrying with Chinese women also acquired in course of time a veneer of Chinese culture. It was the academic, speculative and pragmatic aspects of this culture that were extinct. The new-comers across the frontier knew little of Confucianism or Taoism and their faith was in Shamanism and magic.

From now on, there was a cleavage between North China and South China that was not bridged till 589. For three hundred years no Chinese sovereignty and no classic Chinese culture existed in the North. The two Chinas were launched on different courses of evolution and the history of Buddhism in each has to be separately related.

China split into North and South

Buddhism in North China—In 310 A.D., less than a year before the fall of Loyang to the Huns, there appeared in that city a monk, most probably an Indian, named Fu-to-teng in Chinese. The name is equiparated by Wieger to Buddajaṅgha ('The Thigh of the Buddha').[26] He figures in the Chinese *shu* (official history) of the Chin dynasty and is in several respects, an

[24] See Wright's *Buddhism in Chinese History*, p. 42 and Zürcher's *Buddhist Conquest of China*, p. 84; Fitzgerald's *China—A short Cultural History*, p. 256.

[25] Zürcher's *Buddhist Conquest of China*, p. 49.

[26] See Wieger's *History of Religious Beliefs and Philosophical Opinions in China*, p. 413.

extraordinary figure. It seems that he was an Indian Yogī, a Buddhist by faith, who could by his yogic powers produce striking supernatural effects. To the eyes of the Huns, newly settled in China, he was perhaps undifferentiable from a miracle-working Shaman.

Observing that the Huns, among whom he lived in Loyang, had much faith in magic and thaumaturgy, he showed them some of his feats. Buddhism professed by him came to be associated in the minds of the Huns in North China, through these magic demonstrations, as leading to supernatural powers and potencies and he soon had a large following. To the Hun rulers his faith commended itself for a variety of reasons besides its magic power. In the first place, it was different from Chinese Confucianism or Taoism, which, being Chinese, were at a discount with them; in the second place, it preached an ethic which was not of China but universal in appeal.[27]

Buddhajaṅgha soon established cordial relations with the Hun court. Till his death in c. 349 he was looked upon by the Hun rulers as a sort of spiritual law-giver to them. Buddhism in fact was the first cultured and organised religion presented to the Huns in China, and in North China occupied by them it had not at the time to run the gauntlet of Confucian or Taoist critics who had left the north in a body.

Under the spell of his personality, Buddhism began immediately to spread among the Huns and with a great drive. The Hun Court accepted it; the grandees of the realm patronised it, and it became the faith of the common people. The munificent support it received is evidenced by the great cave-temples of North China,—Yun-kang and Lung-men,—with their many finely carved Buddha and Bodhisattva images,—Chinese art which goes back to the Hun times. "There is a child-like spirituality about them which seems improbable if their makers had been long subjected to the calm and settled Chinese culture."[28]

The kings, however, were autocrats. They were loth to let the Buddhist monk-organisation grow up as an independent body within the body politic. So they converted the Saṅgha into a sort of 'clerical bureaucracy', charged with social welfare work, subservient to the State. It was entrusted with such functions as the due distribution in rural areas of state charities and public donations. The greater monasteries became entrepreneurs for industries of different kinds. They set up water-mills and oil-presses and developed local manufactures,—even established pawn-shops, held auctions and

[27] See Wright's *Buddhism in Chinese History*, 57.

[28] Quoted from p. 15 of a brochure on *Buddhist Sculptures at Yun Kang Caves* by Mullikin and Hotchekis, artists who visited and surveyed the caves. (Pub. by Henri Vetch, Peiping, 1935).

sponsored temple-fairs.[29] In this way they augmented their own resources and were in a position to extend their control and influence in rural areas. This economic function of the Saṅgha as a 'clerical bureaucracy' of the State was a peculiar feature of China's northern Buddhism.

After Buddhajaṅgha, there were three great scholarly monks who made considerable contributions to the development and diffusion of Buddhism in North China.

The first was Tao-an (312-385), a disciple of Buddhajaṅgha. His work lay chiefly in the field of translation and he was the first to reform the current practice of rendering Buddhist concepts by Tao-ist terms which led to much confusion of thought. He had a theory of translation; it was developed later by Kumārajīva in the great translation bureau at Changan of which he became the head, round about 401 A.D.

We have spoken already about Kumārajīva in the context of Mid-Asia and his advent in Changan from there. In the period of confusion which followed the fall of the Hun, the Tibetans had carved out a small state in North China which lasted for some years. Changan was its capital when Kumārajīva was brought here as a war-captive. But the Tibetan ruler Fu Chien knew how to treat a scholar of his stature. He was forthwith appointed director of the Translation Bureau, functioning at Changan over some years past. It was a huge establishment with a numerous personnel. Kumārajīva took up his work with great zest; many of the old Chinese translations of Buddhist scripture which had become archaic in language and obscure in expression were revised and retranslated by him. Assisted by an army of scholars and specialists under his direction, the work of this bureau was carried on by him almost to his dying day and the net outturn of it is put at 300 translated texts. A large number of them is included in the Chinese *Tripitaka*.

Kumārajīva was the greatest translator and teacher of Buddhism of that era. An adherent of Buddhist Mādhyamika philosophy and expounder of Nāgārjuna's doctrine of *Sūṇyatā* (Emptiness), he was approached by some of the most eminent Chinese Buddhist teachers of his time for elucidation of Mahāyānist philosophic concepts and his explanations were taken as authoritative. The correspondence, relating chiefly to the doctrine of the Buddha's *Dharmakāya*, between Hui-yuan (334-417) and Kumārajīva during 405-409 is on record.[30]

Kumārajīva died at Changan in some year after 412, leaving a whole host of disciples and pupils by whom his literary work was carried forward into the next era. He was a half-blooded Indian—his father Kumārāyana

[29] See Wright's *Buddhism in Chinese History*, p. 59.

[30] See Zürcher's *Buddhist Conquest of China*, pp. 226-229 (Text)

being a *Pandita* of Kashmir who had settled in Kucha and his mother, Jivā, a Kuchan, daughter of a local chief. The Chinese who knew that Kumārajīva's father was an Indian cremated him, following Indian custom, at Changan.

Changan fell to the Huns in 316. But, restored as the capital of the cultured and liberal Tibetan ruler Fu Chien, it soon became the most prominent seat of Buddhism in North China.

In 379, the Tibetan ruler had brought Tao-an to his capital where he lived from 379 to 385. From the time of Tao-an's arrival at Changan, a new chapter opened in the history of Buddhism in North China,—"characterised by a new influx of missionaries, scriptures and ideas from Central Asia and India, huge translation projects, state patronage and supervision of them, and the emergence of a body of scriptural and scholastic literature (both Mahāyāna and Hīnayāna), together with a new method of exegesis and a new translation technique".[31] At the centre of this renaissance stood Kumārajīva.

The progress of Buddhism in the north and the south had been on different lines since the Hun conquest. They converged only three hundred years afterwards with the political reunification of 589.

Buddhism in South China........Since mid-3rd century, the scholar-gentry who had monopoly of Han state-service, scared by a sense of insecurity, had been trekking downwards batch by batch to the regions of the lower Yangtse. But the exodus did not become general so long as there was refuge for them in the Three Kingdoms. They made some settlements in the kingdoms of Wei and Wu, specially at Hsiang - Yang (Nanking), capital of the Wu kingdom. It was here that the first Chinese pilgrim to India, Fa-hsien had spent the last years of his life on return to China in 415.

But when the Three Kingdoms were no more and the whole of North China was overrun by the Huns, their position became untenable. They were hunted down and massacred, and had to seek safety further down the country. For the third time since the end of the Han, there was also a mass-emigration of monks into the south. It followed a disintegration and dispersal of the Buddhist community at Changan that took place round 416.[32]

At many places in South China like Hsiang-yang, Lushan and the Shan Mountains, there grew up under their influence, Buddhist centres among the Chinese population. A diluted form of Taoism had prevailed among them so far; now Buddhism began to spread.

Among the early Buddhist monk-teachers, whose activities were mainly

---

[31] *Ibid.* p. 114.

[32] *Ibid*, p. 114.

in the south, the most prominent were Chih-tun (314-366) and Hui-yuan (334-417). Among the Taoist Chinese masses their teachings became immediately effective, though Taoism was not effaced here till Emperor Wu of the Liang (reigned 502-549), a Buddhist ruler, destroyed Taoist temples to make Buddhism the State religion of his domain.

In the south as well as in the north, the Chinese as well as the Hun kings were, generally speaking, Buddhists or patrons of Buddhism. From time to time, however, Buddhism was subjected in both the north and the south to persecution when the old antagonism to it from Confucian or Taoist sources gained enough strength to move rulers to action. The persecution was directed against Buddhist worship and more particularly against Buddhist monkhood. But in spite of large-scale destruction of books, dispersal of monks and the emptying of monasteries, the checks and set-backs failed of their purpose.

Over three centuries the split between the north and the south had continued. There was no intermingling of northern Buddhism with southern. In the south it had passed into the hands of those who represented the 'scholar-gentry' of the old Han times and was being threshed out especially on its philosophic side. The way was being paved for the appearance on the scene of schools of Chinese Buddhist philosophy. In the north it was a more popular Buddhism, mixed up with Chinese ancestor-worship and thaurmaturgy. But by the end of the period of disunion, Buddhism itself had a wide following in the south and the north alike, among both peasantry and the *elitè*. "It thus commended itself to the reunifying dynasty of Sui and to its successor the great Tang as an instrument for knitting together the two cultures. Both dynasties made it a matter of imperial policy to patronise Buddhist establishments and the Buddhist clergy, to sponsor undertakings of piety and to build and support temples in the capital and in the provinces".[33]

The Sui and the great Tang

The political unification of the North and the South was thus preceded by a unification of their common Buddhist culture.

By the year 589, Buddhism was the religion and culture of both the masses and the *elitè* of North China. It had an extraordinary expansion at all levels. the official history records that even so far back as in 405, there were nine families in the north of China that practised Buddhism out of every ten.[34] In the south, there was some time-lag. But under Emperor Wu of the Southern Liang dynasty, it had already become a State religion.

---

[33] Wright's *Buddhism in Chinese History*, pp. 66-69.

[34] See Wieger's *History of Religious Beliefs and Philosophical Opinions in China*, p. 509.

During the Tang period, when the north and the south were united, it was so identified with Chinese culture that Prince Sotoku of Japan, keen on infusing into his people the culture of China, started with founding institutions in his country for the study and dissemination of Chinese Buddhism. The culture of China, to Prince Sotoku's mind, was identical with its Buddhist religion and philosophy.

The Sui dynasty was not long on the Chinese throne. It petered out in 618, yielding place to the Tang which covered the reigns of 21 emperors from 618 to 906, among whom Tang Tai-tsung (reigned 627-649) was perhaps the most brilliant figure. The empire during this period of two centuries and nine decades rose, as regards its internal development and its external relations, to such a position of prestige that to all countries of East Asia, Tang China became the model to copy from in all cultural matters.

Of Chinese civilization under the Tang, Buddhism was the very breath of life. It flourished as never before in China; "supported by lavish donations of the devout, guided by leaders of true piety and brilliance, graced by the most gifted artists and architects of the age, it was woven into the very texture of Chinese life and thought. These centuries were the golden age of an independent and creative Chinese Buddhism".[35]

A Japanese Buddhist monk of the Tendai school named Ennin (794-861) has left us an eye-witness account of Buddhism and Buddhist culture as it prevailed among commonalty in Tang China. His work, entitled *Nyuto-Gubo Junreiki* ('Record of Pilgrimage to China in search of the Holy Law'), is available in an English translation by Edwin Raischauer in two volumes—*Ennin's Travels in Tang China* and *Ennin's Diary* (Ronald Press, New York, 1955).

Ennin had been an abbot of a Tendai establishment on Mount Heie for more than twenty years, but differences of opinion sprang up between him and Enchin, his successor to the abbacy, and the former thought it best to save the situation by leaving Japan temporarily and going on a pilgrimage to China. He sailed for China in 838 and returned in 847. Before his return, he had witnessed the suppression of Buddhism and other 'foreign' religions by Emperor Wu Tsung, a bigoted Taoist, who reversed the accepted Tang policy of complete religious toleration. Buddhism, though originally a foreign religion in China, was at the time too wide-spread in the country to be uprooted and the emperor, by an edict, allowed it to exist though under severe restrictions. The devastation involved in secularising the clergy, demolishing temples and disestablishing convents all over China will be described later. Ennin was an eye-witness to this devastation.

Ennin saw Buddhism in Tang China on its popular side—as it was actually practised by common people in the country. It was then the prevailing

[35] Wright's *Buddhism in Chinese History*, p. 70.

Chinese culture, part and parcel of social life and normal everyday behaviour. Being a foreign monk on tour, what struck him most were the liberal alms-giving to monks by common people, the planting of shade trees along the traveller's paths, construction of bridges across the canals and maintenance of free or low-cost hostels for foreign monks subsidised by local Buddhist congragations. His account raises the picture of a country where life has been transformed to gentleness, charity and loving kindness by the daily practice and culture of Buddhism.

The earlier Tang period was characterised by two great movements among the higher ranks of the clergy—first, direct cultural intercourse with India and secondly, development of some of the schools of Chinese Buddhism.

1. *Cultural Intercourse with India*—China had been receiving Indian Buddhist texts over several preceding centuries from different sources, but among them, works bearing on *Vinaya* made only a child's handful. Among the Han-period translations, *Vinaya* is not represented at all,[36] though later a few *Vinaya* translations were made.[36] In the absence of texts, which were rare, the rules of monastic life were matters of oral instruction in the monasteries, handed down by the *Ācārya* to monks under him. Their scriptural sources were mostly unknown. There was thus no means of ascertaining whether the Vinaya practices of Chinese monks were according to scripture. The leaders of the Buddhist church felt the need to bring direct from India authentic texts, especially those bearing on the regimen of monastic life.

The need was articulated at first by Hui Yuan (334-416), founder of the White Lotus (*Lien*) school, the earliest Chinese Buddhist school, founded at Lushan in southern China. Hui Yuan was not only an apostle of *Dhyāna* (Meditation), but also a reformer of the *Saṅgha* (Buddhist Monkhood). He felt that in respect of both *Dhyāna* and *Vinaya*, the scriptures the Chinese already possessed were incomplete. "The *Dhyāna* methods were not heard about and the collection of monastic rules (*Vinayapitaka*) was fragmentary". As his biographer tells us, he used to urge his disciples, Fa-ching and others, to go in search of scriptures to distant lands. Obedient to the master's wish, the disciples set out for the collection of fresh texts. "They passed through sand and snow, and only after long years they returned, having obtained *Indian* texts which (then) could be translated".[37]

Whether any of Hui Yuan's disciples could in fact reach India at all is unknown. But in 399, Fa-hsien started for India with the same set purpose—to observe at first hand the *Vinaya* practices of Indian monks and to

[36] Zürcher's *Buddhist Conquest of China*, (Text), p. 32.

[37] *Ibid*, p. 246.

acquire texts on *Vinaya*. He obtained a few Vinaya works and brought them to China. There was a time-lag after Fa-hsien's pioneer pilgrimage to India; the need for better knowledge and more texts remained. Of the various motives by which Chinese monk-scholars were impelled in the 6th and 7th centuries to undertake the hazardous journey to India, the desire to reform and improve monastic discipline in China through first-hand acquaintance with the practice of Indian monks and through acquisition of texts on *Vinaya* was the chief one.

The story of the adventures of these Chinese monks of the Tang period is a saga of extreme fortitude and endurance and of braving tremendous perils for the sole sake of religion. In that period, there were both an overland route and a sea-route from China to India. But both routes presented extra ordinary difficulties.

The overland route from China's western border was either across the Taklamakan desert or by a detour round it *via* the Pamirs. It had to be made on horse-back or camel-back, but most of the way on foot. The sea-route was from one of China's sea-ports on the south-eastern coast through the South China Sea and the Indian Ocean. It had to be negotiated in cargo-bearing junks or in tall three-tiered wooden passenger ships into which one had to clamber by a ladder. Though Chinese mariners of the Tang age knew the use of the mariner's compass and the time and direction of the monsoon winds, the unpredictable typhoons along this route were a constant threat of danger.

Among these Chinese pilgrims were some who put on record the experiences of their pilgrimage. Some records can be traced only in scraps of quotations or casual references in Chinese works, known only to Chinese scholars interested in this line of research. Three 'records' (*Chi*), as they are called, have, however, come down to us in a complete form—Fa-hsien's *Fa-Kwo-Chi* ('Buddhist Country Record') for 319-414, Hsüan-tsang's *Si-Yu-Chi* ('Western Country Record') for 630-643, and I-tsing's *Nan-hai-Chi-Kuei-nai-fa-chuan* ('Record of Inner Law sent from the Southern Sea') for 671-695. Besides this work, I-tsing 'sent home' to Changan another work from Java through a friend of his in which he had given brief accounts of fifty-one pilgrims (including himself) who had gone out for study and pilgrimage to India, since the commencement of the Tang Dynasty. These pilgrims were mostly Chinese with a sprinkling among them of monks from Korea and Indonesia and all of them were senior or junior contemporaries of I-tsing. Some of them he met in India. The title of this work, *Ta-Tang-Shi-ku-fa-Kao-sung-Chuan*, rendered in English, is—'Monks of the Buddhist faith who went to the Western Country (India) under the Tang Dynasty'. It is text No. 2066 in the 51st volume of the Taisho *Tripitaka*. The work has not been translated yet, but an abstract of it was made by

Chavannes in French and published in Paris in 1894 under the title, 'Memoire Compose a l 'epoque de la grande dynastie T'ang sur les Religieux Eminents qui allerent chercher la loi dans les pays d'occident, par I-tsing'.

I-tsing concludes the work with this following epilogue :

> 'I, Shaman I-tsing, returned to Srivijaya in South Sea from the Western Country (India), and from there, carrying the map of Nalandā, came back to China. There were previously many noble monks who, without caring for their lives, had gone to the Western Country in search of the Law. Fa-hsien went forth on the difficult and perilous route to the Western Country and Hsüan-tsang also, following his footsteps, went there. Some monks went by the South Sea route. The monks, while journeying by land or by sea-route, remembered all along the traces of the Buddha and prostrated themselves before the law of the Buddha. Arriving in Western Country, they always desired to go back to their motherland to report their experiences to the Emperor. Though it is a great fortune and luck to go out to the Western Country in search of the law, it is an extremely difficult and perilous undertaking. Etc. Etc.'.[38]

How 'difficult and perilous' it was can be realised from the uncoloured realistic descriptions given in their records.

The adventures of the Great Seamen of England of the sixteenth century are said by historians to have been prompted by the 'spirit' of the Elizabethan age. In a different field of activity, those of the Tang-age monks who went out of China to India were also inspired by the spirit of their age. I-tsing speaks of their nostalgic longings to return to China to give their countrymen the benefit of their knowledge and experience. This motive appears in many passages of the *Chi*'s. I-tsing for example inserts in his travel-record a long chapter on Sanskrit books and Sanskrit philology, evidently having in mind the benefit of Chinese translators of Sanskrit works in China. In fact it is not till the dawn of the Tang period that original works in Sanskrit, apart from translations, were drawn upon by Chinese scholars in their expositions of Mahāyānist philosophy.

2. *Development in Schools of Chinese Buddhism*—The Tang period was distinguished also for the development of some important Schools of Chinese Buddhist philosophy that were surviving in that period.

Chinese Schools (*Tsung*) had not come into existence in China under the same urges as the Sects of Hīnayāna Buddhism or the Schools and sub-schools of the Mahāyāna in India. Most of the Indian Hīnayāna sects originated from differences among monk communities relating to the *Vinaya* (monastic *regula*) and the Mahāyāna Schools and sub-schools

[38] See Dutt's *Buddhist Monks and Monasteries of India* (Allen and Unwin, London, 1962) pp. 311-312.

from differences in outlook, standpoint or methodology of their founders. But in Chinese Buddhism, *Vinaya* had no development as in Indian Hīnayāna Buddhism and there was hardly any critical attitude in China towards it. Mahāyāna Buddhism, however, had been cultivated since the scholar-gentry had begun to be interested in Buddhist scripture. But the Chinese interest in it was mostly partial and topical—confined to particular subjects like *Śūnyatā, Dharmakāya*, etc.—out of which no distinct system could evolve. The schools of Buddhism developed on the Chinese soil were not complete, clear-cut and distinctive like the Indian schools. Moulded by Chinese traditions of thought and by the ecclectic and syncretic genius of Chinese exponents, they represent 'Chinese Buddhism' without being in any sense Chinese replicas of Indian sects or schools.

The fundamental difference between Hīnayāna Buddhism and Mahāyāna, grounded on two different Buddha-concepts and on two different sets of teaching was never clearly present to the Chinese mind. The scriptures, from whatever source derived, conveyed the *Buddhavacana* (the sayings of the Buddha) and, accepting all of them as of equal authority, the Chinese mind tried to reconcile them by a syncretic method which resulted in the *Tien-tai,* one of the leading Chinese Buddhist schools.

Besides, the old practice of illustrating Buddhist doctrines from Chinese classics, a stand-by of Buddhist teachers hailing from the scholar-gentry, had a long lease of life and died hard. It was scarcely extinct even when a more discriminative study of Buddhism had been initiated early in the 5th century by Kumārajīva and his school. The practice was responsible for introducing into Chinese Buddhism ideas alien from Indian Buddhism. For example, among the works of Hsia Chao (336-377) is a tract entitled *Feng fa Yao* (Converts' vademecum) purporting to be an exposè of Buddhist doctrines and ethics for the use of Chinese Buddhists. Its explanation of some of the fundamental Buddhist doctrines is curiously modified by Confucian and Taoist doctrines, e.g., *Nirvānā* equated with Taoist Non-activity or the fulfilment of the Taoist quest for immortality. Thus Buddhist *Nirvāna* is described as the state in which one is not born and 'therefore one is not able to die', that is, one attains to immortality. As in Taoism, immortality is regarded as the *summum bonum*[39] of Buddhism also.

The traditional number of 'schools' of Chinese Buddhism is ten.

Two of these schools were directly derived from Indian Buddhist philosophy, viz., the *San-lun* (Three-Treatise School) introduced by Kumārajīva on the basis of the philosophy (*Śūnyatāvāda*) of Nāgārjuna, and the *Fa-hsiang*(Dharmalakṣaṇa School) founded by Hsüan-tsang on the basis of the

[39] This tract is translated in Zürcher's *Buddhist Conquest of China*, Appendix B to Ch. III, pp. 164 ff. See p. 174 for the rendering of *Nirvana*. See also *Sources of Chinese Tradition*, p. 332.

Vijñānavāda of the Yogācāra School. Two others viz., the *Cheng-shi* (Avataṁsaka School) and the *Chu-she* (Abhidharmakośa School), were based on individual texts of Indian Buddhist philosophy. But there were five schools which grew distinctly out of the Chinese mind—*Lien* (oldest of Chinese Schools), Tien-tai, Hua-yen, Ching-tu and Chan. "The common Chinese saying is that the Tien-tai and Hua-yen schools are for doctrine and the Meditation (*Chan*) and Pure Land (*Ching-tu*) schools for practice".[40] It is a pointer to the general ambivalence and fluidity of the Chinese schools. They do not make water-tight compartments: the doctrines easily overflow from one school into another. Thus the Amida cult, which properly belongs to the Ching-tu school, became so popular in China that it was introduced even in the works of Kumārajīva. Intellectual acceptance of the doctrine of *Śūnyatā* is not felt to be incongruous with the desire for rebirth in the promised 'land of bliss' (*Sukhāvatī-vyūha*) through constant repetition of Amida's name.

Some of these Chinese schools were founded or underwent new development during the Tang age. Most schools, however, have "patriarchs", i.e., masters through whom the teachings of the school were transmitted. It is therefore difficult to ascertain when the transmitted teachings were organised into a 'school'.

We have seen that there was a movement for the improvement of *Vinaya* in Chinese Buddhist monasteries. Eminent Chinese teachers from Tao-an to Hui-yan had considered the unsettled condition of Vinaya to be a blot on Chinese Buddhism. The foundation of the *Lu* (Vinaya) school by Tao-hsuan (597-667) in the Tang age was the result of this movement. Both the real founder of the syncretic Tien-tai school, so typical and independent a product of Chinese thought, Chih-kai or Chih-I (531-597), and the third patriarch, Ta-fu-shun (557-589) of the Hua-yen (*Avataṁsa* or 'Flower Garland' School) were of this age. The Chan (Dhyāna) school in the Tang period was divided into a Northern and a Southern one and the head of the southern school was Hui-neng (died 713). The most renowned patriarch of the Pure Land (*Sukhāvatī* School) was Shan-tao (613-681) and lastly, Tantric Chan-yen (True-word School) was founded by Amoghavajra, an Indian monk in China, between 719 and 732. All of them were illustrious names of the Tang age. Of these schools, several were transplanted in Japan at different times and developed independently on the Japanese soil, e.g., Tien-tai (Tendai), Chen-yen (Shingon), 'Pure Land' (Jodo) and Cha'an (Zen). Their developments in Japan will be described in the next chapter.

The set-back to the Buddhism of the Tang period came with the issue of Emperor Wu Tsung's edict in 845 A.D., severely limiting the number of

[40] See *Sources of Chinese Tradition*, p. 332.

Buddhist monks and institutions in the country. The preamble of the edict points to the inordinate prosperity Buddhism has attained to in China and its alleged baleful results :

> "As far as I know", says the Emperor in the edict[41], "in the time of the Three Dynasties, the name of the Buddha was unknown. It is since the Han and the Wei that Buddhist images and books have been introduced into China. In these later times, like a penetrating poison, a spreading weed, this superstition has been propagated to the point of supplanting our natural customs and perverting the morals of our subjects. In the provinces, in the cities, in the two capitals, even in the palace, the Buddhists multiply daily. The Buddhist temples are daily more frequented. The people use up their strength to construct these temples, and their resources to ornament them. Much more, men desert their prince or their parents to serve the monks in these temples or leave their wives to live there as celibates. Truly, never has anything been so opposed to the laws of the empire and the welfare of its citizens. (The emperor points out how this resort to monkhood by common people affects the country economically.) Their temples and convents, incredible in number, rise majestic and splendid, eclipsing the palaces. It is these people (i.e., the Buddhists) who have wasted the wealth and ruined the morals of last dynasties ....I am firmly resolved to put an end to it once for all. All the ministers and governors are of my opinion and press me to act, saying that it is necessary to restore the institutions of the ancients and give the people back their property."

After this preamble, the emperor issues the following order :

> "I therefore order that 4,600 great temples and convents be demolished; that 260,500 monks and nuns be secularised and inscribed on the registers as tax-payers; that 40,000 rural temples scattered throughout the empire, be destroyed; that the millions of acres of excellent land, which these temples, convents and country-temples possess, be confiscated; that their 1,50,000 slaves be freed. As to the Buddhist monks and nuns who have come from abroad, who have until now lived in China as guests and have preached there their exotic doctrines, and as to the Nastorians and Mazdeans, and those people who number in all more than 3,000,—I order that they all be secularised so that they may not again think of amalgamating their customs with those of China. I have issued this edict to eradicate an abuse. Let my wish be carried out."

The emperor's wish was carried out to the letter. Yet Buddhism in China, doomed to death, was fated not to die. It lost undoubtedly the

---

[41] See Wieger's *History of Religious Beliefs and Philosophical Opinions in China*, p. 569.

magnificent position it had held in Tang China during the earlier Tang period, yet under the succeeding Sung dynasty, it had a period of brief revival.

Buddhist Decline in China after the Tang

Buddhism, reaching its heyday in China during the first two and a half centuries of the Tang dynasty (618-906), was in decline in late 8th century.

Sooner or later, the decline was bound to come as Buddhism presented something gritty and indigestible to the Chinese mind. Conditioned by its ancient culture, it must have found Buddhism difficult to assimilate completely at any time.

World-renunciation, institutionalised in the *Saṅgha* and inseparable from the religion, seemed to the Chinese an ideal of life, not only unsocial and therefore unethical, but also an impossible one. How could a man, they asked, renounce the world and still manage to live in it? As a Confucian scholar put it bluntly: "The Buddhists advocate the renunciation of the family and the world. Fundamentally the family cannot be renounced. Let us say that it can—when the Buddhists refuse to recognise their parents as parents and run away. But how can a person escape from the world? Only when a person no longer stands under heaven or upon the earth is he able to forsake the world. But while he continues to drink when thirsty and eat when hungry, he still stands under heaven and sets his feet upon the earth".[42]

Buddhism had always to contend with the 'this-worldly' set of the Chinese mind. Naturally the most virulent attacks on Buddhism were directed against the monk-community. By its reluctance to avow allegiance to the emperor, it seemed also trying to create an 'imperium in imperio', repugnant to the Chinese concept of an imperial State. The Doctrine of Karma which teaches that the fruits of deeds done in this life may be reaped in a life hereafter also seemed illusory to those who were unaccustomed to the idea of *Saṁsāra* (cycle of existences). While the 'apologetic writings' of the scholar-gentry and their interpretation of Buddhist doctrines and ethics sought to bring it into line or unify it with the traditions of Chinese culture, the fact of its being a 'foreign religion' was never completely forgotten. All during the early centuries, while it was spreading among the masses and while the scholars were trying to reconcile it to indigenous cultural traditions, these 'grits' were more or less felt. Questions were mooted——whether Buddhism aimed at the good of human society or insisted only on supramundane value? Whether it intended the well-being and prosperity of people or glorified poverty and privation? Whether its monk-organisation set a right standard of ethical behaviour by ignoring

[42] See *Sources of Chinese Tradition*, p. 533.

social obligations like bringing up families, paying obeisance and loyal service to the emperor and helping to increase the country's wealth?

All these points were raised in a famous memorial addressed to Emperor Hsien Tsung in 819 by the eminent scholar Han Yu (786-824). It is cherished in Chinese literature as a classic piece of prose, though in substance it was a polemic prompted by a proposal to enshrine a body-relic of the Buddha in the imperial palace. Han Yu condemned both Taoism and Buddhism, asserting that the greatest debt of civilization was to Confucianism alone. Buddhism was then the religion of the State and the traducer of it narrowly escaped execution and was sentenced to banishment.

Confucianism had sunk into neglect under the early Tang rulers, but it was once again raising its head. Wu-tsung's edict of 845 on the suppression of Buddhism in China speaks of "loyal ministers of the court and the provinces having lent their aid to the emperor's intentions, submitting proposals that the emperor has found worthy of being put into effect". But it seems that with these 'loyal ministers of the court and provinces,' it was fiscal considerations that prevailed. Their feeling was that, for the country's economic regeneration, the wastage of money and man-power involved in the multiplication of temples and monasteries had to be stopped.

The drive that followed Wu-tsung's edict was ill able to kill Buddhism; it still remained active in the land. During the unsettled period of the short-lived Five Dynasties that rose after the downfall of the Tang as well as in the early Sung period, it made some notable advances.

It was during this later period that some Indian monks whose names are great in the history of Chinese Buddhism—Dānapāla, Dharmadeva, 'Tien Hsi Tsai' and others,—arrived in China from India. They were more translators than propagandists, and what they propagated in China was the Tantric form of Buddhism then gaining ground in India.[43]

In the upper strata of society under the Sungs, the Chinese mind was veering round, not to the old Confucianism, but to a revived and renovated school of Confucian thought, since known by the name Neo-Confucianism. The name is given to it by western scholars. Chinese scholars themselves do not regard it as a new beginning, but simply as a renewal of the old, in spite of its differences which were crucial and outstanding.

Down to the end of the nineteenth century, this Neo-Confucianism held sway over the cultured Chinese mind.

Neo-Confucianism: Its Buddhist borrowings

Its rise was associated with the profound changes in China's social and political scene after the downfall of the Tang. The Tang order was no

[43] See Chou's *Indo-Chinese Relations*, pp. 163 ff.

more: a new one had to be created by the Sung rulers to take its place. They turned naturally to the 'this-worldly' guidance of Confucianism, for the turn of Buddhism towards 'other-worldly' values was unhelpful, even deterrent.

Academies and public schools in the past had been attached to monasteries and the teaching left in the hands of monks. A new type of teaching and educational foundation, not tied to Buddhism, came to take their place under official influence and patronage. This new teaching was canalised in the direction of a revival of Confucianism, which had been by-passed under the Tang. Hu Yuan (993-1049) represents this 'new teaching'. On his work and its effect on young minds, one of his pupils reported thus to Emperor Shen-tsung:

> "Tirelessly and with undaunted zeal, he devoted himself to school-teaching, first in Soochow and finally at the Imperial Academy. Those who have come from his school number at least several thousands. The fact that today scholars recognise the basic importance to government and education the substance and function of the Way of the Sages is all due to the efforts of my master."[44]

The moulders of neo-Confucianism, however, as Wright points out, 'lived in a climate suffused with Buddhism.' "Even the language and the modes of discourse at their disposal had developed in the ages of Buddhist dominance. The new dimensions of meaning in the ancient Chinese classics were dimensions which experience with Buddhism had taught them to seek and find".[45]

The early neo-Confucianists of the Sung era indeed fought Buddhism as though it were a disease in the body politic. The 'disease' was not healed; its contagion spread. The new construct of Confucian philosophy took in certain elements from the very religion it intended to displace, not consciously at all, but because they were floating in the intellectual atmosphere. The Buddhist Bodhisattva ideal and the Buddhist Ch'an doctrine of intuition entered the neo-Confucian ideology.

One of its early founders, the statesman and general Fan Chung-yen (989-1052) had defined a *Chuntze* (Confucian Master) as one who was 'first in worrying about the world's troubles and last in enjoying its pleasures'. He was the ideal man of neo-Confucian conception. We are told that 'this maxim became an article of faith deeply imprinted in the mind of the scholar class.' "As recently as a decade ago (i.e., in the forties of the present century), it was often assigned as an essay topic in modern schools (in China)".[46] The *Chuntze* was the Mahāyānist Bodhisattva in neo-Confucian reconstruction

---

[44] See *Sources of Chinese Tradition*, p. 439.

[45] Wright's, *Buddhism in Chinese History*, p. 90-91.

[46] See Wright's *Buddhism in Chinese History*, p. 93 and footnote 6.

—one whose constant prayer should be this sublime canticle of Śāntideva:

"So long as the sky lasts and the earth remains, let me live to bring to an end the miseries of the world. Whatever misery there is in the world, let all of that settle on me: let the world be happy through the Bodhisattvas' welfare work".[47]

Buddhism of the Ch'an school remained in China for nearly two centuries after Chu Hsi (see *infra*) side by side with the officially sponsored neo-Confucianism. Buddhism was anathema to the neo-Confucianist who would never think of borrowing a doctrine from that religion. Yet a couple of centuries later, under the Ming dynasty, a school of neo-Confucianism, founded by Wang Yang-ming (1472-1529), arose on the basis of the Ch'an Buddhist doctrine of Intuition. It was called the 'School of Intuition' in contradistinction from Chu Hsi's 'School of Reason'. The followers of Wang's school earned later on the opprobrious name of 'wild-cat Ch'an Buddhists".[48]

The immediate effects of the re-risen Confucian spirit in the Sung period, after its complete quiescence during the Tang, may be traced in the new activities it inspired—among officials, in certain re-orientations of old policies and institutions of the State, specially in the fields of land-reform and the civil-service examinations, and among scholars, in revived studies in China's history and ancient traditions of government. In Confucian thought they were believed to be the best guide to government and statesmanship. It was some time later that neo-Confucianism was rounded out as a system of philosophy with a world-view, diametrically opposite to the Buddhist.

The philosopher who raised the new philosophic structure, grounding his system in old Confucian classics, was Chu Hsi (1130-1200). He wrote commentaries on four Confucian classics; they became texts for the civil-service examinations and represented in fact 'the official orthodoxy of the empire' down to the turn of the 20th century. The work of Chu Hsi for the training of a neo-Confucian was based on a short essay, ascribed to Confucius but of apocryphal authorship, entitled *Ta Hsheu* (Great Learning). Setting out a schematic plan for Confucian self-culture, Chu Hsi's work was a key for later developments of neo-Confucian philosophy.

Chu Hsi opposed the Buddhist concept of Void (*Śūnyatā*), which had been in old China a favourite topic in *Chintan* discussions and an outstanding one in works written by Chinese Buddhist philosophers. To Chu

---

[47] See vv. 54-57 in the 10th *pariccheda* of the *Bodhicaryavatara* (The translation is mine). Santideva was an Indian Buddhist monk of the 8th century and a poet of Mahayana Buddhism.

[48] *Sources of Chinese Tradition*, p. 260; MacNair's *China*, p. 260 (University of California Press, 1949).

Hsi, the Great Ultimate was Reality. Reality was motivated by the two cosmic principles—*Yang* (the Male) and *Yin* (the Female). Acting in rhythmic succession and in union with the Five Elements (*Wu-hsing*)—Water, Fire, Wood, Metal and Earth,—they produced the universal order—the visible, the real Ultimate. Reality, as conceived by him, was the product of co-ordination, of which Reason was the basic operative principle. In all things there is Reason and 'the Reason of a thing is one with the Reason of all things.' The school of neo-Confucian philosophy founded by Chu Hsi is therefore called the 'School of Reason'. It is a counterblast to the negativist *Śūnyatā-vāda* (Philosophy of the Viod) of Mahāyānist Buddhism.

After a brief revival between the fall of the Tang and the installation of the Sung in power, Buddhist philosophy practically ceased to develop in China, while neo-Confucianism entered on a long course of development. It passed through several stages of re-thinking and re-adjustment in the hands of Chinese scholars of successive generations, Wang Yang-ming (1472-1529), Ku Yen-wu (1613-1682), Tai Tung-yuan (1724-1777), Kang Yu-wei (1858-1927) and others.

Having passed its peak period under the Tang, Chinese Buddhism definitely ceased to be creative. Several Buddhist schools coalesced with others or became extinct, only the Tien-tai and the Cha'an were carrying on. Late in the Sung period, Eisai, the pioneer of Zennism in Japan where it has since flourished most, went to China. He found Zen to be the only form of Buddhism flourishing in that country and he returned to Japan in 1191 a full-fledged Zen master of one of its two current schools, viz. the *Lin-chi* (Japanese— *Rinzai*).

Buddhism in China, however, never came to a doomsday. Efforts were made, in the later centuries by Chinese Buddhist scholars, and by voluntary associations and academies founded by them, for its spread and promotion. But in these centuries it was drained of both its popular urge and its creative vitality.

At the same time, it lingered on in folk-religion. It got mixed with other faiths and evolved a heterogeneous pantheon. "As early as the eleventh century a Buddhist monk had combined the worship of Confucius, Buddha and Lao-tzu in a single cult, and many temples of the Sung and later periods had special halls for the worship".[49] Wright quotes from a 1948 report on the popular cults of one country of China to the effect that only 19.7 per cent of the local cult units were identifiably Buddhist, and a number of deities in these were tending to be confused with those of non-Buddhist origin.[50] Evidently the common folk, following folk-ways in their

[49] See Wright's *Buddhism in Chinese History*, p. 100.

[50] *Ibid.* p. 101 and footnote 14.

religion, were untouched by the influence of Buddhist teachers.

Since the acceptance of Communism as their national faith by the Chinese, both Buddhist teachers and Confucian scholars may be said to have become *functus officio* in that country. Both Confucianism and Buddhism are relegated now from living faith to a place in the old and antiquated scholarship of China. Against this form of scholarship, the most strident voice in the early years of Communism in China was raised by Lusin, the great wit and 'leftist' writer of the country who died in 1936. He was strongly opposed to the study of both Buddhist and Confucian literature and, describing how Buddhist literature became part and parcel of China's national heritage, he refers wittily to what he believes to have been a Chinese characteristic: "There is a favourite way with those who know old literature. When a new idea is introduced, they call it 'heresy' and must bend all their efforts to destroy it. When that new idea after hard struggle has won a place for itself, they then discover that 'it's the same thing as what was taught by Confucius'. They object to all imported things, saying that this is 'to convert the Chinese into barbarians', but when the barbarians become rulers of China, they discover these barbarians are also descendants of the Yellow Emperor".[51]

If this be a true reading of Chinese mentality, how clearly it shows the way in which Buddhism was at first taken and later transmuted to suit their own faith and culture by the Chinese people !

---

[51] See Lin Yutang's *Wisdom of China* (published by Michael Joseph, 1948 Ed.) p. 502 for this aphorism of Lusin.

Chapter X

JAPAN

Korea and Japan in Ancient History

The civilization of Japan is not of venerable antiquity: its beginnings do not go back much beyond the end of the 6th century, A.D., when Prince Shotoku, regent for Queen Suiko, opened Japan's cultural intercourse with China. It had been preceded by her relations with Korea from where Japan had her first introduction to Chinese culture and Chinese Buddhism.

Korea had been a sort of outpost of the ancient Chinese empire. Since the 1st century, A.D., it had been known to the Chinese as the 'principality of Chosen'—a commandery under China's imperial way. At the turn of the 5th century, it was divided into three kingdoms under the hegemony of the kingdom of Silla. Korea had the Chinese type of society, a Confucian system of government and a culture dominated by Chinese Buddhism. The southernmost Korean kingdom was Paikche, known to the Japanese under the name of Kudara. It was not difficult of access from Japan, only a short voyage distant from the island of Kyushu in western Japan.

Since primitive times, there had been interminglings of people between western Japan and Korea. They are recorded *passim* in the *Nihongi* and the *Kojiki*,[1] and in the latter work a tradition is recorded that at the commencement of the 3rd century, A.D., Empress Jin-gu of Japan conquered Korea.[2] These chronicles of ancient Japan are, however, wholly legendary until the commencement of the 5th century, A.D.

The Kudara (Paikche) kingdom in the earlier half of the 6th century was in trouble, being hard-pressed by neighbouring Silla. The Kudara king solicited help from Japan and sent an envoy to the Japanese court in 552 A.D., with presents which included a Buddha-image and some sacred writings, hoping perhaps that, if the Japanese court could be induced to

---

[1] These two national chronicles of ancient Japan are available in translation. *Nihongi* (Chronicles of Japan) was completed in 720 A.D., eight years after *Kojiki* (Records of Ancient Matters) had been presented to the Japanese empress Gem-miyo. The scope of the two chronicles is the same. The 'Chronicles' carry the narrative down to 700 A.D.; the 'Record' stops at 628 A.D.

[2] For Jingo's conquest of Korea, see Chamberlain's English translation of the *Kojiki*, pp. 281-282.

accept Buddhism, it would cement friendship between the two countries[3].

The Japanese emperor was charmed by the grace, poise and beauty of the Buddha-image, but, unwilling to institute a worship that had no sanction in the national Shinto faith, he made it over to the head of the Sogo clan to which he himself belonged, with instruction to instal and preserve it. The image, unfortunately, was regarded more as a talisman than an object of worship, and when after its installation some natural calamities ensued, it was discarded and thrown away into a moat.

In 584 A.D. a member of the Sogo clan received two other images from Korea. He erected a temple to enshrine them and appointed a Korean priest to do the rites of worship. But there was a further disaster in the form of an epidemic and the votaries of Shinto came to the temple and again threw the images away. But the act had no effect on the incidence of the epidemic. The Emperor, recognising that the installation of the images could not have been its cause, agreed to allow the Sogo clan to continue the worship. Thereafter Korean priests began to arrive in Japan as officiants and it so happened that they found Prince Shotoku (b. 574-d. 622) among their disciples. He had not been called to the regency yet. He was wedded to learning and soon acquired such proficiency in Buddhist scripture that it is said he used to explain the Chinese Buddhist texts, brought by the priests from Korea, to his mother Empress Suiko. When Shotoku assumed regency in his twenty-first year, he had already come under the spell of Chinese culture and Chinese Buddhism.

From Korea, Buddhism came not only with its texts, its priests and its new doctrines, but also with rudiments of some specialised learning and some arts and crafts till then unknown in Japan.

Two entries in the *Nihongi* for the years 588 and 602 A.D. corroborate this.[4] In 588, it is said that the 'land of Paikche' sent envoys and, along with them, Buddhist priests to the Japanese court with a present of Buddhist relics. Perhaps in expectation that *stūpas* would be raised over the relics, two temple-carpenters and a man 'learned in the art of marking braziers and chargers', a painter and also men 'learned in pottery', were sent from Korea. The entry for 602 A.D. is to this effect: a Paikche priest (name given) arrived and presented by way of tribute books on calendar-marking, on astronomy and on geomancy, and also books on the 'art of invisibility and magic'. It is not clear, however, whether they were Taoist books or texts of Tantric Buddhism. At this time three or four pupils were selected and made to study under these Korean priests. One studied the art of calen-

[3] See Aston's English translation of *Nihongi*, Vol. II, p. 66. Also see *Sources of Japanese Tradition* (Columbia University Press, New York 1959), p. 93.

[4] See *Sources of Japanese Tradition*, p. 95

dar-marking; two studied astronomy and the art of invisibility; and one studied magic. 'They all studied so far as to perfect themselves in these arts.'

It is evident that in these budding years of Japanese civilization, when no distinctive Japanese culture existed, the impetus to its development on certain lines came from Korea. Korea itself was a wholly sinified country, dependent for her own culture on China.

Shotoku and 'Nara' Buddhism

There is no room for doubt that Shotoku was an ardent Buddhist by personal faith. But his imperial status made obligatory some ceremonial allegiance to the national faith, Shinto. The imperial throne of Japan rested on its mythology of the divine descent of the Mikadoes in an unbroken line and their divinely ordained authority over the people. So Shotoku turned to Shinto when state rituals and ceremonies were concerned and Shintoism was never disavowed by him.

Of the sayings fathered on him, one is that "Shinto is the root of a tree; Confucianism its stem and branches, and Buddhism the flower and the fruit".[5] Whether he ever cherished such a syncretic notion in his own mind is difficult to say. Where he represents Buddhism as a cult in the sculpture and paintings of his temples, he does not admit any of the Shinto deities, thus keeping Shintoism and Buddhism apart. But he is said to have initiated a great national festival 'in honour of the Shinto deities of Heaven and Earth'.

Though bound to Shintoism in the exercise of his official functions, his mind was steeped in Buddhist philosophy. During 604-605 A.D., he wrote commentaries on three leading Buddhist *sūtras*: only one of them survives in a holograph copy, preserved with pious care in the Horyuji temple built by him. Shotoku himself gave lectures on the *sūtras* at his court and also to the public outside, and it is said that on the latter occasions he used to drape himself in Buddhist robes over his royal attire. The Horyuji was annexed to the palace and housed a conventual college where the study of Buddhist philosophy was carried on. Here the Prince pursued his own studies and wrote his commentaries on the *sūtras*. Near it was an octagonal temple called the 'Temple of Vision' (*Yumedono*) housing a most delicately executed image of Kannon (the Chinese Goddess of Mercy). It was worshipped in solitude by the Prince. Nearly seven centuries later, here came also another great Buddhist leader of Japan, Saint Nichiren, the much persecuted founder of the 'Lotus Sect', to meditate and seek the blessings of the goddess.

---

[5] See Anesaki's *Prince Shotoku: the Sage-Statesman of Japan* (published from the Horyuji Temple, 1959), p. 47.

The remnants of the religious edifices built by Shotoku are still to be seen at Nara and Osaka. The first one built by him was the 'Temple of the Four Heavenly Kings' (*Shitennoji*) at Osaka. It was not a mere temple for worship, but a conglomerate structure housing an academy where Buddhist studies were carried on along with the cultivation of music, dance, architecture and the arts, and had, annexed to it, a herbal pharmacy, a hospital and an asylum for the destitute. The other great edifice was the Horyuji, built in memory of Shotoku's father. Here also was a college for Japanese students of Buddhism. The buildings are largely planned and decorated with sculpture and mural paintings. But the models are all Chinese and there is nothing distinctively Japanese about them. It is not till we come out of the Nara to the Kyoto period in Japan's history that the expression of Japanese genius becomes at all perceptible.

For the stabilization of Buddhism, the Prince raised a priestly hierarchy in the capital, the members of which, however, did not always feel bound to confine their interest to matters of religion. They took active part in the discussion of politics and affairs of State and tried to influence State policies.

Shotoku stood for the progress of his country. But the idea of progress entertained by him and the emperors of the Nara period after him cannot be characterised as 'nationalistic'. They wanted to produce in the country a true copy of Chinese culture and Chinese society and they embarked on a course of sinification of Japan, political and cultural, believing that to be the only way to advance civilization in the country. In the legends about Shotoku in the *Nihongi* and the *Kojiki*, reference is made to a 'Constitution of Seventeen Articles' which Shotoku is supposed to have drawn up for Japan.[6] It was not exactly a Constitution, but rather a conspectus of Buddhist and Confucian ideas that he wished to see introduced into the Government of the State. But expert opinion is inclined to assign the document to a period later than his reign. Even this 'Constitution' fathered on him shows that Shotoku's idea of progress was more of cultural advance than political amelioration.

He believed in complete sinification of Japan as the only way of progress for the country as it was conditioned in that age. Japan had known China so far through the medium of Korea, but Shotoku initiated direct cultural intercourse with China and formulated the idea, which was worked out by his successors, of sending Japanese scholars to that country for training. Buddhism appeared to him to be the most important aspect of Chinese culture and he desired to establish it in Japan. By the time of Shotoku, most of the schools (*Tsung*) of Chinese Buddhism had already developed, and out of the traditional ten schools, as many as six were represented in the Nara hierarchy.

[6] A summary will be found in Anesaki's *Prince Shotoku: the Sage-statesman of Japan* (pub. from Horyuji Temple, 1959), Sec. 6. But see Sansom's remarks on its authenticity in *A History of Japan*, Vol. I. pp. 51-52.

What these six specifically were is not definitely known[7]. But Buddhism at Nara was in fact completely sinified Buddhism, taken from scriptures in Chinese, interpreted variously in the different Chinese schools, and mixed with China's indigenous philosophies,—Confucianism and Taoism. Prince Shotoku himself had a Korean priest, Eji-hosshi, as his own teacher and spiritual guide.

Shotoku succeeded in establishing a strong and broad-based tradition of Buddhism in the country. By the end of 624 A.D—that is, only two years after his death—there were in Japan, we are told, 46 monasteries with 816 monks and 569 nuns.[8] Monks who lived at Nara basked in the sunshine of imperial favour, were as keenly interested in ecclesiastical matters as in State politics, and, by the combination of imperial favour with diplomacy and intrigue, the Nara hierarchy became a power almost superior to the State.

The Todaiji : its History

The successors of Shotoku were from the Sogo clan. This clan had been, as we have seen, the first in Japan to embrace Buddhism. The Sogo emperors after Shotoku kept up the traditions of his reign. The sinified Buddhism initiated by him prevailed; the intercourse with China was kept up, and the Todaiji, the biggest of Japan's ancient temples, was built by one of his successors with all-out nation-wide effort. It was the wealthiest and most influential religious establishment of the Nara period and the history of this temple is an interesting study in the early co-operation in the service of Buddhism between the Japanese emperor and the people.

Shortly before its foundation, an outbreak of small-pox had ravaged the country. For such calamities, according to Japanese political theory, the emperor and his government were not exempt from blame.

Emperor Shomu, who was then on the throne, thought fit to issue an edict in 743 A.D. declaring that, as men do not seem 'to enjoy the grace of Buddhist law' everywhere in the land, the emperor had taken a vow to erect an image of Lochana Buddha in gold and copper and that he wished to make the utmost use of the nation's resources in metal for casting the image and in levelling the high hill on which the temple was to be raised. The Lochana (Sanskrit. *Avalokana*—Overseeing) Buddha, as the presiding deity of the universe, is represented in the *Kegon* (*Flower-Wreath*) *Sūtra* as sitting on a lotus-throne of a thousand petals, each of which is a universe. The establishment projected was meant to be both a sanctuary for the image

---

[7] They were probably Sanron, Joyitsu, Hoso, Gusha (or Kusha), Kegon, and Ritsu,—— See *Nihon Bijutsu Zenshi*, Vol. I, p. 42 ('History of Japanese Art'), published Tokyo by Bijutsu Shuppansha.

[8] See Sansom's *A History of Japan*, Vol. I, p. 64.

and a seminary of monastic learning, specially in the scripture of the Kegon school. The combination of a sanctuary with a seminary was in the approved Nara tradition.

As an example of the prevalence of Shintoism side by side with Buddhism, the legend that for the imperial vow ratification was sought and obtained from the Shinto Sun-goddess at Ise is apposite. It is related in the section on 'Shinto and Ryobu Shinto' in the present chapter.

When at length, after a few years' efforts, the obstacles from lack of funds and necessary skill were overcome, the great bronze image, 53 feet high, stood complete. But gold for the purpose of gilding it was short of requirement. Happily, however, the precious metal was discovered in the province of Mutsu in Japan and the emperor celebrated the discovery with a function within the temple, declaring:

> "This is the word of the Sovereign who is the servant of the Three Treasures (i.e. the Buddha, Dharma and Saṅgha) that he humbly speaks before the image of Lochana. In this land of Yamato, since the beginning of heaven and earth, gold, though it has been brought as an offering from other countries, was thought not to exist. But in the east of the land where we rule, gold has been found. Hearing this, we were astonished and we rejoiced, and feeling that this is a gift bestowed upon us by the love and blessing of Lochana Buddha, we here received it with reverence and humbly accepted it, and have brought with us all our officials to worship and give thanks".[9]

Popular enthusiasm over the discovery is reflected in a poem composed in 749 which calls upon all people to stand solidly behind the emperor.[10]

Cartloads of gold were conveyed over a long distance from Mutsu to Nara and the image was complete with the gilt on. It was the image of the 'Buddha with the Overseeing Eyes', and the eyes, the most significant feature of the image, had to be 'opened' (i.e. traced in outline with gold) with brush and paint at the installation. This 'eye-opening ceremony' was entrusted to an Indian monk hailing from China. He subsequently became the abbot (*Sojo*) of the Todaiji and served in that capacity at Nara for several years till his death in that city at the age of fifty-six in 760 A.D. The story of 'Baramon Sojo' is told in the Appendix.

By an imperial edict of 741 A.D., emperor Somu decreed the establishment of a number of monasteries (*kokubunji*) and nunneries (*Kokubunniji*) in various parts of the country. The Todaiji was placed at the head of them all.

---

[9] See *Sources of Japanese Tradition*, pp. 98-99.

[10] Sansom's *A History of Japan*, Vol. I, p. 94.

Transition to the Heian Period

Nara was priest-dominated. It is supposed that one of the main reasons for shifting the capital from Nara to Kyoto in 710 A.D. was to save affairs of State from the muddling interference of priests. The atmosphere of Nara had become academic, more fit to be a religious than a political centre. The situation was disliked by the successors of Shotoku. With the transfer of the capital to Kyoto, a new chapter opened in Japanese history: it is called 'Heian' after the old name of Kyoto.

The spirit of the first eight decades of the Heian period is summed up thus by Sansom: "It is scarcely possible to exaggerate the achievement of learned monks expounding the scriptures, the fruitful work of practitioners of all the arts, the sudden ripening of a rich and varied culture".[11] What disappeared from the scene was the State policy of sinification and the State's overmuch preoccupation with ecclesiastical affairs.

The rulers of the Heian period found society suffering from various economic ills and were more concerned with social amelioration and economic reforms based on Confucian principles. The study of Confucian philosophy became more worthwhile than that of the Buddhist *sūtras*. Not that the State turned secular: the building of Buddhist temples and the sending out of Japanese monk-scholars to China continued. But the actual promotion of Buddhism in the ways it had been done in the days of Shotoku and his successors was not undertaken as a primary concern of the State.

Buddhism,—rather its Chinese version—had been intensely cultivated at Nara. But it was by and large an academic affair. It is when we come to the Heian period that we see Buddhism diffused among common people, and one hundred years after the foundation of the Heian capital, there is evidence that some of the Buddhist ideas and doctrines were playing a considerable part in every aspect of social life. Buddhism met with no opposition and no hostility as it had encountered in China.

On the whole Heian Japan was not the same as old Japan. No longer in the shadow of Nara's academic Buddhism and its all-controlling priesthood, the upper strata of Heian society developed a different type of culture. Though not exempt from superstitions like exorcism and belief in auspices, it was a culture free and refined and uninhibited in aesthetic pleasures. The life of the court and the aristocracy of this period is fully reflected in the well-known classic of Japanese fiction, *Genji-monagatari*.[12]

Buddhism, however, held its place. The patronage of the court to Buddhism especially of the Fujiwara Regents, suffered no abatement; the study

---

[11] Sansom's *A History of Japan*, vol. I.p.219

[12] It is a voluminous novel, as all Japanese works of fiction are, written by a court-lady Mursake Shikibu (978—1025 A.D.), describing the life of an imperial prince Genji of the Heian peirod.

of Chinese literature was encouraged and the cultural intercourse with China continued. But under the Chinese top-layer a Japanese form and quality, different from the Chinese though based upon it, was manifesting itself in literature and the arts.

Genji-monagatari shows also how the influence of Buddhism has already seeped into all strata of society. The Japanese mind has seized particularly on the basic Buddhist Doctrine of *Karma.* It is unmistakable from the numerous references and allusions to it in the story of Genji. On the effect of this on Japanese culture, Sansom remarks: "Whatever argument there may be about the place of Buddhism in Japanese life, there can be no doubt that the adoption of this one idea, which is entirely foreign and has no indigenous counterpart, brought about a truly revolutionary change in the moral outlook of the Japanese people. It was perhaps more an addition than a change, since neither the native cult nor the Confucian ethical creed had anything to say about past or future lives, or about the spiritual needs of the individual or his view of human destiny".[13]

Tendai and Shingon

The *Kojiki* refers to six schools of Chinese Buddhism, out of its traditionary ten, as being represented in the ecclesiastical community of Nara. Some of these Chinese schools still exist in Japan, though they do not seem to have undergone after-developments on Japanese soil.

But two other Chinese schools were introduced in the Heian period which were of far-reaching influence. They were the Tendai (Chinese—*Tientai*) and the Shingon.

The former was a syncretic school of Chinese origin; the latter a Chinese version of Indian Tantric Buddhism which had been introduced into China in the first quarter of the 8th century by two Indian monks from South India, Vajrabodhi and Amoghavajra.

The founders in Japan of the two schools were respectively Saicho (767-822), posthumously known as Dengyo Daishi, and Kukai (774-835), posthumously Kobo Daishi. The latter was also an accomplished Chinese scholar in both religious and secular literature. Besides versions of Chinese Buddhist scripture, he wrote a learned treatise on Chinese prosody. He is said to have learnt Tantric Buddhism from a Chinese disciple of Amoghavajra.

We need not dilate on the specific doctrines of these two schools. But they certainly acquired a certain Japanese flavour on their transplantation in Japan, and also had what may be termed a new spiritual orientation. This 'new orientation' is indicated by the kind of setting and location in which the two schools chose to run their establishments.

---

[13] See Sansom's *A History of Japan,* vol. I p. 220.

At Nara the city had been the venue of Buddhist activities. The monk community there was exposed to secular and political influences, unwholesome in the conduct of spiritual life. Both Saicho and Kukai preferred the aloofness, the silence and the solitude of mountains: their idea of a man of religion was that of a recluse and solitary. Both Chinese and Japanese art traditionally represent a religious devotee as such an one,—a person all alone with Nature. The tradition of it goes back in Japan to Saicho and Kukai. Even before the shift of the capital to Kyoto, Saicho had selected Mount Hei, several miles out to the north-east of the city, to build a shrine and a monastery in which religious fraternities could develop in sequestered surroundings. Kukai likewise founded monasteries on Mount Koya still farther off from Kyoto and more difficult of access. These shrines and monasteries, though far removed from the city, attracted official patronage and grew into large-scale and expanding establishments governed by rules and regulations for admission, residence, etc. framed under State authority.

The two establishments flourishing separately on the mountains of Hei and Koya, were filled with Japanese Buddhists from far and near. They became the most prominent seminaries of Buddhist learning in their time.

Tendai was a sort of eclectic Buddhism originating in China, which accommodated in one system the doctrines of several Buddhist schools. It became the nidus from which different texts of Buddhism were drawn later and sects arose in later times in Japan based on one or another of these texts.

Centering round the great temple of Enryaku, the Tendai establishment on Mount Hei was the premier institution for the cultivation of Tendai philosophy—the *Tientai* of China. It was a liberal philosophy,—liberal even to the extent of recognising the gods of the Shinto pantheon and investing them with the character of Bodhisattvas. There were several active Shinto shrines on Mount Hei testifying to the Tendai recognition of Shinto deities. Tendai Buddhism was in fact a mansion of many chambers in which diverse and mutually exclusive doctrines of different schools could find shelter and accommodation. Creative minds like Genshin, Honen, Shinran, Eisai, Dogen, Nichiren and a host of others, who came here to study Tendai, carried away from this intellectual store-house concepts and doctrines on which they founded new faiths and philosophies. It was State-endowed and State-sponsored.

Its end, however, was tragic in the extreme. After nearly eight centuries of existence, with many interim changes of fortune, the establishment in 1571 had 3,000 buildings and 20,000 inmates.[14] In that year it fell to the revengeful wrath of the Japanese General Nobunaga who, ambitious to bring all Japan

---

[14] See *Sources of Japanese Tradition*, p. 314.

under his sway, met with stout opposition from the monk community. He never came near the fulfilment of his ambition, but wreaked a terrible revenge on Mount Hei, setting fire to all temples, halls and monks' quarters and putting all the monks to the sword. The site, full of ruins, is now given over to picnickers and holiday-makers from Kyoto.

Shingon with its establishment on Mount Koya was an esoteric cult. The establishment enjoyed great prosperity for six centuries and consisted of seven thousand temples and monasteries centring round the Kongobuji temple founded by Kukai in 819. The buildings on Koya were several times destroyed during the period of monastic warfare (see *infra*) until the great fire of 1888 involved it and left only about a hundred buildings standing.

The method of instruction in Shingon doctrines was based mainly on figures and diagrams which had to be drawn with meticulous care and exactness, and in this process Shingon became the nursery of old Japanese painting. Kukai was an artist himself and considered art to be the proper medium of spiritual learning. "The secret of the *sūtras* and commentaries", said Kukai, "can be depicted in art, and the essential truths of the esoteric teaching set forth therein. Neither teachers nor students can dispense with it. Art is what reveals to us the state of perfection".[15] Kukai was in fact an artist sublimated to sainthood by his inborn artistic urge. "For Kukai whatever was beautiful partook of the nature of the Buddha."[16]

The development of Shingon in Japan shows more clearly than anything else how in the Heian period the Japanese were not content to take Buddhism exactly from a Chinese stereotype. They developed it in ways dictated by Japanese spirit and temperament. The core of Shingon was what are called the 'Three Mysteries'. The 'mysteries' had been worked out in Indian Tantric Buddhism to a system of *maṇḍalas* (circles) each representing a cosmos. This Tantric doctrine of *maṇḍalas* had been conveyed by the Indian monk and teacher Amoghavajra to Hui-Kuo, Kukai's master in China, and imparted by the latter to Kukai. But the Japanese disciple in expounding it gave it an orientation, not towards magic spells and formulae or the sexual significance to which Tantrism degenerated in India, but to what was congenial to Japanese spirit and temper,—love of the beautiful, aestheticism and art.

In the next century, however, both the establishments were involved in calamity of a peculiar nature.

Being located in lonely places and possessing rich treasures, they needed strong guards for safety. These guards of monasteries, who counted among

---

[15] See Coates and Ishizuka's *Honen: The Buddhist Saint*, p. 323.

[16] See *Sources of Japanese Tradition*, p. 142.

them a number of monks who had betaken themselves to this occupation, developed afterwards into irregular bands of soldiery known as *Sohei.* The maintenence of these Sohei bands—monks to outward seeming, but soldiers by occupation—was an experiment fraught with danger. It tended to breed war which it actually did. During the 11th century, the raiding of a monastery by its rivals became an all-too-frequent spectacle. How it affected the minds of the people in regard to current Buddhism and its approved institutions is little known by outward expression. But it must have stirred a feeling of discontent with—perhaps something of revulsion to—the set and institutionalised forms of prevailing Buddhism. Pampered by State patronage, it was torn by internecine feud. At any rate, the prevalence of such a feeling rationalises the rise about the turn of the 11th century of some dissident faiths breaking with the old established monastic order. Vigorously growing and gathering strength, these faiths swept over the whole country in the centuries following.

Amidism: the Religion of the Common Man

Of these emergent faiths, Amidism or the 'Pure Land' cult was in the 12th and the 13th centuries most popular and most widely propagated in Japan.

Amidism had first developed in China, somewhat early in the history of Chinese Buddhism, on the basis of Chinese versions of three Mahāyāna texts of Indian provenance—the 'Sūtra on Boundless Life', the 'Longer and smaller Sukhāvatī Sūtra' and the 'Sūtra on Meditation', of which the last has no known Indian original.

These works present two inter-dependent conceptions,—first, of an *ideal* land, a sequestered and refulgent Land of Bliss (*Sukhāvatī-vyūha*) and, second, of Amitābha (Lord of Infinite Light) who has undertaken to admit to this land all, without distinction of rank or merit, who would show their faith in Amitābha by constantly invoking him by name.

The Land of Bliss is imagined as a land of illimitable light "where each flower sends forth thirty-six hundred thousand-millions of lights and from each light comes out thirty-six hundred thousand millions of Buddhas".[17] Conceived in such superlative terms of endless splendour and magnificence, it is also spiritualised: being equiparated with the 'state of Nirvāṇa,—the Buddhist concept of a state in which all the grossness of life vanishes and only enlightenment is left.[18]

The concept of 'Amitābha's vow', as his undertaking to the faithful to

---

[17] *The Shinshu Seiten* (compiled and published by the Honpa Hongwanji Mission of Hawaii, 1727 Fort Street, Honolulu, Hawaii, second print, 1961), p. 38.

[18] "It is like the uncreate and is like Nirvana itself.—*Ibid*, p. 35.

admit them to the 'Land of Bliss' is termed, stems from the fundamental Mahāyānist doctrine that the Buddha as Bodhisattva keeps vigil in this 'Land of Bliss' till all creatures on earth attain salvation (Japanese—*Ojo*). The dual concept of a 'land of bliss' (Japanese—*Jodo*) and of the Saviour waiting to admit the faithful is elaborated in the exegetic commentaries. The 'Vow of Amitābha' is named the 'original vow' and is expanded into 48 articles of which the eighteenth is most relevant. It runs thus: 'Any being in the ten quarters of the earth who calls upon my name at least ten times a day shall be born into my land'.[19] The 'pure-land cult' or Amidism is founded on these two interlinked concepts—the 'Original Vow' and the 'Land of Bliss' where Amitābha waits to welcome the faithful in.

This cult was developed in China and one of its leading Chinese exponents, Zando (Chinese name—Shan-tao, died in 681), is frequently cited as an authority by Honen in his works.

Honen was the first to popularise it in Japan. He pointed out that, while in other schools of Buddhism the way to salvation is through strenuous self-effort—through earnest study and through strict mental and moral discipline which ordinary men are not capable of—here was for them an easier way which demanded only faith in Amida, sincerity of heart and the taking of his name.

It was a simplified faith, but in its immediate spread among the masses and the hold it retained on the mass mind, its simplicity was aided by an escapist longing in the minds of people who were witnesses at the time of the bloody clan-feuds through which Japan was emerging from the Kyoto to the Kamakura order.

The life and teachings of Honen may be read in Coates and Ishizuka's *Honen, The Buddhist Saint: His Life and Teaching*, compiled by Imperial Order and published from Tokyo, Chionin, in 1925. Honen was not exactly the initiator of Amidism in Japan : he had pioneers—Kuya (903-972), a monk of Mount Hei, who founded what was called 'circulating Nembutsu' (*Yuzu Nembutsu*) and went about singing with his followers:

"He never fails to reach the Lotus Land of Bliss,
Who calls, if only once, the name of Amida;"[20]

Genshin (942-1017) who, also a painter, wrote a work on *Ojo-Yochu* (Essentials of Salvation) which had a wide circle of readers in mediaeval Japan; and Ryonin (1072-1132) who travelled all over the land inviting everyone to join him in 'circulating Nembutsu'. Dancing, painting, music, sculpture and tract-writing had all been pressed before Honen into Amidist propaganda. But in other cults Nembutsu had been regarded in those

[19] See Coastes and Ishizuka's *Honen:The Buddhist Saint*, pp. 363-364.

[20] Quoted in *Sources of Japanese Tradition*, p. 193. These are two lines only from the song.

days as only an accessory practice.

It was Honen's achievement to place 'Pure Land' Buddhism on the basis of philosophy in his work, *Senjakushu,* He had been a scholar of Mount Hei and he collected in this work scriptural passages on the 'Original Vow' of Amida. He claimed superior merit for the invocation of Amida by recitation of his name in the formula—*Namu Amida Butsu* (Salutation to the Amitābha Buddha!). Holding that it was the only proper and authentic means of access to the Pure Land, he called upon people to reject the other ways: they were man-made, while this was recommended by Amida himself. "I throw aside those practices", said Honen, "that are not included in Amida's vow, nor prescribed by Sākyamuni, nor having the endorsement of the Buddhas of all quarters. I now throw myself only on the Original Vow of Amida..............I give up my own foolish plans of salvation and devote myself to the practice of the mightily effective discipline of the Nembutsu".[21] As to how many times a day the salutation to Amida must be made, his answer was that it might begin with ten thousand, and then go on to twenty, thirty, fifty, sixty, to even a hundred thousand. Everyone should, in his own heart and according to his own will, determine the number of recitations within these limits.[22] Rosaries were used to help counting. The same doctrine, it is interesting to note, prevails in certain forms of Hinduism even today and is known as *Nām-Jap* (Meditating the Name).

Nembutsu was the token of absolute self-surrender to the mercy of Amida. As said by Honen's disciple Shinran: "It is because of Amida Buddha and because his light nurtures us that Nembutsu comes to our lips........ The Nembutsu is neither practice nor virtue. As it is not practised through one's own will or power, it is no practice; as it is not perfected by one's own will or power it is no virtue. It solely arises from the other-power and has nothing to do with Self-power. Hence no practice and no virtue to one who practises it. Such was the word of our Master (Honen)."[23]

Men and women had absolute equality in this school and the rule of celibacy for monks was not recognised There were nuns of this school and there is an old Jodo nunnery still functioning at Kyoto. A 'History of Jodo Nuns' has been published from this institution in 1961.[24]

Jodo (Pure Land) is the name by which the sect was called after it had been organised by Honen's disciple Shinran (1178-1262). On the basis of

[21] Coates and Ishizuka's *Honen: The Buddhist Saint.*

[22] *Ibid*, p. 423.

[23] The *Shinshu Seiten*, p. 267.

[24] The Japanese title is—*Jodoshu Niso-shi.* It is the compilation of a committee,—published in 1961 from Kyoto. The second chapter is the longest in the book, containing the biographies of Jodo nuns from olden times to 1960.

his master's teachings, simplified and modified here and there, the sect he founded is better known as the Jodo Shinshu sect. The date of its foundation is taken to be 1224 in which year appeared *Kyogyo-Shinsho*, Shinran's exposition and systematization of the Nembutsu cult. Shinran describes himself as one believing in what was handed down to him by the old masters and his writings are generally expository in character.

The Amidism of the Jodo sect represents a new orientation of Japanese Buddhism. It had started as a 'teaching Buddhism' at Nara—a kind of academic Buddhism, demanding much earnest study in its metaphysics and philosophy and calling for severe mental and moral discipline. It was transformed by Amidism into a 'praying' Buddhism. Yet, however simple the faith, Honen and Shinran had to delve deep in the scripture to find for it the exact spiritual sanction.

We have dealt at some length with Amidism and the Jodo sect which was its product, because no school of Buddhist thought ever became so intimately and widely popular in Japan. Other schools were for the elect and the initiate; this was for the common man. Even in the social and political revolution of the Kamakura period that followed, while Zen Buddhism spread among the upper classes of society, the Shoguns and the Samurai,—Amidism remained the faith of commonalty.

In the after-years the Amidist school had to run the gauntlet of other Buddhist schools and Honen himself to suffer persecution and banishment. But the Jodo sect to this day is active in Japan with its stand on the creed that "we become Bodhisattvas when we believe in the Buddha's Original Vow and call the Nembutsu".[25] There are today 10 Jodo sub-sects in Japan.

Nichiren: Founder of a 'Nationalist Buddhism'.

Somewhat unique among Japanese Buddhist sects is the sect of Nichiren. The other sects were founded on Chinese texts and the teachings of Chinese masters. Nichiren took his stand on his personal conviction that Japan's destiny was linked with the acceptance of '*true* Buddhism' and that she was destined to propagate and establish it in the world.

Nichiren (1222-1282) was the son of a fisherman, but his mind was not in the family occupation. Right from his youth, the question why Buddhism should have so many and such different interpretations by sectarians disturbed and haunted his mind. In search of the particular scripture which represented Buddhism truly, he betook himself at the age of twenty-one to the great Tendai institute on Mount Hei. The belief grew increasingly strong within him that the 'Lotus Sūtra' (*Saddharma-puṇḍarīka*) alone was

[25] See *Jodo Shinshu* (*An Introduction to the Authentic Pure-Land Teaching*), Preface, (published by the Otani University, Kyoto, 1961).

the depository of pure and genuine Buddhism. The other *sūtras* and commentaries were regarded by him as perversions of it, with the possible exception, as he conceded, of Saicho's interpretations of the doctrines of the Tendai.

Nichiren came to believe that he was divinely appointed to fight and destroy all heresies against the doctrines of the *Lotus Sūtra.* Relying on a prophecy of ancient tradition that Buddhism would collapse in the world after a specified tale of centuries and re-rise in a purified form through the lips of the Buddha, he arrogated to himself the function of this resurrected Buddha of the future. Nichiren was a nationalist and his mind was set on saving the future of his country: that future, as he believed, was at stake so long as perverted forms of Buddhism kept battening on official favour. Wishing that the State should encourage and foster true Buddhism, if the future of the country was to be assured, he addressed several letters on this topic to the political and ecclesiastical authorities of the time. The result was that Nichiren was regarded as a fanatic and kept under surveillance and finally prosecuted. He was sentenced to death, but for some reason or other the sentence was not carried out. The legend is that at the moment of execution, the executioner's sword, struck by lightning, dropped from his hand. But though he escaped death, he had to suffer imprisonment and exile more than once and this he did bravely without flinching.

A strange thing, however, happened to restore him for a time to official favour. There was a prophecy on record to which he had drawn official attention that unless Japan saw her way to adopting 'true Buddhism', she would be exposed to attack by a foreign power. Sometime after Nichiren had warned officials of this possibility, the prophecy seemed fulfilled by Kubla Khan's invasion of Japan in 1271. There was dismay in the ranks of government; a Ninno service[26] was held and divine powers were invoked to protect the realm. Nichiren also was asked to join the Ninno service 'as an appointed priest'. But he curtly declined,—he was no seeker of official favour.

A large number of polemical and dissertative works was produced by Nichiren. The original manuscripts of these works are preserved as holy relics at the Taiseki Temple. But the works are now available in print in four volumes compiled by the Rissho University of Tokyo and published in 1952-1959.

Among them is the *Rissho Ankoku Ron* which means 'the establishment of the Legitimate Teaching for the security of the country'. The prophecy

---

[26] "This service included readings from the *Ninno Kyo* or Sutra of the Benevolent King, which treats of the duties of monarchs and the protection of States. It was a regular part of court ceremonial from 800 or thereabouts"—Sansom's *A History of Japan*, Vol. I p. 441, footnote 4.

of a foreign invasion of Japan (which turned out to be the Mongol invasion) was first made in this work. The only way to avert it, Nichiren had declared, was to adopt as basic what he regarded as the Buddha's 'true teaching', viz., the *Lotus Sūtra.* In his time the most popular religion was Amidism and he had directed in *Senjakushu* his sharpest attacks on Honen and his manifesto of Nembutsu. To replace Honen's formula of *Nemu Amida Butsu,* he invented a new one, *Namu Myoho-renge-Kyo* (Salutation to the *Saddharma-puṇḍarīka Sūtra*). Out of the experiences of his own life, he preached to his followers the value of suffering and he believed himself to be the Buddha as described in the *Lotus Sūtra, i.c. Sadāparibhūta* ('the ever-chastised one') and yet at the same time *viśiṣta-caritra,* 'one of Superb Action'.

Nichiren was no nationalist in a political sense, except that be believed that Japan at some future time would be the centre of a regenerate Buddhism and head of the Buddhist world. His mission, as he felt, was to convert Japan, and the whole world through the mediation of Japan, to the 'true teaching' of Buddhism.

The saint who was the 'son of a fisherman' is now deified and worshipped by his followers as the only 'True Buddha'. His worship is conducted in the great Nichiren establishment, Taisekiji, at the foot of the sacred Fuji-san mountain. A temple houses his carved image and manuscripts in his handwriting are preserved as sacred relics and shown on festival occasions to the faithful.

The spirit of deified Nichiren,—fiery and fanatical, bent through all sufferings to save his country by the restitution of the Buddha's true Teaching, —influences to this day the sect he founded. Its members in Japan, moved by a spirit of nationalism, are active in all fields of national life. Its action arm is an organisation named Sokagakkai, which is trying to spread the message of Nichiren to other countries and is energetic in all spheres of national welfare, including political activities. Perhaps the Nichiren sect is the most 'this-wordly' of all the Buddhist sects of Japan.

The Cult and Culture of Zen

The shift of the central government from Kyoto to Kamakura in 1192 was through a bloody revolution that saw instituted the Sogunate, the feudal system of mediaeval Japan, and its government known as the Bakufu. Kyoto remained just a ceremonial capital where the emperor had his residence.

It was at Kamakura that Zen Buddhism started to propagate itself first among the Shoguns (feudal lords) and the aristocracy. Its pioneer was Eisai (1141-1215). He had brought to Japan from China both Zen and Tea,—both to be assimilated later in the culture of Japan.

Buddhism came to be looked upon as Japan's national religion by the Japanese by the middle of the 12th century. It had by then acquired a 'this-worldly' bias: it stood for prosperity in this world no less than for happiness in the next. It was supposed to be linked with the country's destiny. Both Nichiren and Eisai regarded Buddhism as the securest standby for the people in times of difficulty and distress, though they differed regarding the form of Buddhism best for the country. Both Nichiren's *Rissho Ankoku Ron* and Eisai's *Kozen Gokoku Ron* stress this temporal value of Buddhism as the nation's ultimate source of strength. Nichiren belonged to no recognized school, but Eisai had come back from China a full-fledged master of Zen.

He settled under the patronage of the Hojo regents at Kamakura, the new capital. Moving in high society, he started in this capital city to bring about a *rapprochement* between the Shogun rulers and the Zen sect.

It was an age of rank militarism. Yet strangely enough, it was among the ruling warrior-class that Zennism first began to spread. Eisai's conversion at Kamakura of the Shoguns to the faith was ably seconded by another Zen-master Muso Soseki (1275-1351) who was known as the 'National Master of Seven Reigns'. Power changed hands quickly in those unsettled times, and Soseki carried on his ministrations during seven reigns, greatly honoured at court and eminently successful in cementing alliance between Zennism and the war-lords and aristocracy. The famous Zen monastery at Kamakura, Tenryuji, was erected in his honour by the first Ashikaga Shogun, Takauji (1305-1358).

The question what affinities there could be between the warrior-class and the meditative religion of Zen has often been posed, but there is no satisfactory answer. Yet it has to be considered that the most cultured among the Japanese of this age belonged to this class. They were warriors by profession, not shrinking from its incidental cruelties, but were at the same time inheritors of Japanese culture,—aesthetes by taste and temperament. Perhaps they were led by their ingrained aesthetic sensibilities to see in Zen trends of thought and attitudes to life that held possibilities of enriching life with new forms of aesthetic experience.

Anyway Zen was so favoured by the top men of the Bakufu that during the Ashikaga Shogunate, known as the Muromachi Era (1338-1573), Zen priests led foreign missions, controlled educational institutions and occupied all cultural offices in the State. Zen had little to do with art or aesthetics, but through its organised official influence it inculcated among the intelligentsia of Japan standards of taste and principles of social behaviour, while stimulating at the same time certain special and distinctive trends of thought and feeling about individual and social life. In fact, Zen teaching prepared the soil out of which flowered in that age the art-forms and aesthetic principles which have become Japan's cultural heritage.

The common people since the 12th century had remained adherents of Amidist Buddhism and the Pure Land cult; the rulers and warrior-class, including the Shoguns and the Samurai, from the 13th century to the 19th, held Zennism,—a long epoch of five centuries during which most of the typical art-forms of Japan came to birth. "The influence of this (Zen school)", says Sansom, "has been so subtle and pervading that it has become the essence of her (Japan's) culture. To follow its ramifications in thought and sentiment, in letters and behaviour, would be to write inexhaustibly the most difficult and most fascinating chapter of her spiritual history......'[27]

"What is Zen?"

Since Dr. Suzuki first introduced Zen Buddhism to the western world in his *Essays* in 1927, the question, 'what is Zen?', has never been laid to rest. It crops up persistently in all books on Zen which have been written since. Perhaps only the Zen practitioner, who has undergone its discipline in a *Zen-do* (Zennist meditation hall) is capable of finding the answer. But the outsider's reactions to Zen are bound to be irreconcilably different. Much of Zen—both its faith and its discipline,—may strike him as absurd, even grotesque, justifying Arthur Koestler's depreciatory account of it in his challenging work, *The Lotus and the Robot*. The fact, however, is that the Zen system, both as faith and as practice, scarcely becomes understandable unless looked at in its own light and from its own peculiar standpoint. A sizable literature on Zen is now available, and Dr. Suzuki, the pioneer of our knowledge of Zennism, has himself produced more than a hundred titles in English which we have drawn upon rather freely in the following pages.

Zen is a Japanese equivalent for Chinese *Cha'an* which in its turn is a phonetic form of Sanskrit, *Dhyāna* (Meditation). Its obvious meaning is absorption in one's inner self,—withdrawal from the world into one's deeper consciousness,—and the Buddha himself is said in the canon to have practised it in his solitary hours. But although *Dhyāna* is represented as an essential practice in spiritual living, there is no 'school' of *Dhyāna* in Indian Buddhism. But a '*Dhyāna*' school was founded in China under the inspiration of an Indian Buddhist saint who landed in Canton in 527. His personality and life-story are heavily shrouded in legends from which one historical episode has emerged into the dynastic histories (*Shu*) of both the Wei and the Liang. It is of his interview at Nanking, early in his career in China, with the Chinese Emperor. The latter spoke to him of his own outstanding services to the holy cause of Buddhism in his realm, to which

[27] Sansom's *A History of Japan*, Vol. I, p. 329

the former's reply was: "Where everything is emptiness, nothing can be called holy". The emperor, amazed and astounded, asked: "Who is he who tells me thus?" "I do not know", replied the saint and left the audience hall. The saint of such curt manners and brief speech is known as Dharmabodhi or Bodhidharma in China and as Daruma in Japan.

He wrote no books, went on no missionary tour, recommended for study to his disciples only a single scriptural text, *Laṅkāvatāra Sūtra*, and died, wrapped in meditation with his face constantly to a wall, in the Shao-lin monastery outside the outskirts of Loyang. But he left a large number of disciples, among whom was the principal Chinese disciple Hui-ke, the actual founder of the *Cha'an* school in China.

The *Cha'an* school had had about six centuries of development in that country before the visit of Eisai, its pioneer in Japan. He had found Buddhism of that school widely prevalent in China and, having studied and practised it, came back to Japan in 1197. Along with the practice of *Cha'an*, he introduced into Japan a new beverage, tea, the drinking of which, at first a ritual concomitant of Zen, became in later times a social ceremony in Japan, not obsolete yet.

Zen relies on no scripture, though it cherishes records of the lives and teachings of the great Chinese and Japanese Zen masters, drawing upon them to illustrate Zennism and to collect *Koans* (See *infra*). It relies instead on the personal transmission of its truth from master to disciple. This is done under a system, the specialty and singularity of which is that it negates the faculty of Reason as a means of approach to truth. Truth, on the other hand, the Zennist believes, bursts of itself on the consciousness that has received 'enlightenment' from the practice of Zen discipline.

There are three key-terms in Zen discipline. They do not open wholly, but throw a little ajar, the closed door that Zen presents to the uninitiated mind. It is necessary first to seize on the connotation and significance of these terms, for they act as sign posts to indicate both the goal and the way of Zen discipline.

Three Zen terms

(i) SATORI (Enlightenment)—The attainment of *Satori* is the aim and object of Zen discipline; it is defined by Dr. Suzuki as "acquiring a new view-point for looking into the essence of things".[28] Much has been written on the subject by modern exponents of Zen, but the essential mystery of it remains. The mystery lies in its absolute unpredictability, the lightning-like suddenness with which it comes and in a moment illumines the Zen practitioner's entire range of consciousness. It cannot be 'acquired'

[28] *An Introduction to Zen Buddhism* (Rider and Company, London, Reprint, 1960), p. 88.

but it comes in a flash like an outbreak in the mind, ushering in the dawn of a new insight. By this insight, one knows things not by the normal, static and discriminative means of cognition, but things *as they really are* in their eternal flux, released from time and space and all conceptual distinctions. It is an experience so unique and individualistic and so rooted in the individual consciousness that it is incapable of being imparted by one to another.

Among Zen masters, there was some difference of opinion whether Satori was 'sudden' or 'gradual'. But its pre-condition was recognised by all of them to be a rigorous, well-guided, special mental discipline. It is to receive this discipline that a trainee has to betake himself to a Zen establishment and place himself under a Zen master.

The discipline consists in bringing about a complete transformation of his existing mental make-up,—first emptying the mind of all *ideas*, even to their last vestige, as illustrated in the following story. A pupil asked his master, 'Zen emphasises the need of expulsion of every idea. Am I right when I have no idea?' The master replied, 'Throw away that idea of yours'. 'I have told you that I have no idea. What can I throw away?' Said the master in reply: 'You are free of course to carry about with you that useless idea of no-idea'.[29] In the second place, the discipline consists in turning the wholly emptied idealess mind, one-pointed on the solution of a given *Koan* (Riddle).

A Chinese Zen master of the 13th century describes the disciplinary process thus :

> "The *Koan* I ordinarily give to my pupils is:
> 'All things return to the One; where does the One return?' I make them search after this. To search after it means to awaken a great enquiring spirit for the ultimate meaning of the *Koan*. The multitudinousness of things is reducible to the One, but where does this One finally return? I say to them: Make this enquiry with all the strength that lies in your personality, giving yourself no time to relax in this effort. In whatever physical position you are, and in whatever business you are employed, never pass your time idly. Where does the One finally return? Do not give yourself up to a state of doing nothing; do not exercise your fantastic imagination, but try to bring about a state of perfect identification by pressing your spirit of enquiry forward, steadily and uninterruptedly. You will be then like a person who is critically ill, having no appetite for what you eat or drink. Again you will be like an idiot with no knowledge of what is what. When your searching spirit comes to this stage, the

[29] Christmas Humphrey's *Zen Buddhism* (William Heineman Ltd., London, 1949), p. 138.

time has come for your mental flower to burst out".[30]

The 'bursting out of this mental flower' in all its unpredictability and suddenness is a *Satori*. It is the consummation of what is called *Zazen* (See *infra*).

In *Satori* a consciousness that was latent so long, floats up to the surface of the mind: the process may be started by the rap of *shippe* (vide *infra*), a shout or a blow, the utterance of a joke or a paradox or by silence itself. But its effect is to transform for a man his entire world-view, putting him at a point from where he has an unexpected insight into his own nature and the nature of reality. It opens to him at a knock that inscrutable world of Kegon philosophy named *Jiji Muge Hokkai* in Japanese (*Jiji* meaning 'things'; *muge*, 'without hindrance'; '*hokkai*' 'the material universe', 'the *Dharmadhātu*': that is, the universe in its primordial condition where no distinction existed between thing and thing, and all things were interconvertible, interfused and confluent.[31]

Approaches to an experience of the same kind, of a 'universal oneness', have been made by poets and saints of different countries and times of which instances are given in the popular pages of Suzuki, Ruth Sasaki, Christmas Humphreys and other modern writers on Zen. But it is Zen only that recognises fully that the experience of 'oneness' may come *not* through conclusions of intellectual thinking, not through the musings of metaphysics or philosophy, but through sudden emergence of a level of consciousness latent in each individual,—so deep-lying that none of our names or concepts of things is able to reach it. The experience shuts out all discrimination. "When the mind discriminates, there is manifoldness of things; when it does not, it looks into the true state of things" (Suzuki).

The realities of the world do not change for the man whose consciousness has risen to this 'true state of things'. Only the things take on a new meaning for him which is not in their outward showing. He comes back to the world after *Satori* and sees its realities, but with eyes that have seen into their fundamental oneness.

> "A master says : Before a man studies Zen, mountains are mountains and waters are waters. But when he obtains a glimpse with the truth of Zen, through the instruction of a good master, mountains are no longer mountains, nor waters waters; later, however, when he has really reached the place of Rest (i.e. has attained *Satori*), mountains are again mountains, and waters are waters" (Suzuki).

Satori is the aim of Zen; "it is its *raison d'etre* and without it Zen is no

---

[30] Suzuki's *Essays in Zen Buddhism* (*Second Series*) (published by Rider and Company, London, Second Impression, 1958) pp. 121-122.

[31] See Ruth Sasaki's *Zen*: *A Religion* (published by The First Zen Institute of America Inc., New York, 1958), pp. 14-15.

Zen".[32] The importance of *Zazen* and the *Koan* exercise is only ancillary. Each course of *Zazen* may result in a *Satori* which is a sudden 'enlightenment' of consciousness. But before one can habitually perceive things (*Jiji*) in the light of *Satori*, one has to discipline one's mind by solving a large number of *Koans* (vide *infra*).

(ii) ZAZEN (Seated Meditation)—It means 'meditation' (in its special Zen connotation) for which a particular sitting posture is prescribed. It is not the mere concentration of mind on a self-chosen subject, but a complete course of meditation,—intense, 'one-pointed', directed straight to the solution of a Koan set by a Zen master.

In a Zennist institution, a hall or dormitory, called *Zen-do*, is appointed in which the practitioners sit in rows in perfect stillness, in a particular sedentary posture, with their minds attuned to the highest key of intensity. A supervisor is present with a stick, about one and a half feet long, called *Shippe*, made of a split bamboo tied up with a rattan, and he raps with it anyone who may seem to be slipping down from the requisite level of mental intensity.

Dr. Suzuki points out the difference between meditation in its ordinary sense and the Zen meditation, *Zazen*. The former implies a subject and an object, but the latter is a very different kind of exercise,—it is a kind of self-immersion in 'universal life-activity',—something like existentialism in practice.

> "To meditate, a man has to fix his thoughts on something......Meditation is something artificially put on; it does not belong to the native activity of the mind. Upon what do the fowls of the air meditate? Upon what the fish in the water? They fly; they swim......Zen just feels fire warm and ice cold; because when it freezes, we welcome fire. The feeling is all in all, as Faust declares; all our theorisation fails to touch reality. But the feeling here must be understood in its deepest sense or in its purest form. Even to say that 'this is feeling' means that Zen is no more there. Zen defies all concept-making".[33]

(iii) KOAN (Riddle-solution Exercise)—The Japanese word, *Koan*, comes from Chinese *Kung-an* which means a 'public document'. The sense perhaps is that of an open standard of judgment by which one's correct Zen understanding of things may be tested. It is of the nature of a question-paper set at a public examination. Usually a *Koan* represents some saying of an old Zen master or a question propounded by him or some attitude or gesture of his, culled from his biography, and offered to the Zen practitioner for interpretation or solution.

---

[32] Suzuki's *Introduction to Zen Buddhism*, p. 95.

[33] Suzuki's *An Introduction to Zen Buddhism* (Rider and Company, London, Reprint 1960), p. 41.

It is said that there are 1,700 *koans* which a Zen practitioner must solve correctly before he can qualify as a master.

In the Zennist system a *koan* is given by the master (*Roshi*) to a Zen practitioner to meditate on and solve and produce his solution to the master at a formal interview (*San-zan*).

The 'public document' is in the form of a riddle propounded in such terms that no solution of it is possible by the process of mere reasoning. Reason is kept at bay; intuition at large. It is only when the practitioner's intuition is most precisely aligned to that of the author of the riddle that the *Koan* begins to take a meaning.

Almost all *Koans* in Zen repertory will appear hopeless, nearly nonsensical, to a mind conditioned to seek the solution of a problem by step-by-step reasoning. A *Koan* halts the process at the very start. It may seem to contain a premise and a conclusion, but with no conceivable nexus between them, or posit a state of things without any conceivable correspondence to reality. All *Koans* are deliberately and emphatically 'anti-rational'.

A popular *Koan* may be cited for an example. It is of classic derivation, having been propounded by the great Chinese Zen master Hakuin (1683-1768), about 'the sound of one hand'. The master is said to have stretched out one hand to the pupils and bade them describe its *sound*.[34] It is commonsense that until both hands are clapped no sound can be produced. Seemingly a fantastic notion, the master must himself have been conscious of the possibility or reality of the 'sound of one hand', and the only way of solving the *Koan* was to bring up by a process of *Zazen* the level of one's own consciousness to that of the master's.

The *Koan* practice, borrowed from the Chinese Zen masters, is the only valid teaching in the Japanese Rinzai school of Zen. Dr. Suzuki, who is of this school, remarks: "To seek Sotori without a Koan is like boiling sands which will never yield nourishing rice".[35] But Dogen (1200-1253), from whom the later Soto school of Zen derives, rejected the practice on the ground that it was not the true Buddhist way: "By reflecting upon various 'public cases' (*Koan*) and dialogues of the patriarchs, one may perhaps get the sense of them, but it will only result in one's being led astray from the way of the Buddha. Just to pass the time in sitting straight, without any thought of acquisition, without any sense of achieving enlightenment—this is the way of the Founder".[36]

Zen and Japanese Culture

[34] *Ibid*, p. 109.

[35] Suzuki's *Essays in Zen Buddhism* (Second series) (published by Rider and Company, London) Second Impression 1958, p. 123.

[36] See *Sources of Japanese Culture*, p. 253.

It was not till the close of the 'middle ages' of Japan that culture was available for commonalty in the country. The Edo Period (1615-1866) came in when the old clan-feuds had petered out and peace was back again. It was a period of multiplication of printing presses when book-trade was brisk and a number of schools functioned to dispense liberal education. But before the Edo period, culture in Japan had always been the preserve of a class or a closed community. This was the old culture-tradition of Japan: it held ground till a new order was established in the 17th century.

As culture was treated as a 'preserve', the exclusive property of the *elitè* of society, its characteristic type was determined by the major interests or the habitual inclinations of its custodians. Thus the sinified Buddhist culture of the Nara period, proceeding from the Buddhist priesthood, was different from the care-free, sensuous and sophisticated culture of the Heian when it was in the hands of the gay nobility and the *jeunesse doree*, the type of whom is Prince Genji, hero of the most representative romance of this period. Likewise the Zennist-aesthetic culture of the Shogunate period was moulded by the feudal lords (*Shoguns*) and the feudatory warrior chiefs (*Samurai*) who held the stage of history in mediaeval Japan.

Of these different culture-types, it is the mediaeval 'Zennist-aesthetic' that has passed into Japan's cultural heritage, and in speaking of the special traits and distinctions of Japanese culture, we refer most often to the arts, customs, institutions and conventions that grew up in the mediaeval period. Their vitality is due perhaps to the fact that this mediaeval culture was most typically Japanese, most representative of the native genius. Aestheticism was its very soul.

It took shape and prevailed under the Shogunate, that is under the mediaeval social and political order, attaining its spring-tide and flowering maturity under the Ashikaga Shoguns,—in what is called the 'Muromachi Period' (1334-1573) of Japanese history. As in previous periods, this culture was the preserve of the upper classes, the Shoguns (Feudal lords) and the Sammurai (Warriors in feudal relations to them). They were adherents of Zen Buddhism, while among commonalty, the older Amidist faith prevailed.

The political and social history of these centuries, however, reveals a picture in which an advance in culture or refinement of life would seem an incongruity, uncongenial to the historical setting.

It was not a peaceful, but a much distracted age in which clan pursued clan with long and ruthless vendetta,—one in which the 'sophistications and refinements of life' of the previous Heian period, so well reflected in the *Genji Monogatari*, were replaced in the upper classes by 'a general turbulence, a wild ebullient tenor of life with a background of danger and stark brutality.'[37] Those classes which were the privileged custodians of this culture

[37] See *Sources of Japanese Culture*, p. 253.

—the Shoguns and the Samurai,—were involved in bloody feuds sparked by mutual jealousies, personal rivalries and lust for power. From the brutalising effects of these feuds, what redeemed them was their Zen Buddhism.

Coming under its influence, the age grew Janus-faced as it were—one face turned to cultural and aesthetic refinements and the other to the excitements of war. Those who suffered most from the unsettled war-torn condition of the country, that is, common men on lower rungs of society, clung in despair to the cult of Amida, which promised to the faithful, after their hopeless miserable life of the present, rebirth in Amida's 'Land of Eternal Bliss'.

Yet the Shoguns and the Samurai, who carried on the incessant internecine warfare of this age and made intolerable the life of the common man, were not men without culture or the finer sensibilities.

The Shogun, involved in intrigue and preparing for feud, was by no means a moralist, but he was an aesthete more or less by taste and temperament. The Samurai was not just a war-toughened warrior; he had caught the refining influence of Zennism; on his sword-hilt often appeared as a token the picture of the founder of Zen, Bodhidharma (Daruma in Japanese) with his swarthy face, staring eyes, shaggy beard and gnarled limbs. The 'stark brutality' of his profession was mollified by the adoption of a code of knightly behaviour known as *Bushido* (Way of a Warrior). How his love of Nature, a Zennist trait, remained unspoiled by a life of constant soldering is expressed exquisitely by a representative of this class, a prince of Shirakawa, in a book of jottings of his random thoughts:

> "Though they come stealing to your bedside in the silent watches of the night, drive not away, but rather cherish these: the fragrance of flowers, the sound of distant bells, the insect hummings of a frosty night.
>
> "Though they may wound your feelings, these three only you have to forgive: the breeze that scatters your flowers, the clouds that hide your moon, and the man who tries to pick quarrels with you.".[38]

No wonder that the Samurai warrior was looked upon as 'the glass of fashion and mould of form' in mediaeval Japan.

It cannot be ascertained how many among the Shoguns and the Samurai were actual practitioners of Zen, but Zennism, apart from its practical discipline, inculcated its own idealistic view of life and its own scale and standard of life's values. True to the genius of the race, the Japanese deduced from them an 'art of living' that represented the aristocratic culture of the time. Zen, as we have remarked before, had little to do with art or

[38] Quoted from Inazo Nitobe's *Bushido* (1938 Ed.), p. 49.

aestheticism, but in Zennism the Shoguns and the Samurai discovered principles to guide them in the pursuit of both life and art. Their 'art of living' may indeed be described as a distillation from the philosophy of Zen.

The Ashikaga Shoguns (1335-1573) as rulers enjoy no good odour in Japanese history. But in their patronage of art and culture, they were the Medici of feudal Japan. It was under this Shogunate that painting, porcelain, faience, lacquer-work and demascening attained to the finest beauty of design and workmanship, while in the fine arts, the *Noh* drama and the classical *Bugaku* music were developed under court patronage. The tone of culture was set by some of the Shoguns themselves who commanded wealth enough, though by questionable means, to indulge in the most expensive luxuries.

Yet, as we are told, "they loved thatched cottages as simple as those of the peasants, but whose proportions were designed by the highest genius of Shojo or Soami, and whose pillars were of the costliest incense-wood from the farthest of Indian islands; even whose iron-kettles were marvels of workmanship by Sesshu".[39]

This aesthetic type of culture became in that age the aristocratic culture of Japan—the Daimyo hiding his costliest art-collections in the treasure-house and bringing out only one art-object at a time to satisfy his aesthetic sense; the Samurai keeping his blades of wonderful workmanship in plin unpretentious scabbards, and people wearing their costliest stuffs as under-garments.

What was 'aristocratic' culture in the middle ages is now the common heritage of Japanese culture. It is summed up in the Japanese term of aesthetics, *Shibhumi,* for which there is no foreign equivalent. It means the appreciation of beauty that is quiet and subdued, natural and deep, simple without crudity and austere without severity, avoiding, instinctively as it were, self-consciousness and ostentation. Something parallel to Japanese *Shibhumi* appears perhaps in Keats's aesthetic approach to the Grecian urn, "the foster-child of silence and slow time".

Through all the art-forms that originated in mediaeval Japan, we find *Shibhumi* diffused.

These art-forms have not lacked interpreters, technical and historical, since Ernest Fenellosa. The forms recognise no principle or rule of scale—greatness or smallness being immaterial to the expression or exercise of art in Japan. From large painting on silk or paper in Indian ink, in colours or in monochrome, to the making of *inros* and *netsukis* (minute landscape or seascape on button or small lacquered wooden plate), from largely planned landscape-gardening to the miniature *bonsuki* (imitation garden on

[39] Longford's *Japan* ('Nations of Today' series), p. 107 (quoting Brinley).

wooden plate), from the ornate eves and sweeping curves of a Buddhist temple to the barest simplicity of a Shinto shrine or a tea-cottage, Japanese art is supremely regardless of scale measurement.

Grandeur is therefore alien to all its forms. Being dependent for effect on range and scale, it is not reconcilable to the Japanese aesthetic sense, which is habitually repelled by what in its nature is striking and self-assertive. The Japanese are no doubt great builders of ships, railways and skyscrapers. But these are utilitarian constructions. Where art is concerned, the Japanese, as Dr. Nitobe observed, "are great in small things".[40] The elements of the grand and the grotesque in the art and architecture of Nara, Heian and even of later periods are unassimilated, dictated more by the spirit of imitation of the Chinese than by spontaneous temperamental preference.

The art-forms that are characteristically Japanese have grown from a soil impregnated with Zennist ideas and they smack perceptibly of the soil.

There are two terms *Sabi* and *Wabi* in Japanese aesthetics— the former related to the verb, *Sabiru*, meaning 'to grow rusty'—hence suggesting the taking of pleasure in what is 'old' or 'faded';[41] the latter interpreted by Dr. Suzuki as "the aesthetic appreciation of deficiency or poverty". It is illustrated in this *Haiku* by Bode poetising what seems but a paradox.

> "In my hut, this New Year's time there is nothing—which means that in it there is everything".

Sabi and *Wabi* are not distinguishable, for in Zennist notion they are aspects of the same fundamental quality.

The manifestation of *Wabi*, in both life and art, lies in that kind of expression which, by its very reticence or incompleteness of form, becomes infinitely suggestive or symbolical, and which, by its bare solitariness, fills and enriches with significance the emptiness around it. *Wabi* was the practice of the Zen masters; by a mere explosive sound, an uplifted finger, a simple poise of the body, a twist of the lips or even by utter silence, they were wont to convey an infinitude of meaning and significance.

Some legends of mediaeval Japan will serve to show how *Wabi* was taken up and practised in Japanese culture.

In the 16th century, the morning glory was a rare plant in Japan. Rikyu, the leading aesthete of Japan of that time, had planted a whole garden with morning glory which used to attract admiring crowds of visitors. The great warrior and statesman Hideyoshi, a friend of Rikyu's, expressed a desire to see the flower and was invited by Rikyu. When the visitor turned up, he was surprised to see no trace of the flower anywhere. The whole garden

[40] Nitobe's *Lectures on Japan* (delivered in America, 1932-33 and published in 1936), p. 319.

[41] See *Sources of Japanese Tradition*, pp. 286-287.

had been levelled and strewn with sand and pebbles. He was then conducted to the tea-room, where, lo, in the alcove (*Tokonoma*) was an old bronze vase—only one,—holding a vine of morning glory with a single white blossom nestling in a few green leaves wet with dew.

Another Japanese aesthete Iyehara Jizen was the owner of a famous flower-vase of bamboo which bore the name Onjoji. It was a fashion in Japan in those days to christen with names tea-pots and flower-vases of artistic distinction. Jizen had promised to show the flower-vase to a friend and for that purpose invited him to tea. A special tea-house was constructed for the occasion in which no bamboo-work was visible and all bamboo clumps growing along the garden-path and in the vicinity were cut down and removed. All this was done to secure for the visitor the greatest possible intensity of aesthetic feeling for the solitary bamboo flower-vase set in the alcove.

In different ways illustrative of the *Wabi* principle are (i) the aestheticized simplicity of the Japanese tea-ceremony, (ii) the traditional 'thrifty-brush' mode of Japanese painting which was probably of Chinese derivation, with its large suggestive blank spaces on cloth or silk, (iii) the quality called *Yugen* of the Japanese *Noh* drama, (iv) the typical Japanese domestic architecture and its interior decor, and, lastly (v) the elemental quality of Japanese Haiku poetry. One may indeed say that the masterpiece of Japanese painting, Miyamoto's sketch of a singing bird on a dead branch, Rikyu's showing of a single spray of morning glory to General Hideyoshi and Basho's typical *Haiku* on a frog splashing into an ancient pond are all inspired by the same spirit,—the *Sumiye* ('thrifty-brush' painting), the *Chao-no-yu* (tea-ceremony) and the *Haiku* are unified by the same quality, call it *Sabi* or *Wabi*.

We have quoted Suzuki's interpretation of Zennist meditation as a kind of self-immersion in the universal life-activity of Nature. If the interpretation be right, which none but a Zennist meditator can judge, Nature as presented in Haiku poetry is just Nature as perceived in this way of meditation. The poet's ego is drowned completely in the moment's perception: there is an utter absence of the subjective element. It is not the transcript or impression or, far less, an interpretation of Nature, but just—snow falling on the sacred mount Fujisan, the cherry blossoming, the mist or rain over landscape or bay, cicadas buzzing, birds chirping and fireflies twinkling, —all the life-activity of Nature in which the poet himself is immersed.

Two Zen-inspired Literary Forms

Two forms of literary art originated in Japan during the Shogunate period—the *Noh* drama (14th century) and the *Haiku* poetry (17th century).

The *Noh* drama as a literary form was evolved out of the old song-dances of Japan by a distinguished actor and writer Kanami (1337-1384) and his son Zeami (1363-1443) who both enjoyed the patronage of the third Ashikaga Shogun, Yoshimitsu. In addition to his dramatic activities, Zeami composed a number of works in which he explained the nature of the *Noh* play and the aesthetic principles governing it.[42]

The *Noh* theatre has its standardised stage-arrangement and stage-properties, among which are masks of different kinds, orchestral music, songs and dances. There are different schools of *Noh* with their own repertories. The plots are drawn from both Japanese and foreign sources, being mythical or legendary, fantastic, historical or contemporary. Apart from its artistic and dramatic significance, the *Noh* drama "is of paramount historical interest in as much it reflects, as no other Japanese work does, the feelings, thoughts, beliefs, superstitions and aspirations and in short the moral and intellectual life of the people during one of the stormiest periods of its history".[43] Derived from these mixed source materials, the Buddhist themes are outstanding in *Noh* plays and Zen saints and Zen masters are prominent among the *personae.*

But the play is not presented as a mere entertaining spectacle. Instilled into each is a kind of symbolism —a suggestion that more is meant than meets the eye and the ear —and this is achieved not only by the action of the play but also by intervals of "no-action".

Zeami in his exposition of *Noh* insists that all parts of a *Noh* play—the action and the actors, the plot and the dialogue, the mime and the song—should be instinct with what he calls *Yugen.* It is a Japanese aesthetic term untranslatable by a foreign equivalent. In the *Noh* play it implies symbolism—of the kind that leads the mind into realms of thought and feeling not immediately conveyed by the play itself. *Yugen* is implicit in many forms of mediaeval Japanese art, but the *Noh* theatre was the medium which carried it to its highest effect. It was what Zeami consciously aimed at in his own plays.

In parts of his exposition of *Yugen*, Zeami shows the influence of Zen teachings. He emphasizes for instance the 'no-action interval' of the *Noh* play when "dancing, singing, movements and the different types of miming"

---

[42] For the history and aesthetics of the *Noh* drama and English translations of ten *Noh* plays, see *The Noh Drama*, a work compiled by the Japanese Classics Translation Committee of the Nippon Gaku-jutsu Shinkokai and published by Tuttle Company from Tokyo (Second Printing 1961). For specimens of *Noh* drama, translated into English, see O' Neill's *A Guide to Noh*, published by Hinoki Shoten. It contains short summaries of about 240 plays from the repertories of different schools of *Noh*. See also Umeyo Hirano's *Buddhist plays from Japanese Literature*, published by The CIIB, Tokyo, 1962.

[43] *The Noh Drama*, Intro., p. xv.

are in abeyance, but the spectators' tension of mind is not relaxed. "The actions before and after an interval of 'no-action' must be linked by a state of 'mindlessness' in which one conceals even from oneself one's intent".[44] This suggests undoubtedly the spirit of *Zazen*. In another work Zeami expounds the 'Nine Stages of *Noh*'. Each of these stages is introduced with a sort of *Koan*, e.g., 'At midnight in Silla, the sun shines bright', 'snow covers a thousand mountains—why does one lonely peak remain unwhitened?' 'The sun sinks in the bright mist, the myriad mountains are crimson' etc.[45] Zeami's intention evidently was to bring the *Noh* play into line with Zennism, although in his writings on the *Noh* aesthetics he betrays the influence also of the Tendai and the Shingon.

The *Haiku* form of poetry took birth in Japan much later—in the 'Genroku Era' when aesthetes—then a class by profession—used to set the tone of cultured society. The originator of Haiku was Basho (1644-1694) who took his name, Bamboo, from a bamboo-hut in which he lived in a village of Japan. Basho and the poets of his school produced a mass of Haiku poems, but the first one composed by him has become a prototype of this form—the well-known Haiku:

"An ancient pond,
A frog jumps in,—
The sound of water".[46]

This Haiku has been variously interpreted both by Japanese and by western scholars. But one is left wondering whether Basho really intended this Haiku to be a symbolical presentation of Zennism itself—the frog jumping into the pond standing for the rap of a *shippe* and the sound of water, the sudden upbreak of *Satori*. All genuine Haiku follows this type.

'The moment is all'—is its formative principle; the momentariness is the essence. Stretch the moment, it loses its distinctive Haiku quality. And the supreme value of "the moment" was distilled into Zennism from a doctrine of Kegon philosophy that everything, sentient or non-sentient, represents just at the moment of its appearance the concentration of all time and space. "In you and in each one of them (i.e., sentient or non-sentient beings) *at this moment* is all time and all space".[47] Dr. Suzuki

[44] *Sources of Japanese Tradition*, p. 291. (Translated from Zeami)

[45] *Ibid.* pp. 292-293

[46] In Japanese the syllables are as follows :

"Furu ike ya
Kaeru Tobikomu
Mizuno Oto."

It is not clear whether it was one frog or many frogs that splashed into the pond. The singular and the plural have no formal distinction in both Chinese and Japanese.

[47] Sesaki's *Zen—A Religion*, p. 17.

thus amplifies the concept: "The philosophy of intuition takes time at its full value. It permits no ossification, as it were, of each moment. It takes hold of each moment as it is born from *Śūnyatā*. Momentariness is therefore characteristic of this philosophy. Each moment is absolute, alive and significant. The frog leaps, the cricket sings, a dew-drop glitters on the lotus-leaf, a breeze passes through the pine-branches, and the moonlight falls on the murmuring mountain-stream".[48]

Haiku can grow and flower out of Zennism alone: it is not capable of being transplanted to any other soil.

Japanese civilization has the knack of never allowing traditions to die. Whatever veneer it may assume through the impact of changing times and compelling circumstances, its substance is still a composite of traditions gathered from the historical experiences of the nation. So it is that Buddhism of different schools and different epochs from Nara downwards still survives in a multiplicity of sects and sub-sects; the art-forms developed in mediaeval Japan are still in practice, and life at the domestic level is still traditionally Japanese. The *Noh* plays still attract full houses and Haikus are composed even today. There have been several renewals of culture in Japan in her transitions from Nara to Kyoto, from Kyoto to Kamakura, from Kamakura to Edo (Tokyo), each shift of the capital betokening a new beginning. But Japan's break with the past has been political, social or economic, but rarely intellectual or cultural. Japanese civilization loses its character if we excise from it its aesthetic quality and that quality has been the contribution of Buddhism to native genius. "All the earliest manifestations of art in Japan (if we except certain prehistoric objects and some pre-Buddhistic metal work) in building, sculpture, painting, embroidery and calligraphy were due directly or indirectly to the introduction of Buddhism. Indeed it is scarcely possible to imagine Japanese civilization without the influence of Buddhism, for its aesthetic quality is one of its essential characteristics".[49]

Shinto and Ryobu Shinto

Shintoism had been the religion of Japan long before the introduction of Buddhism from Korea. Perhaps it was no more than a bundle of primitive beliefs implemented by some rituals until, under the impact of Buddhism, it was organised as a religion and called by the name of *Shinto*. Its meaning is 'the way of the gods' contra-distinguished from *Buppo* which means 'the way of the Buddha'. In any case, it is difficult to define what Shintoism had been exactly like before it came under the influence of Buddhism. In

[48] Suzuki's *Buddhism in the Life and Thought of Japan*, p. 27 (Cited in Humphrey's *Zen Buddhism*, pp. 107-108).

[49] Sansom's *A History of Japan*, vol. 1, P. 64.

its after-development, Shinto became Japan's 'national' religion. It had its own deities and shrines, its distinctive rites and ceremonies, its national festivals and forms of worship.

Shinto has no scripture, but the *Nihongi* and the *Kojiki*, which are the ancient chronicles of the country, are regarded by the Shintoist in the same light as the *Purāṇas* by the Hindus. They contain the mythology and cosmogony which invest the land of Japan and the ruling house of the Mikado with the sanctity of divine origin and descent. There is besides the liturgical collection called the *Norito*. The opening passage of the Shinto classic *Jinno-shotoki*, written by the consummate Shinto scholar Katabatake Chikajusa (1295-1354), sums up thus the Shintoist's peculiar regard for his country: "Japan is the country of the gods. The Heavenly Ancestors laid the foundation of the country; the Sun-goddess transmitted the long imperial line.................For this reason Japan is called the country of the gods".[50]

This Shinto myth, which isolated Japan and her Mikado, in the eyes of the people, from the rest of the world and its sovereigns, was revived in all its strength in the 18th century. It obtained in that century such hold on the Japanese mind that it continued to be cherished till Japan's defeat in the Second World War and occupation by the Americans. The 'Shinto Directive', issued by the Occupation on the 15th December, 1945, directed the division of the Shinto religion into State Shinto and Shrine Shinto. The former which had centralised the religion round the house of the Mikado and the imperial family was abolished; only the latter, i.e., the rites of worship at a shrine or in private household, was allowed to remain.[51] The 'Shrine Shinto' is practised all over Japan even to this day.

There are indigenous histories of Shintoism written in different epochs. They give clear evidence of the absorption, in course of its development *as a religion* over the centuries, of Confucian as well as Buddhist thought in a considerable measure. It is said that the Chinese influence on Shinto goes back to the reign of Emperor Ojin (C.270 B.C.) when two Korean priests came from Kudara (in Korea) and were appointed tutors to Prince Uji. When the Prince became Emperor Uji, he was, as some scholars hold, apotheosised as Hachiman, the Shinto god of war.[52] The influence of Buddhism on Shinto also started early,—in the Nara period (645-793 A.D.) about the time when the Todaiji Temple was founded in the reign of Emperor Shomu.

[50] Cited in *Sources of Japanese Tradition*, p. 274

[51] See Bunce's *Religion in Japan* (Tuttle and Company, Tokyo. Third printing, 1959), Chapter II on "Impact of Occupation on Japanese Religions".

[52] See *Studies in Shinto and Shrines* by Ponsonby-Fane, Ponsonby Memorial Society, Kyoto, (Revised Ed. 1953), pp. 44-45.

Shintoism has often been described as the 'worship of the *Kami*'—again a term which has no foreign equivalent. But to call Shintoism '*Kami*-worship' is an oversimplification, presenting it only on its external ritualistic side. On the other hand Shinto is a developed cult: it conglomerates in its substance materials from both Confucian and Buddhist sources and they are amalgamated with the native elements of the cult.

Thus, ancestor-worship and the concept of filial reverence in Shintoism came probably from Chinese Confucianism, as expounded in the Chinese classic *Hsio Ching*, a discourse in eighteen chapters by the Buddha to his disciple Tsang;[53] the idea of mental and moral purity as distinguished from physical and ceremonial purism, and also to some extent the Doctrine of *Karma*, were the contributions of Buddhism. But Shintoism's most characteristic and congenial expression is its attitude towards what are called *Kami*, 'superior beings', to whom we owe all the benefits in this life. An old Shinto saying thus differentiates Buddhism from Shinto: "The two systems run concurrently—Buddhism being looked for for favours to come, and the Shinto deities revered for favours received".[54]

It is difficult to define the character of these deified 'superior beings' of Shinto. Their general name *Kami* means just 'upper' or 'superior'. The foremost scholar of the Shinto revival of the eighteenth century, Motoori Norinaga, (1730-1801), writes thus on *Kami:*

> "I do not yet understand the meaning of the term *Kami*. Speaking in general, however, it may be said that Kami signifies, in the first place, the deities of heaven and earth that appear in the ancient records (i.e., *Nihongi* and *Kojiki*) and also the spirits of the shrines where they are worshipped. It is hardly necessary to say that it includes human beings (i.e., those great ones of the earth who have been deified). It also includes such objects as birds, beasts, trees, plants, seas, mountains, and so forth. In ancient usage, anything whatsoever that was out of the ordinary, possessed of superior power and was awe-inspiring, was called Kami. Eminence here does not refer merely to the superiority of nobility, goodness or meritorious deeds. Evil and mysterious things, if they are extraordinary and dreadful, are called Kami. It is needless to say that among human beings who are called Kami, the successive generations of sacred emperors are all included. The fact that emperors are called 'distant Kami' is because, from the standpoint of common people, they are far-separated, majestic and worthy of reverence. In a lesser degree we find, in the present as well as in ancient times, human beings who are Kami. Although

[53] This work, first published by a Chinese emperor in 722 A.D., has an English translation by Legge in Vol. III of the Sacred Books of the East series.

[54] See *Studies in Shinto and Shrines*, p. 51.

they may not be accepted throughout the whole country, yet in each province, each village, and each family there are human beings who are Kami, each according to his own proper position. The Kami of the divine age were for the most part human beings of that time and, because the people of that time were all Kami, it is called the Age of the Gods (Kami)".[55]

Evidently the Kami do not belong to a homogeneous pantheon, but hail from diverse sources. Hence they are indefinite in character and indeterminate in number. They are collectively designated as 'the Spirits of Heaven and Earth'. The 'spirits of heaven' are the figures of Shinto mythology that appear in the *Nihongi* and the *Kojiki*. They are given anthropomorphic representation when installed in shrines or in images.

But the 'spirits of the earth' are unlimited. There is an ancient liturgy in Shinto literature, a 'Prayer for Harvest', which used in ancient times to be chanted ceremonially first in the imperial palace and then at all Shinto shrines and Buddhist temples in early spring, approximately at the vernal equinox.[56] The Prayer is addressed not only to the 'gods of the harvest', but also to other groups of gods, such as the 'gods of growth', the 'gods of the wells', the 'gods of the gateways', the 'gods of the islands', the 'gods of the farms, uplands and streams', and finally to the supreme Sun-goddess, the presiding deity of Shinto faith. There is no doubt that in the conception of these gods, animism had a large part. It shows also how easy it was to extend and widen the Shinto pantheon,—to add other gods from various other sources. This facility offered an opening for a rapprochement between Buddhist worship and Shinto, when Buddhism was established in Japan.

The early Buddhists of Japan (of the Nara period) were anxious to make Shinto part and parcel of Buddhism,—to identify Shinto deities with Buddhist. The first attempt in this line is said to have been made when the great Todaiji temple to Lochana Buddha was in course of construction. It has come down in the form of a legend which is a late one and of Buddhist provenance. It is said that Emperor Shomu was anxious to obtain permission from the Shinto gods to build this Buddhist temple. He despatched Gyoki to the premier Shinto Shrine at Ise to consult the great goddess Amaterasu Omikami. The emperor's emissary had sat in meditation for seven days and nights at the door of the shrine when the door suddenly flew open and an oracular voice declared: 'The Sun (Amaterasu Omikami) is in the state of becoming a Buddha'. The emperor on getting this report sent a

[55] Cited in *Sources of Japanese Tradition*, pp-2324.

[56] Sansom's *A History of Japan*, Vol. I. p. 78-79.

second emissary to the shrine who also reported that he had heard a voice declaring, more definitely this time: 'The Sun is the Buddha Vairochana.'[57]

The oracle heard at Ise began in a century's time to unfold its cryptic meaning. It was at the time when the Buddhist establishments on Mounts Hei and Koya were started under Saicho and Kukai.

Saicho and Kukai allowed Shinto temples to stay within these establishments; the Shinto priests began to officiate at Buddhist worship as well as Shinto, and, accepting Shinto gods as Bodhisattvas, tried to work out between Shintoism and Buddhism a viable unity. They enunciated the doctrine that the Bodhisattvas of Buddhism and the Kami of Shintoism were alike *gongen* (i.e., manifestations of the Buddha) and, as such, equally worshippable. So the worship in their establishments was 'in two parts' (*Ryobu*), —Shinto worship in Shinto shrines and Buddhist worship in Buddhist, and the priests belonging to the two religions formed one body. Thus the Shinto Kami and the Buddhist deities began to keep house together. Their long co-existence led at the close of the 10th century to the emergence of a syncretic form of faith to which the name *Ryobu* Shinto (Two-part Shinto) was given.

Though the name was not invented in their own time, both Saicho and Kukai had given practical demonstrations of their acceptance of the Ryobu cult. There was a small shrine to the Shinto god Oyamaguino Mikoto on the top of Mount Hei and Saicho had it rebuilt on a grander scale at the foot of the mountain adding another Shinto god to keep the other company.[58] Kukai was the incumbent of the Toji temple and he himself adopted the Shinto god Inari as its tutelary deity. He used to officiate there, and several other Shinto shrines are said to have been founded by him.[59] At the ordination ceremony held in the Euryakuji, the first Buddhist temple built by Saicho on Mount Hei, Shinto priests used to be invited to take part. These two great Buddhist saints seem to have recognised no difference in merit between Shinto worship and Buddhist worship.

Ryobu Shinto never became a sect of Shintoism, but it introduced into Japan's religious history a principle of co-existence between the two major faiths of the land. The old rivalry between national Shinto and imported Buddhism wore out. Arnold Toynbee was struck with a phenomenon he had observed in Japan[60]: "In Japan you see the Shinto gods accepting the position of guardian of the gate to some Buddhist shrine. You can't imagine the pre-Christian pagan priests and the Christian clergy working

---

[57] The legend is given in *Studies in Shinto and Shrines* at pp. 63-64.

[58] *Studies in Shinto and Shrines*, p. 71.

[59] *Ibid*, pp. 71-72.

[60] Toynbee's *Comparing Notes—A Dialogue across a Generation*—Weidenfeld and Nicolson London, 1963).

together like this in a present-day English village". It is from Ryobu Shinto that the phenomenon derives.

During the 18th and the 19th centuries, Japan went through a vigorous revival of Shintoism. Perhaps it represented a resurgence of nationalist sentiment in a country, virile and vigorous, lying too long in the shadow of Chinese culture.

Shintoism was closely studied during these centuries by scholars in Japan. Its ideas, specially about Japan's unique status as 'the country of the (Shinto) gods' and the divine origin of the imperial line, were energetically propagated. The propaganda high-lighted the nationalistic (or as detractors call it, chauvinistic) aspect of Japan's national religion. The *Nihongi* and the *Kojiki*, the storehouse of Shinto mythology, were sought to be purged of their foreign (i.e., Chinese) accretions and a 'School of National Learning' functioned and flourished.[61]

This revivalist movement was called '*Fukko*', a return to the past. It aimed at the recovery of 'true Japan' from under her centuries' encrustations of the borrowed learning and civilization of China, and this true Japan, to the minds of the revivalists, was expressed in her national Shinto. The most prominent literary exponent of this movement was Motoori Norinaga (1730-1801).

The Shinto propaganda under official sponsorship had some temporary reaction on Buddhism. Shinto prevailed, and Buddhism temporarily receded to a secondary place; but the spirit of Ryobu Shinto had by then allayed the old rivalry between the two. A Shinto god was eligible then to receive worship from a Buddhist as a Bodhisattva or Buddha-incarnation (*Gongen*). In fact the most popular god of Shintoism, the war-god Hachiman, is regarded in a dual aspect,—as a Bodhisattva by the Buddhist and as a mythological god of the Shinto pantheon by the Shintoist.

Hachiman-worship has an interesting history. The name literally means 'eight banners'. The Buddhist identified the 'eight banners' with the Buddhist 'Noble Eightfold Path' (*Ārya Ashtāṅgika Mārga*) and Hachiman in his eyes was identical with the Buddha upholding the eight principles. Long way back in the Nara period he was worshipped as such by the Buddhist and regarded as the guardian god of Buddhism. A great shrine to Hachiman was erected at Kyoto on the removal of the seat of government there from Nara. He was the tutelary deity of the then most powerful Minamoto clan, and when the military government Bakufu was established at Kamakura, the clan erected a shrine to him, as the eight-banner-carrying patron of military men. He is still worshipped in Shinto shrines, but now as a

[61] See *Sources of Japanese Tradition*, pp. 507 ff.

peaceful god.[62]

Is Japan a Shinto country or a Buddhist one?—the point-blank question is sometimes put by foreigners. But Buddhism since the Nara period has become as 'national' to Japan as the native Shinto.

In the countryside of Japan Shintoism prevails, though perhaps not so widely or deeply as *Nat*-worship in Burma. The primitive character of both Shinto and *Nat*-worship is indicated by their alliance with astrology and other cognate popular forms of superstition. There are about 110,000 Shinto shrines in round number in rural Japan as against 75,089 all over the country. The Shinto shrines were formerly (that is, before the American occupation after the last World War) under the control of the Home Ministry of the Japanese Government and the ministrants in many of these temples were officially appointed priests who had received scholastic training in Shintoism.

By the side of a Shinto shrine, one may frequently see today a Buddhist temple controlling the shrine and Buddhist priests coming to conduct the shrine-worship. As one enters through the *tori* (gateway) of a Shinto shrine, what first catches the eye is the accumulated heap of offerings in kind of various sorts, mostly from traders, farmers, handicraftsmen, shop-keepers and peasants. It is obvious that on these classes of society Shintoism retains a strong hold. The spirit of Ryobu Shinto, however, prevails and no sense of higher or lower obtains in respect of the two distinct forms of worship.

Both Buddhism and Shintoism have each a large number of sects and sub-sects in Japan. But there is one non-Buddhist and non-Shinto sect which may be noticed in this connection. It is known as Tenrikyo. It does not call itself a sect, though its members wear a special uniform as a mark of distinction. The Tenrikyo has a mythology of its own, altogether different from the Kojiki mythology and its only object of worship is its deified foundress—a lady who in life was a woman of saintly character and remarkable activities. Born in 1798 and expired in 1887, she started her

---

[62] The following interesting extract is from Bunce's *Religions in Japan* (pp. 124-125): "Hachiman shrines are generally thought of as being dedicated to the god of war. But Hachiman has now become a fishing and agricultural deity......In the Nara period Hachiman was made the guardian god of Buddhism. Later he was identified with the Buddha Amida, and his name was said to symbolize the eightfold path of Buddhist morality......Hachiman is sometimes inaccurately described as the god of war, but there is no denying the fact that Hachiman shrines have been militaristic. Their popularity in war time is sufficient evidence of this. But the present transformation of Hachiman into a peaceful god is in accord with pantheistic practices".

missionary career with a new religious cult, non-Buddhist and non-Shinto, in her forty-first year. The rituals and practices of the cult of Tenrikyo are, however, strongly reminiscent of some Shinto rituals and symbols. The symbolical presence of the Foundress is betokened in the temple dedicated to her by the Shinto symbol of a mirror. Ritual songs and dancing are regularly offered. For its philanthropic and educational work, this band of Tenrikyo adherents is well-known in the area where it functions. Its imposing temple service is attended daily by scores of devotees from Tenri and its neighbourhood and it concludes in the magnificent assembly hall with the universal joint prayer—"Sweep away all evils, and save us, O Parent, Tenri-o-No-Mikoto !"

A short *History of Tenrikyo* (issued by Tenrikyo Kyokai Honbaiz Tenru, Japan in 1956—3rd edition in 1960) gives the history and the doctrines of Tenrikyo as propounded by the Foundress.

APPENDIX—ON BARAMON SOJO (THE BRĀHMAṆA ABBOT)

During my sojourn in Japan in October, 1962, I first heard of 'Baramon Sojo' (Brāhmaṇa Abbot) of the old Todaiji Temple at Nara. I proceeded to make enquiries about this Indian monk who officiated at the 'eye-opening' ceremony of the great image of Lochana Buddha at the Todaiji. He had come to Japan in a ship from China.

Later when I visited Nara and was cordially received by the head-priest of the Todaiji, I asked him whether there existed any original document on 'Baramon Sojo'. He replied that a 'Succession Record' of the abbots of the Todaiji, marked 'Essential Documents', was preserved in the Shoto-in of the Genkoji temple. I then made bold to make a request to the venerable head-priest to supply me with a copy of the portion of the record relating to 'Baramon Sojo'. He was kind and gracious enough to grant my request, and so I was enabled to have the following English translation of the record made for me by a research scholar of the Tokyo University:

> "Baramon Sojo was a saint from South India. For the purpose of seeing Gyoki (*Mañjushrī*) he came here to Japan in the 19th year of Tenpyo (747 A.D.). He arrived at the Naniwa harbour in the Settsu Province (now in Osaka prefecture). People around the harbour, seeing many foreigners on board, approached the ship in five boats, about ten men in each. They put questions to the foreigners but could not understand their replies. Then the headman of the district arrived and made enquiries of them, but failed to make out their answers. Finally came the Imperial messenger at the request of the provincial governor and he wrote his enquiries in Brāhmi characters and passed them on. Baramon Sojo wrote in reply: 'I come from South India.

I am a Brāhmaṇa. I have come to Japan from China on pilgrimage'. The imperial messenger, on return to the court, informed the authorities. The emperor Shomu and his ministers were surprised and pleased at the coming of a learned Indian from China and organised a party to greet him with special envoys, priests and musicians. The Brāhmaṇa priest landed along with ten disciples and, having seen the procession of priests marching in two lines with Gyoki Bosatsu in the rear, he caught him by the sleeve of his garment and said: 'I once met you, Venerable Sir, many years ago. I have been eagerly looking forward to seeing you again and hence I have come to greet you'. Both, exceedingly pleased to meet each other, exchanged the following *Waka*-poems:

Brāhmaṇa:	How happy I am again in your presence: You are the Japanese Mañjushrī, whom I once met and parted from at Kapilavastu.
Gyoki-Bosatsu:	We once met each other in the presence of Sākyamuni on the Gridhrakūṭa and today we have the pleasure of meeting again. This, I believe, is evidence of everlasting truth.

(Note: This meeting at Kapilavastu and at Gridhrakūṭa in the presence of Sākyamuni is not to be taken in a literal sense. It is a meeting in spirit,—not a physical meeting.)

These *waka*-poems used to be widely chanted by people and have come down to the present time by oral tradition.

"The Brāhmaṇa priest presented to the emperor, through the kind office of Gyoki, textiles, tin-made articles, 5 sets of incense-burners 100 leaves of *Talapat* (palmyra-leaf) manuscripts in Brāhmī writing, 2,000 grains of the Buddha's body-relics, and various other things which were Indian products. The emperor distributed them to different Buddhist temples and most of them are preserved in the Shoto-in of the Genkoji temple.

"The Brāhmaṇa was warmly received by the emperor who supplied him with attendants and made arrangements for his boarding and lodging.

There is a supplementary record about the Indian Brāhmaṇa priest, in which his Indian name Bodhisena occurs, in the Dianji temple (Dianji-Bodai-Deraiki). It is reproduced here in translation, somewhat abbreviated:

"Since Hironari Tajibinomahito was despatched by the Japanese Court as Messenger-in-Chief to the Tang Court of China, three years or so had elapsed. Nashiro Onakanoomi, the deputy-messenger, and Genbo, the research-student, had already left Japan in the fifth year of the Tenoyo (734 A.D.). In 737 A.D., they returned to Saigon and there the ship took on board Bodhi (sena) who hailed from

South India, the Japanese priest Doyo who had studied in the Tang country (China), and Buttetsu, a Buddhist priest from Cambodia.

Bodhisena was a priest from Kapilavastu. He was skilled in meditation and had an earnest desire to propagate the Law of the Buddha. While in India, he had been eagerly looking forward to seeing the Mañjushrī Bodhisattva. He happened to meet a holy man in a dream who told him that the Bodhisattva resided in the Tendai-san of Shinton (China). He wanted to start for the Tendaisan, the mountain on which the Tendai sect had its seat in China, to have an opportunity of worshipping Bodhisattva Mañjushrī. At that time Buttetsu, the Cambodian monk, was back from northern India. He had learnt the Buddhist doctrines since his youth and was skilful in magic. He was in search of *Cintāmani*, the superb gem of the Nāgarāja (King of Serpents), and was for that purpose sailing over the ocean. As it happened, his ship was blown off by a storm to the coast of South India. Here in South India, Bodhisena and Buttetsu had met and the former accepted him as his *guru* (spiritual guide). Both started together along the rugged route across the deserts for the Tang country (China).

Note:—They seem to have been together in China and both Bodhisena and Buttetsu left on a boat at Saigon for Japan)......

Bodhisena resided at Chuin (name of a monastery) of the Dianji temple. Emperor Shomu valued him highly and greatly honoured him.

In the 15th year of Tenpyo (744 A.D.), the casting of the big Buddha statue (Lochana Buddha of the Todaiji) started and the ceremony of its installation was performed in the fourth year of Shoho (753 A.D.).

The 'eye-opener' was Bodhisena.

In order to celebrate the occasion, the emperor commanded the functionaries of the main Buddhist temples to give a performance of Chinese music. The Cambodian priest Buttetsu was ordered to act as conductor-in-chief of the Gogaku Music of the Japanese imperial court and was requested to teach artistes Cambodian dances like the 'Bodhisattva dance', etc."

In the "essential documents of the Todaiji temple" is included a document purporting to be a request by Emperor Shomu to Bhodhisena to perform the 'eye-opening ceremony':

"The Emperor Shomu thus requests the Brāhmaṇa priest Bodhisena: We are going to purify the Todaiji by abstinence and hold the celebration of the Vairochana Budha. After that, will be opened the Eyes of Infinite Light and Love. I am very tired and not in good health. Even in doing the routine work of daily life, I feel some difficulty. But

I do not know any person other than you who can draw the eyes of the image on my behalf with the writing brush. I heartily request you to perform the function as the 'eye-opening' priest. Please do not decline".

Konjaku-monogatari (Ancient Tales) is an old work of fiction in Japanese published in five volumes in 1957-1962 by Iwonami Shoten in Iwanami Koten Bungaku Taikai (Japanese Classical Literature series). In its third volume, published in 1961, at pp. 70-71, there is a brief account of Baramon Sojo. The 'ancient tales' in this collection are said to have been collected by Dainagon Minamoto (1003-1077 A.D.) from travellers who used to pass in front of his house at Uji near Kyoto. The tales are placed under three heads, Indian, Chinese and Japanese. Baramon Sojo figures in one of the Japanese tales. His life-story in the tale does not differ substantially from what we find in the "Essential Records". He is said to have resided in the Daianji Temple and passed away from this world, 'facing westwards (towards India?) with folded hands and without changing countenance' in 760 A.D. An "Eulogy" on him was composed in 773 A.D., by Shuei, a disciple of his who acted as his personal attendant.

Finally I consulted at the Kyoto University, with the help of an American research-scholar, the article on Bodhisena in the Japanese *Bukkyo Daijiten* (The Great Buddhist Dictionary), compiled by a commission of scholars, presided over by Dr. Mochizuki (Ist Ed. in 1936; revised Ed. in 1960). The following life-sketch of Bodhisena is given in Vol. v, pp. 4670 ff:

"His Indian name was Bodhisena. He is reputed to be either a South Indian or having come from Kapilavastu. He was a Brāhmaṇa and his clan-name was Bharadwāja...At some unspecified date he went to China on a pilgrimage to Wutai (a mountain in China where the spirit of Mañjushrī is supposed to reside). While in China he met some members of Japanese Embassy there. One of the members of the embassy was a learned Japanese monk. He asked him to go to Japan to which Bodhisena agreed. This was in 735 A.D. Leaving for Japan, he landed at Kyu-shu (an island in the south of Japan). Shortly afterwards, he went to Settsu (near Kobe) where he was met by a delegation appointed by the emperor, to welcome him, led by the Buddhist monk Gyoki. They came to Osaka (modern name) and were greatly honoured there. From there Bodhisena went to Nara, the capital city, and was lodged at the Daianji Temple. There he gave recitations from the *Avataṁsa Sūtra*. He was very skilled in *mantras* (magic formulae). He was invested by the imperial court with the title of *Sojo* (Arch-priest) in 751 A.D. In the following year (752 A.D.), when the Great Buddha statue was completed, he was invited by Gyoki to preside over the installation of the image. In 754 A.D. Chienchen (Japanese Gan-jin, meaning 'one that sees the truth') arrived from China. On his arrival, Bodhisena housed him at the Todaiji. Bodhisena died in 760, probably at Nara, at the age of 56". (The article is followed by a list of works in Chinese and Japanese in which Bodhisena is mentioned).

The exact term of Bodhisena's tenure of abbotship at the Todaiji is not known,—it must have been not less than half a dozen years. The Todaiji Temple was an illustrious centre of learning and especially of studies in Kegon philosophy at the time. Monks from different parts of Japan resorted to it. The presence of an Indian abbot there must have stimulated curiosity to know about India. Prince Shinnyo, son of Emperor Heizei, is said to have become a monk and was at the Todaiji carrying on studies in Buddhism. He went thereafter to China in 861 A.D. in the company of another Buddhist monk. He had all along cherished the desire to worship Buddhist places in India, but at the start of his Indian pilgrimage in 864, he vanished at Laos. The story is that he was killed by a tiger at Laos.

There are also legends of other Japanese monks who tried to go to India on pilgrimage but, for one reason or another, were prevented from undertaking it. The first Japanese monk who is said to have been able to do the Indian pilgrimage successfully was one Shimaji in 1873.[63]

Chinese pilgrims to India used to take both the sea-route from South China Sea and the overland route through Mid-Asia. But sea-voyage from Japan to India opened only in modern times. Perhaps the failure in the past to open intercourse with India was due to the Japanese sea-men's lack of knowledge of the monsoon winds which was possessed by most Chinese sea-men of the Tang Dynasty. In any case, a cultural intercourse between Japan and India could not be started, such as commenced between China and India after Fa-hsien's pioneer pilgrimage to India overland.

[63] He is mentioned as the first monk to come to India from Japan in *Nihonno-Bukkyo* by S. Watanable (in Japanese) published by Iwanami Shinsho, Tokyo, 1958 (Ch.... 'In Quest of Truth', pp. 22-24). The source of information, however, is not given.

The Tenryugi Temple of Kyoto, headquarters of the Rinzai (Zen) Sect. It was founded by Takauji, the first Ashikaga Shogun. A rock—garden and a pond in front.

24. *Nanzenji Temple at Kyoto. Part of a former imperial palace turned into a Zen Buddhist templ*
in 1291. The garden of sand and stone conveys a Zennist symbolism.

25. A modern Japanese-style inn in Kyoto. It was designed by a noted architect of Japan in 1960. Between the opposite corridors, the two patterned moss-covered patches of ground are for decoration.

26. *The garden of Daisen—in a sub-temple of the Daitonuji temple of Kyoto, was founded in the early 16th century. The garden, divided by a corridor, is a typical example of the 'dry landscape' style with sands and rocks of different sizes and shapes.*

27. *A beautiful Kyoto temple with a pool of water decorated with rocks of different sizes in front.*

Chapter XI

TIBET

Limitations on our Knowledge of Tibet

Tibet to the north of India across the eastern Himalayan range is situated on the world's highest tableland. The country is known to us by that name, but it is strange to its own people. Its old historiographers and present inhabitants call it by a descriptive name, *Pod Yul* or *Khong Yul* (Land of Snow).[1]

By reason of its geographical isolation, the extreme severity of its climate and lack of facilities for internal travel, it has been a somewhat 'forbidden country' to foreigners all these years. The Chinese held a nominal suzerainty over it and the *Ambams* (Deputed Governors) from China and their entourage only could demand right of entry within its bounds: other foreigners had to assume for entry into Tibet the disguise of Tibetans. For them hospitality was scant, for the sort of zenophobia, concomitant of a strictly inbred society with no external contact, used to lurk in the Tibetan mind. Yet in their rigid seclusion, the Tibetans developed a culture,—it was necessarily inbred, peculiar to them,—and a form of Buddhism which is *sui generis*. The fate of both is in the lap of the gods at the present moment. On the strength of their lapsed or obsolete suzerainty, the Chinese Communists rule the country and plan to remould, 'according to their heart's desire', existing life and society of the subjugated people.

Some historical instances on record seem to suggest that during the 17th century and most part of the 18th, Tibet was not an *officially* 'forbidden' country. Entry was not barred to Christian missionaries and adventurous travellers from Europe[2] nor perhaps to Indians from the south of the Himalayas. But the country outside the capital Lhasa had not heard for centuries the footfall of a foreigner, friend or foe. It was not till 1904 that the seclusiveness of Tibet was broken in upon by a military mission sent by the British Government of India under Colonel Younghusband. It

---

[1] "As for the name Tibet, it may be interesting to know that it is a word unknown in the Tibetan language. Its origin is not clearly traced, but Tibetans ignore it completely. They call their country Pod Yul and themselves as *Pod-po*"——Alexandra David-Neel (*My Journey to Lhasa*, Penguin Ed. 1940, pp. 15 and 225). The name *Khong Yul* occurs in indigenous historiography.

[2] Instances of this are given in David-Neel's *My Journey to Lhasa* (Penguin Ed.), p. 10. footnote.

formally opened Tibet to the outside world. This event at the time was metaphorically described as 'the Unveiling of Lhasa'.[3]

More 'unveilings' came later when some Orientalists from Europe as well as a few Indian scholars embarked on the task of introducing Tibet to the world—its language, its culture, its system of religion, its religious literature. While the European Orientalists engaged themselves mostly in philological studies, the Indian scholars were keen on the exploration of the religious literature of Tibet which preserves in translation a number of Indian Buddhist works long lost in India. The foremost among this band was the intrepid itinerant Hungarian scholar, Csoma de Koros (1784-1842) who compiled, among other works, a Tibetan Dictionary and a Tibetan Grammar. Tibetan studies progressed after Csoma de Koros's initial labours. But the achievement of greatest consequence of this early band of scholars was the recovery from local lamaseries of a large assortment of manuscripts, several of which have now been translated and published. To the succession of these European Orientalists and Indian scholars —from the Hungarian savant Csoma de Koros to the Indian pandit Rahula Sankrityayana (expired only a few years ago)—we owe the raw materials of our knowledge of the history, the language, and the surprising wealth of the religious literature of Tibet.

Young husband himself brought from the monasteries of Lhasa, Drepung and other places a large assortment of Tibetan manuscripts. His collection is now stowed away in the India Office Library in London; other manuscripts are dispersed in German, Russian and other libraries of the Continent; the Tibetan encyclopaedia in two parts, the *Kanjur* and the *Tanjur*, is happily in print and more easily available. Consisting of 4,569 texts, the whole has been carefully catalogued by Japanese scholars of the Tohoku Imperial University of Japan.[4] These works, once known only to learned lamas, are now available to students of Tibetan and they have laid the foundation for systematic studies on Tibet. Tibetology represents now a recognised part of Orientalia. Since the turn of this century, Tibetologists have multiplied in both Asia and Europe and the number of Tibetan manuscripts, edited, translated and published by them is yearly on the increase. Tibet is no longer a geographical expression nor a land of mysteries as she had been to foreigners over centuries past.

Tibetology, however, is not more than half a century and a decade old and has not advanced far enough yet to give us a clear and consistant picture of the country's social evolution or political history. Though Tibet had been

---

[3] This was the title of a book published in England shortly after Younghusband's mission. It contains a reference to the missionaries and explorers from Europe who had been in Tibet in 17th and 18th centuries. See David-Noel's book *My Journey to Lhasa*, Penguin Ed. 1940, pp. 9-10.

[4] *A Complete Catalogue of the Tibetan Buddhist Canons* (1934) and *Catalogue Index*.

in different periods of Asian history a political and military power, holding under it large parts of the oasis-states of Mid-Asia, a portion of China (Changan) and parts of Mongolia and Manchuria, the forces that worked at the root of that power are unknown. Nor can they be discovered from the indigenous histories of Tibet of which we shall make mention at the end of this chapter. The historiographers were monks in a Kingdom where the State was a theocracy and the religion to them was identified with the State and the country. Its political affairs or social conditions were, in their view, nothing apart from the fortunes of the religion. The result is that Tibet's secular history up till now is known just in shreds and patches that are neither integrated nor brought into correlation.

In other Buddhist countries, where history is richer and ampler in contents we can see more clearly how Buddhism acted in the life of the people and how it fitted into their regional history. But this dynamic view is difficult to attain in respect of Tibet in the absence of continuous history. The development of Buddhism in Tibet, however, can be fitfully traced, mostly through the story of its conflict with Bon till its reform and final establishment by Atisha in 11th century.

Bon—Its renovation under Buddhist Impact

Bon was Tibet's pre-Buddhistic cult. It became an organised religion only in later times under the influence and impact of Buddhism. Between Bon and *Tāntric* Buddhism which had grown strong in India at the time when the Tibetans took Buddhism from this country, there were certain outstanding affinities, specially in the mythology of deities controlling human affairs. The Tibetan mind was pre-conditioned by the Bon cult to accept the *Tāntric* form of Buddhism. But its establishment in the country did not ring the death-knell of Bon. It was not given up, but a conflict betweeen the native cult and borrowed religion inevitably ensued. It went into final decline only in the 11th century, when the Indian Pandit Atisha undertook a reformation of Tibetan Buddhism and effected its separation from Bon. Yet Bon exists in Tibet even today.

The term Bon is of uncertain derivation and meaning. Originally it was a regional form of the pre-cultural 'animistic-Shamanist cult', wide-spread in primitive times 'in Inner Asia including East and West Turkestan, Mongolia, Manchuria, Tibet and even China'.[5] It was transformed into the national religion of the Tibetans in about a century of the introduction of Buddhism by a reformer of Bon known as Shen-rab, meaning 'the most excellent of Shamans'. He is regarded as the founder of the Bon religion of Tibet and his legendary biography is sketched in a work called *Ser-myig*.[6]

[5] See Helmut Hoffmann's *Religions of Tibet* (Allen and Unwin, 1961), p. 15.

[6] A synopsis of the first twelve chapters of the book will be found in *Ibid*, pp. 85 ff.

Significant of the formative influence of Buddhism on Bon is the fact that the life-story of this founder of Tibetan Bon reproduces the main episodes of his career from the Buddha-story of the *Lalitavistara*.

Under Buddhist influence, Bon became a cultured religion: no longer the primitive unorganised Shamanism out of which it had originated. The *Bon-po*, adherents of renovated Bon, adopted some of the institutional features of Buddhism; they had their own priests who lived in monasteries under rules similar to the Buddhist; they cultivated Bon philosophy, mysticism and magic lore and were a body parallel to the Buddhist monkhood (*Saṅgha*). But coming thus far near to Buddhism, it never coalesced with it. Fundamental differences remained. The Bon world-view and the Buddhist were never at one; Bon had divinities in its pantheon drawn from Shamanist sources and also a mythology about them; it did not recognise the Buddha who had no place in its theology or pantheon; Bon classical language was not Sanskrit but a regional dialect of Tibet.

Suffering spells of persecution at the hands of Buddhist kings, the adherents of Bon in this renovated form managed to survive in Tibet and, supported by the feudal nobility, it gathered strength enough to give fight to Buddhism in the fateful religious struggles of the 7th and 8th centuries. Bon-po families exist even today in the northern and eastern regions of Tibet, though from the western regions, they were ousted in the eleventh century (see *infra*).

Introduction of Indian Tāntric Buddhism

At the time of its first introduction into Tibet from India in the 7th century the Buddhist religion had already passed into a decadent form in India. At this stage its main plank was neither the moral and spiritual discipline of the Hīnayāna nor the idealistic philosophy of the Mahāyāna. From the two previous *Yāna's*, it distinguished itself by the name Vajrayāna (The cult of the thunder bolt): It was a system founded on esoteric beliefs, rites and practices mainly drawn from the *Tantras*.

The *Tantras* are a special branch of Indian religious literature with slender basis in the scriptures of the Hīnayāna or the Mahāyāna. The staple topics of this literature are magic, demonology, exorcísm, alchemy and allied beliefs, supplemented by a mass of formulae for invoking the terror-striking deities of the cult or averting their attentions. But it is by no means purely thaumaturgical : it is grounded on a mystic philosophy concerning unseen powers that dominate human life and the means to control them which gives a somewhat realistic background to Bon concepts of supernatural and mystical powers.

A saint and practitioner of Vajrayāna from Kashmir introduced Indian Tāntric Buddhism into Tibet in the 7th or the 8th century and he is said to have introduced also the Indian monastic system and the

Lamaist hierarchy. Till the recent Chinese occupation of Tibet, this hierarchy of Lamas had been the main stronghold, and the impregnable tradition of Tibetan Buddhism. This missionary of Vajrayāna Buddhism from Kashmir was named Padmasambhava (Lotus-born)—called Guru Rimpoche in Tibetan. It is difficult to define what his actual achievement as a Buddhist missionary in Tibet was, besides laying the foundation of the institution of monachism in Tibet. Perhaps he did no more than give to the native Bon religion a Buddhist-Tantric system of expression. His teachings and his life-story, mostly made up from legends, marred also by many anachronisms, may be read in Evans-Wentz's rendering in *The Tibetan Book of the Dead* and *The Great Liberation*.

The first Buddhist monastery in Tibet was built by Padmasambhava at a place called Sam-Yas. It is said that on this occasion he was accompanied by two distinguished scholars from Nalandā, India's premier Buddhist University of the time, one of whom Śāntarakṣita was named the first High Priest of the new establishment. The other was Śāntarakṣita's disciple Kamalasila about whom the legend is that he died a martyr, having been murdered by his opponents out of spite after he had won a victory over them in a religious debate. This first seat of Tibetan Buddhist monkhood is said by Tibetan historiographers to have been built on the plan of the great monastery at Odantapura founded by the first Pāla king of Eastern India Gopāla. It became in course of time the first predecessor of thousands of lamaseries, great and small, scattered all over Tibet.

The religion Padmasambhava gave to Tibet must have been a sycretic cult, one compounded of Bon and Indian Tantric Buddhism, to which Hoffmann gives a distinctive name, 'Padmaism'.[7] Padmasambhava was believed to have secreted many texts of the cult in clefts of rock or underground which, being discovered later, a special sect called *Nying-ma* developed on their basis. The sect however is regarded as heretical by Tibetan Buddhists. 'Padmaism' passed for Buddhism in Tibet till the religious reformation initiated by Atisha in the second half of the 11th century.

The old Bon religion itself in spite of the set-back received from Buddhism remained independently side by side with it. But the latter was accepted as the religion of the State. The principal supporters of Bon were the conservative feudal nobility which was ill-disposed to Buddhism. In the religious history of the country the main contentions were always between the native religion and the one imported from India.

The Beginnings of Literacy and Literature in Tibet

Sometime after the introduction of Indian Tantric Buddhism, a progressive and enterprising king surnamed Srong-btsan-gampo (Skt. *Sarala-ugra-*

[7] See Hoffman's *The Religions of Tibet*, pp 5 ft.

gambhīra, meaning 'simple, strict and profound') was on the Tibetan throne (620-649). It was in his time that Buddhism was declared as Tibet's State Religion, and simultaneously a Tibetan script was introduced and the beginnings of literature were made. The script was a modified form of Indian script, nearly allied to the Bengali script.

Tibet was then in contact with both China and India. For matters political it had its face towards China and for religious, cultural and ecclesiastical matters towards India. It had till then no script or written language of its own,—it is said that it had instead a system of making twisted knots in strings to represent figures and words. The king, a man of understanding, had the intelligence to realise that no progress in any direction was possible for his kingdom without the aid of a written language. So he sent his prime minister, Thonmi, to India to study the Indian alphabetic system and help develop a written language. Thonmi stayed in India (Kashmir and Magadha) and returned to Tibet with Buddhist texts and grammatical textbooks, and, back home, he spoke to the king in such high terms of the Buddhism and Buddhist culture of India that the king had no hesitation in declaring that religion to be the State Religion of his kingdom.

The legend is that king Srong-btsan-gampo had two queens, one a Nepalese and the other a Chinese, and it was mainly due to their insistence that the king made this declaration giving to Buddhism an acknowledged status in his realm. Anyway, these two ladies have been apotheosized in Tibet as incarnations of Goddess Tārā,—one the Green Tārā and the other the White Tārā. Their portraits appear again and again in temple paintings, and a temple dedicated to the queen from Nepal (Bhrikuti Devī—the Frowning Goddess), stands it is said, to this day in Lhasa.

The script brought from India, slightly modified, and the language reformed for literary use on the model of Sanskrit were employed in rendering Buddhist texts in Tibetan. The translations accumulated since the time of Srong-btsan-gampo and slowly swelled to the great dimensions of the *Kanjur* and *Tanjur* collections. The texts are products of both Indian and Tibetan monk-scholarship,—from works of the ancient Mahāyānist *ācāryas* of India to late Tantric texts of Vajrayāna Buddhism,—with a few interspersed translations of Sanskrit literary classics like Kalidasa's *Meghadūtam* and Dandin's *Kāvyādarśa.* The activity of translation was not confined to the Buddhists. While the Buddhists translated from Sanskrit texts, the Bon-po adherents of Bon did it from a dialect called *Zang-zung* spoken round the Kailas mountain in the area which had served as the cradle and then the nursery of Bon. By the end of the 9th century there was a great mass of Tibetan religious literature, both Bon and Buddhist.

Struggles between Bon and Buddhism

The 8th and 9th centuries in Tibet were a period of religious struggle in which the main contention raged between Bon and Buddhism, besides a Chinese school known as Hva-shang Mahāyāna, an off-shoot of Chinese Ch'an Buddhism and Taoism, which had established a footing in Tibet.

The nobility of the realm formed the main buttress of sovereignty in the country. But while the kings were mostly supporters of Buddhism, the nobility was conservative and wedded to the cause of the native Bon. Nor was Buddhism universally popular. Since Srong-btsan-gampo it had always been allowed to co-exist with Bon, but there were those who disliked and even hated it. Its Tāntric rites evoked a strong protest from one of the queens of Tibet, Queen Tshe-spong-bza, who wrote some verses on Buddhist Tāntric practices, describing them as "not religion, but the evil that comes to Tibet from India".

The strong Bon-Buddhist dissensions that filled two centuries of Tibet's history had important political repercussions. They served to break up the unity of the country, driving a wedge between the authority of the sovereignty and the power of the nobility. It was a case of Buddhist kings *versus* Bon nobles. Among the kings, the most out-and-out champion of Buddhism was Ral-pa-chan (A.D. 817-836) and its most bitter opponent, his brother, Lang-dharma (A.D. 836-840). The latter, on coming to the throne, persecuted the Buddhists and lost his life at the hands of an assassin. There was no longer an established State Religion. The confusion in the ecclesiastical world resulting from the sovereign's distribution of favours and benefices at haphazard between one religion and another acerbated more and more the tension between king and nobility. It weakened the political structure of the country which began to disintegrate and finally broke up before long into a number of small independent principalities. The authority of the central government was so reduced as to be hardly operative outside the capital. A period of complete religious and cultural stagnation followed.

But even in this dark eclipse of Buddhism there were some heroic spirits who sought to rekindle its light in the land: among them was Ye-shes-od, a Buddhist monk-king who embraced martyrdom. After Lang-dharma's persecutions, there actually came about a revival of Buddhism in Tibet,—in 70 or in 108 years, according to different authorities.

Atisha in Tibet : Reformation of Tibetan Buddhism

Ye-shes od had come to the throne towards the end of this troublous period. He was more interested in the philosophic teachings of Mahāyāna Buddhism than in the *tantras* current in Tibet and he was anxious to

[8] See Hoffmann's *The Religions of Tibet*, pp. 76, 78.

[9] *Ibid.* p. 70

propagate the higher Mahāyāna teachings in his realm. But only in India were they available. He, therefore, chose twenty-one young Tibetans and bade them proceed to that country and master these teachings. Only two returned, and Rin-chen (958-1055 A.D.), the youngest of the party, distinguished himself later on as an assiduous translator of Mahāyānic texts and obtained the title of *Lo-chen* (Great Translator).

Mahāyāna Buddhism now appreciated in value among Tibetan Buddhist scholars. Its best exponents however were to be found in eastern India at the famous centres of Buddhist learning like Nālandā and Vikramaśīlā. So several missions were organised by the king with the object of persuading some Indian scholars to come to Tibet for the reformation and revival of Buddhism.

These missions were a heavy drain on the resources of the State and king Ye-shes-od had to go out himself prospecting for gold to replenish his depleted treasury. On the way he was captured by the king of Garlog. A ransom was put on his head at his weight in gold and his nephew, Chen Chub, who succeeded him on the throne, tried to collect the amount of gold demanded. But the stock fell short. He met the captive king in prison, but the king instructed the nephew to desist from efforts to ransom him and advised him to spend the gold already collected in attempts to bring an Indian Buddhist scholar to Tibet. The king was murdered in captivity, but the nephew, who also was a monk-king, made a determined effort to carry out his unfortunate uncle's last wish.

So he despatched another mission under Nag-tso to India which succeeded in bringing from Vikramaśīlā its head-abbot Dīpaṅkara Srījñāna, equally famous for his learning in the *Tontras* and in Mahāyāna philosophy. Chan Chub had died in the meantime, but his successor gave Dīpaṅkara a rousing welcome on his arrival at Tholin, capital of Tibet at the time. Arriving in Tibet in 1042 A.D., he was installed at the head of the ecclesiastical organisation and spent 13 years in the country, dying in Nethan in 1054 A.D.[10]

Two names outstanding in Tibet's intercourse with India are Padmasambhava (Tibetan—Rimpoche) and Dīpaṅkara Srījñāna (Tibetan—Atisha). While the activities of Padmasambhava are wrapped in legends, those of the latter belong to history, and in all Tibetan histories of Buddhism are dwelt on at large. There are also independent biographies of Atisha, one of which was written by his chief Tibetan disciple Bromton. Padmasambhava is credited with having first established 'Lamaist system' in Tibetan Buddhism; its systematic organisation was part of the religious reforms carried out by Atisha. After a long run of nine centuries, the

[10] For the Tibetan cultural missions to India and Atisha's career in Tibet, see Dutt's *Buddhist Monks and Monasteries of India*, Appendix II of Part V, pp. 367 ff.

hierarchy stands now on the brink of ruin at the hands of the present Communist Chinese rulers of Tibet. The expulsion of the Bon religion from Central Tibet was also due to Atisha's missionary activities. He had aimed to bring the whole country under the banner of Buddhism. "His work was crowned, so to speak, when, after his death, the king of Western Tibet called a 'Dharma' or Great Council in the holy place of Tholin where Atisha had been first received in Tibet and where to this Council priests came from Western, Central and Eastern Tibet." [11]

Tibetan Buddhism after Atisha

The history of Buddhism in Tibet after Atisha is mainly the history of the growth of a number of sects. The first of these sects was the Kadam-pa, founded by Atisha's disciple and biographer Bromton. It means 'the sect which adheres to the *Kadams* or authoritative sayings of the Master' as recorded in his work *Bodhipatha-pradīpa.*[12] The history of the sect is given at large in Chapter V of the 'Blue Annals' (See *infra*) under the caption 'Joborji (Lord) Atisha and his Spiritual Lineage'.

Buddhism's heyday in Tibet was the years Atisha stayed in the country. To this day he is worshipped by the Tibetans as an incarnation of god Mañjuśrī, the Buddhist god of learning. Out of the sects that came into existence in the after-centuries, appeared a number of saints and sages, eminent ecclesiastics, pandits and monk-historiographers and a few religious poets of whom the most distinguished was Milarepa. He was a famous saint and mystic poet, who is represented in Tibetan paintings and woodcuts as trying, with the palm of his hand cupping the right ear, to catch the faraway 'voices of silence'.

Some of the monk-scholars of Tibet wrote historical works on the origin, development and progress of Buddhism before and since its introduction into Tibet from India. They are not 'histories' in our modern sense, but may be called 'church-histories', drawing mainly upon tradition and folk-lore about saints and religious teachers and the birth and growth of Tibetan Buddhist sects. But they contain at the same time valuable references to episodes of secular history. The following works of this category, given in order of chronology, have been printed and published so far :

(1) 'History of Buddhism' in two parts by Bu-ston Rin-po-che (A.D. 1290-1364) : translated into English by Dr. Obermiller (Heidelberg, 1931-1932).

---

[11] Hoffmann's *The Religions of Tibet*, p. 122.

[12] It is a work much valued by Tibetan Buddhists. See Dutt's *Buddhist Monks and Monasteries of India*, p. 366 and footnotes.

(2) The 'Blue Annals' in fifteen books by Gos lo-tsa-ba (A.D. 1392-1481), completed in 1478 : translated in two parts by George Roerich and published by the Asiatic Society of Bengal (Calcutta, 1949).

(3) 'History of Buddhism' by Lama Tāranātha (b. 1573), completed in 1607 : translated into German by Schiefner.

(4) 'History of Buddhism : Its Rise, Decline and Downfall' (*Pag-sam-jon-zang*) by Sumpa Khanpo Yese Pal Jor, completed in 1747 : edited with a List of contents and an Analytical Index by Sarat Chandra Das (Calcutta, 1908).

To these is expected to be added the 'Chronicle of Tibet' by the Fifth Dalai Lama surnamed 'The Great' (A.D. 1615-1680) whose reign was perhaps the most brilliant in Tibetan annals.[13] It was in his reign that Tibet became finally a 'theocratic state' with sovereignty (in both State and Church) vested in the Dalai Lama. His 'chronicle', relating to the historical development of Tibet based on official archives, is one of great value, not being a record merely of ecclesiastical events. But in spite of all the greatness of the Fifth Dalai Lama, he may be said to be the harbinger of the misfortune that Tibet groans under today, for it was this fifth Dalai Lama who established those relations with China which have now proved so disastrous for the country. His recognition of China's suzerainty over Tibet has supplied the excuse to the present communist rulers to come and mop up gradually its traditional culture of many centuries.

The 'church-histories' hardly open any outlook on the broader aspects of Buddhism in Tibet which concern the growth of social norms, traditions of art and culture and the peculiar Tibetan outlook on and attitude towards life. The impact of Buddhism must have been determinant on the national aspects of life through the centuries from the 7th on.

[13] There was an announcement in the *East and West*, the organ of the ISMEO of Rome, that Prof. Tucci had this book on hand for translation. But it has not come out yet.

LIST OF BOOKS CONSULTED

ANESAKI:

Prince Shotoku, the Sage and Statesman of Japan (Hariyugi Temple, Nara, 1959)

ASTON:

English Translation of Nihongi. 2 vols. (Japan Society of London, 1896)

BEAL:

Buddhist Records of the Western World (one-volume Popular Edition)

BIDNEY, D:

Theoretical Anthropology (Columbia University Press, New York, 1953)

BUKKYO DAIJITEN:

The Great Buddhist Dictionary in Japanese. Revised Edition, 1960

Bulletin of the School of Oriental and African Studies (University of London)

BUNCE :

Religions in Japan (Tuttle and Co., Tokyo; Third Printing, 1959)

BUSCH :

Thailand (Asia Library, 1959)

BUTTINGER, JOSEPH :

The Smaller Dragon (Pub. by Frederick Praeger, New York, 1958)

CADY, JOHN F:

South-East Asia : Its Historical Development (MacGraw Hill Inc., New York, 1964).

CARTMAN:

Hinduism in Ceylon (Gunasena and Co., Colombo, 1957)

CHAMBERLAIN:

English Translation of the Kokiji (Asiatic Society of Japan, vol. X)

CHOU:

Indo-Chinese Relations (Allahabad, U.P., India, 1955)

COATES AND ISHIZUKI:

Honen, the Buddhist Saint (Kyoto, Chion-in, First Edition, 1925)

COEDES :

'*Documents on the Political and Religious History of Laos*' (in French, in the DEFEO, Vol. XXV)

COEDES :

Recueil des Inscriptions du Siam

COEDES :

Les Stats Hindouises de indochine et d'indonesie

COEDES :

Inscriptions du Cambodga (6 vols; Paris, 1937—1854).

Complete Catalogue of Tibetan Buddhist Canons and Complete Catalogue Index (Tohoku Imperial University, Sendai, Japan, 1934)

COON, CARLTON, S:

The History of Man (Jonathan Cape, London, 1955)

CORAL REMUSAT:

L' Art Khmer (Paris, 1940)

CULAVAMSA:

(Continuation of *Mahavamsa.* Text and Translation by Geiger.)

CULLAVAGGA:
(in Oldenberg's *Vinayapitakam*. Vol. II.)

DHANINIVAT, PRINCE:
A History of Buddhism in Siam (Bangkok, 1960)

DIPAVAMSA:
(Ed. and Tr. by B. C. Law, Ceylon Historical Journal, 1959)

DUTT, S:
The Buddha and Five After-Centuries (Luzac and Co., London, 1957)

DUTT, S:
Buddhist Monks and Monasteries of India (Allen and Unwin, London, 1962)

Epigraphia Zeylanica (Ceylon)

Epigraphia Birmanica (Rangoon)

FITZERALD C. P:
China—A Short Cultural History (Cresset Press, London, 1942)

Genji Monogatari (trans. into English by Waley; pub. by Constable, London, 1927, in 3 vols.)

Glass-Palace Chronicle (trans. by Tin and Luce, Rangoon, 1960)

GROUSSET:
In the Foot-steps of the Buddha (George Routledge, 1932).

HALL:
History of South-east Asia (MacMillan and Co., London, 1961).

HIRANO, UMAYO:
Buddhist Plays from Japanese Literature (CIIB, Tokyo, 1962).

HIRTH:
Ancient History of China (Columbia University Press, New York, 1911)

History of Ceylon (2 vols. Colombo University Press, Colombo, 1959)

Historians of South-east Asia (pub. by School of Oriental and African Studies, University of London, Oxford University Press, 1961)

HOFFMAN, HELMUT:
The Religions of Tibet (Allen and Unwin, London, 1961)

Hsio-ching (English Translation by Legge in Vol. III of the Sacred Books of the East)

HUMPHREYS, CHRISTMAS:
Zen Buddhism (William Heinemann, London, 1949).

HOERNLE:
Manuscript Remains of Buddhist Literature, etc. (Clarendon Press, London, 1916)

Jodo Shinshu (Otani University, Kyoto, 1961)

Jodoshu Nisco-shi (compiled by a committee and published from Kyoto in Japanese)

Journal of Burma Research Society (Rangoon)

Journal of the Siam Society (Rangoon)

Kao-sen-chuan ('Lives of Eminent Monks' in three series as collected in the 50th vol. of the Taisho edition of Chinese Tripitaka)

LAW, B. C:
Historical Geography of Ancient India (Societie Asiatique de Paris, Paris, 1955)

LE THANH KTRI:
Le Vietnam, Historie et Civilization (Paris, 1955).

LONGFORD:
Japan (in the Nations of Today series)

MACDONALD, MALCOLM:
Angkor (1958)

Mahāparinibbāna Suttanta (Tr. in S.B.E. Vol. XI.)
Mahāvagga (in Oldenberg's *Vinayapitakam*, Vol. I.)
Mahavamsa (Trans. by Turnour and Geiger.)
MAJUMDAR, R. C:
Suvarnadvipa (Calcutta, 1938)
Inscriptions of Kambuja (Asiatic Society of Bengal, 1953)
MAY, REGINALD LE:
The Culture of South-east Asia (Allen and Unwin, London, 1954)
MULLIKIN AND HOTCHKIS:
Buddhist Sculptures at Yun Kang Caves (pub. by Henri Vetch, Peiping, 1935).
NANAMOLI, BHIKKHU:
The Path of Purification (pub. by R. Semaga, Colombo, 1956)
Nihon Bijutsu Zenshi ('A History of Japanese Art': pub. by Bijutsu Suppansha, Tokyo)
NITOBE:
Lectures on Japan (1936)
No Drama
The Noh Drama (Compiled by the 'Japanese Classics Translation Committee' and pub. by Tuttle and Company, Tokyo, Second printing, 1961)
O'NEIU:
A Guide to No (pub. by Hinoki Shoten)
Polonnaruva Period ed. by S.D. Saparamandu (Special Issue of the Ceylon Historical Journal, 2nd Ed. 1958)
PONSONBY-FANE:
Studies in Shinto and Shrines (pub. by Ponsonby Memorial Society, Kyoto; Revised Ed. 1953).
RADHAKRISHNAN, S:
Comparative Studies in Philosophy presented in honour of his Sixtieth Birthday (New York, 1950).
RAHULA, W:
History of Buddhism in Ceylon (Gunasena and Co., Colombo, 1956).
RAY, N. R:
Theravada Buddhism in Burma (pub. by University of Calcutta).
Samanta-Pasadika (Simon Hewavitarne Bequest Series, Colombo. Extracts in Oldenberg's *Vinayapitakam*, Vol. III.)
Sansom: *A History of Japan* (2 vol., London, 1958-1960).
Sāsanavamsa (Ed. by B. C. Law).
SASAKI, RUTH:
Zen—A Religion (pub. by the First Zen Institute of America Inc, New York, 1958).
Shinshu Seiten (Compiled and published by the Honpa Hongwanji Mission of Hawaii. Second Print, 1961).
STEIN, A.:
On Central Asian Tracks.
Sources of Japanese Tradition (Columbia University Press, New York, 1959).
Sources of Chinese Tradition (Columbia University Press, New York, 1959).
Subha Sutta (in Majjhima Nikaya, Further Dialogues of the Buddha, *ii*).
Suttanipata (in Khuddaka-mikaya, English trans. in S. B. E., Vol. X).
SUZUKI, D. T.:
Essays in Zen Buddhism (Second Series, Rider and Co., London, 1958).
An Introduction to Zen Buddhism (Rider and Co., London, 1960).

Buddhism in the Life and Thought of Japan (Rider and Co., London).

TA KUAN :

Memoirs of the Customs of Cambodia in Pelliot's edition in BEFEO, *ii*, 1902, pp. 123—177.

TEMPLE, R. C. :

The Thirty-Seven Nats (London, 1906).

THAI VAN KIEM :

Vietnam, Past and Present (Saigon, 1957, published under the Vietnamese Department of National Education and the National Commission for the UNESCO).

TOYNBEE :

Comparing notes: A Dialogue across a Century (Weidenfeld and Nicolson, London, 1963).

WATANABE :

Nihon Bukkyo (In Japanese; pub. by Iwanami Shinsho, Tokyo, 1958).

WATTERS AND RHYS DAVIDS :

On Yuan Chawng (Royal Asiatic Society, London, 1905)

WEIGER, REV :

A History of the Religious Beliefs and Philosophical Opinions in China (Translated from French by E. E. Warner and pub. by Hsien-Hsien Press in Peking, 1927).

WOODMAN, DOROTHY :

Making of Burma (Cresset Press, London, 1962).

WRIGHT :

Buddhism in Chinese History (Oxford University Press, 1959).

ZURCHER :

The Buddhist Conquest of China, Two vols. (English translation from German, E. J. Brill, Leiden, 1959).

INDEX

(*Names of Books and Authors are italicized*)

C

D

E

F

G

H

I

L

M

N

O

P

T

U

V

W

Y

Z